D1211984

KEMAL KURSPAHIĆ

AS LONG AS SARAJEVO EXISTS

Translated by Colleen London

THE PAMPHLETEER'S PRESS
STONY CREEK, CONNECTICUT

Published by the Pamphleteer's Press

10 9 8 7 6 5 4 3 2 1

Library of Congress Catalog Card Number
96-071334

ISBN 0-9630587-7-0

Cover by Barbara Marks and Toki Design
Book Design by Toki Design

Manufactured in the United States of America

THE PAMPHLETEER'S PRESS
P.O. Box 3374
Stony Creek, Connecticut 06405
Tel/Fax (203) 483-1429

To journalists around the world who have struggled and died for freedom of expression—in war and peace.

Acknowledgments

THIS BOOK IS ABOUT that courageous group of men and women—the journalists of *Oslobodjenje*—whose commitment to their profession and to a pluralist, multiethnic Bosnia-Hercegovina was translated into a unique form of resistance to the ultranationalist warriors who laid siege to their city and rent their country from end to end. By refusing to put their pens down, even at the risk of their lives, they proved once again that ideas and ideals are not ephemeral things and cannot be obliterated by guns. They have my admiration and my gratitude for the inspiration and support which made it possible for me to carry out my duties as editor-in-chief through six of the most difficult years in the newspaper's history.

I also owe a great debt of gratitude to my wife Vesna, and my sons Tarik and Mirza, for their encouragement and support in the darkest, most desperate days even when, fearing for my life, they could not but ask, "why?" I hope this book will help them understand the reasons for the sacrifices that we as a family—and the three of them in particular—had to make in those years when I was unable to be a better husband and father.

My special thanks go to the Nieman Foundation at Harvard University and its curator Bill Kovach, the Robert R. McCormick Tribune Foundation, and Charles T. Brumback and Vivian Vahlberg for providing me the opportunity of writing this book and of working as *Oslobodjenje*'s U.S. correspondent without any cost to the paper.

As the former editor-in-chief of *Oslobodjenje* I would like to express my appreciation for all those institutions in the United States that came forward with assistance for the paper, such as the National Endowment for Democracy, the Soros Foundation, the International Media Fund, and the Freedom Forum. I also thank those American institutions that honored *Oslobodjenje* with their awards, such as the Nieman Foundation, the Rothko Chapel in Houston, the University of Missouri in Columbia, the International Women's Media Foundation in Washington, D.C., and the World Press Review in New York.

The same goes to numerous European press organizations, and most of all—to the Reporters Sans Frontiers and their Director Robert Menard, for their tireless efforts to help keep *Oslobodjenje* alive.

My personal thanks go to the numerous groups and individuals across the United States who have continued to demonstrate their sincere concern for the fate of Bosnia over the past few years and who invited me to speak at their universities, synagogues, churches and cultural centers. Here I must mention Sharon Silber, Jack David Marcus, Meryl Zagarek, and other members of JACOB (Jewish Ad Hoc Committee on Bosnia); Ed Herbert, Barry Afergan, Glen Ruga, Roger and Joyce McNeil, Sharon Machlis Gartenberg, and others among Bosnia's friends in Massachussetts; Anwar Kazmi of the American Muslims Friends of Bosnia; Professor Joshua Goldstein of the Washington, D.C. Committee for Bosnia; Patrick McCarty of the Bosnian Student Project in St. Louis, as well as many, many others.

I am especially grateful to two of the finest writers on Bosnia—Christopher Hitchens and Roy Gutman—for agreeing, respectively, to write the foreword and the introduction to this book. Since the beginning of the war in Bosnia both have made an enormous contribution to the American public's understanding of the conflict in the Balkans. Hitchens's extraordinary columns and Gutman's excellent reporting on the war crimes in Bosnia (for which he received the Pulitzer Prize) are representative of the best in journalism.

I would like to thank Annie Leibovitz for her kind permission to use one of the photographs she took during her visit to Sarajevo. I also thank Glen Ruga and Frank Ward for agreeing to the reproduction in these pages of some of their compelling photography of Bosnia at war. Danielle McClellan, Managing Editor at the Pamphleteer's Press, guided the manuscript through the final stages of production with expert care and great professional skill.

And, finally, as the author I owe my very special gratitude to Rabia Ali for her intellectual support and great editorial contribution to this book; to Lawrence Lifschultz for his determination to have *As Long As Sarajevo Exists* published; and to Colleen London for her work on the translation of my original manuscript from Bosnian into English.

CONTENTS

FOREWORD

CHRISTOPHER HITCHENS

At a conference of activists (and others) in solidarity with Bosnia, held during the hard post-Dayton winter of 1995–1996, I sat on a panel with Mira Baratta and David Gelber of ABC News. Ms. Baratta was the foreign-affairs attaché to the Robert Dole campaign, and Mr. Gelber had been instrumental in the airing of some network "specials" during the prolonged torture of Sarajevo. Both of them had done a great deal more for the people of Bosnia-Hercegovina, in other words, than I had. The large audience, which had stuck by the Bosnian cause through the heat and burden of the day, was intensely preoccupied with the question of Muslim "fundamentalism"—never a slow subject in American discourse. Questioner after questioner inquired why "the media" (this to Mr. Gelber) or "the politicians" (this to Ms. Baratta) routinely referred to the government and people of Bosnia as "the Muslims." And every questioner had his or her answer implicitly ready. Wasn't it self-evident that Bosnians were Bosnians, irrespective of faith or confession or parentage, and that this had been the motive and energy of the movement in solidarity with their cause? Well, wasn't it?

Well, of course, I was much used to dealing with this question, often in more hostile or more ignorant forms, from countless seminars and rallies and private discussions. How many times had I pointed out that the Serbian and Croatian aggressors were never described as "the Christians" or, more accurately in each respective case, as the "Orthodox" or "Roman Catholic" forces. "Christian Orthodox forces renewed their bombardment of Sarajevo today . . ." In your dreams. The only difference on this Washington occasion was that some actual Muslims, devout at least in point of their garb, were seated near the front. In their interjections, they seemed to imply that being Islamic ("fundamentalist" or not) was the main point of their commitment. Politeness was the solvent that prevented this amusing distinction from surfacing at the conference. (Politeness and the iron law that states that there shall be no unseemly or "divisive" discussion of politics at any American political gathering.)

Had I had time—there is never time—this is what I had jotted down to say. I kept it schematic for my own sake as well as that of others.

One: If the Muslims of Bosnia-Hercegovina had long practiced and enforced the sharia law, this neither would nor should have provided any pretext, however faltering, for their extirpation. They had the absolute right to their own faith and obedience, under any conditions, and without any conditions. If, like Christian Armenians or observant Jews, they made themselves obnoxious to their neighbors and fellow countrymen by their religious practice, then all the more reason to defend the right to the difference. If it had been found that they wanted forcibly to proselytize their neighbors, as the Armenians weren't able to do and the Jews didn't care to do, then even this would not begin to justify genocide.

This might appear to be an elementary statement, but in the rhetoric of more than one speech I had detected an occluded corollary, and I didn't care for it. "The Bosnians are being slaughtered and deported for being Muslims," one would hear, "and they are really secular. See them eat pork. See them drink loza. They aren't really Islamic at all. They even intermarry." This trope has begun to wear me down. Of course none of those uttering it would have uttered the unspoken corollary; that if they really were Muslims then the whole butchery might be somewhat more understandable if not excusable. I had simply registered, as a committed atheist and secularist, that if it was my community that was being defended in this rhetoric I would have felt a slight queasiness as much at the implied reservation as the trumpeted broad-mindedness and generosity.

Two: There are fundamentalists in Bosnia, both domestic and foreign, who think that a clerical and/or a party-state is a good idea. They may have been taught this by their party-state forebears, or by some of their international allies, or they may have always harbored the notion. In any event, they are entitled to the sinews of self-defense just as they are entitled to advice from outsiders about the lessons of history. A clerical state for Muslims would ghettoize Bosnia-Hercegovina within Europe, and a party-state run by a "Muslim" party would be the counterpart of great-power partition, however much it proclaimed its sovereignty and "integrity." But one should still not preach to the victims as if they were co-responsible in beginning a war which threatened their (and only their) survival as a post-Yugoslav people.

Three: Those of us who declared for Bosnia at the outset were perfectly well aware that there are moral risks involved in taking any side in a war. We would not have been entitled, having taken the stand that we did, to complain later if some action of the Bosnian government had put "us" in an awkward position. We should certainly have looked foolish running to protect our own unsullied reputations in what we had called a war for survival. It would of course have been pardonable, if not in fact essential, to hold the Bosnians to their own standard on human rights. But there could have been no advance conditions of that sort. ("One bad story about maltreatment of Serbs, and I withdraw my signature and compose a righteous letter to the editor of the evenhanded Warring Faction Post . . .") Nonetheless, it deserves to be said that the Bosnian government and its armed forces never did put any of us in such a position. I prefer to think that this was because neither their cause nor their culture necessitated the waging of a racist type of war. This was part of the point in the first place, and to begin with.

Four: There were and are those, in Bosnian politics and society and journalism and academic life, who took and take seriously the idea of Bosnia for the Bosnians, and who carried the idea not just in their heads and minds but in their bodies and in their families. As the Dayton carve-up took hold, and as the military and national and (my own coinage) "uniformist" forces were rewarded, the next phase would be the struggle within each partitioned statelet for the control over moral and intellectual and civic life. Given the precedents and given the nature of the war, it seemed that only in Bosnia-Hercegovina was there likely to be any very spirited opposition to the new dispensation. And at least in Bosnia-Hercegovina, those arguing for pluralism of any kind could argue that they were using at least the proclaimed rhetoric of the government. A Serb or Croatian dissident had no such privilege.

I therefore ended my tersely written and undelivered intervention with a kind of double-entry bookkeeping that was not supposed to be tricky. Solidarity with Bosnia and Bosnians and indeed Bosniaks was unconditional. But I reserved a little of my personal solidarity for those who, as in all societies, see the importance of the non-sectarian Enlightenment and see it as important not just for "others" but for themselves. (And also, it might be added, not just for themselves but for "others".) I expected, and expect, to be doing a little work with them and for them against some of their former allies and in favor of an open society, a free press and a nondenominational state.

I hope and trust that I would have come to this conclusion on my own. And after a couple of visits to Sarajevo and other centers of Bosnian resistance I felt that both solidarities were confirmed in my own mind. But I was enormously assisted, and reinforced in my convictions, by the author of these ensuing pages. Kemal Kurspahić knows in practice what it is like to fight on more than two fronts at one time. As you will see, he has been engaged on several. First came the struggle to emancipate the Yugoslav press from the dead hand of one-party rule. To describe this rule as "Titoist," by the way, is often a mistake. Kurspahić's depiction of mediocre conformism and place-seeking and time-serving shows that may of the apparat did not possess even Tito's rather formal and rigid concept of "Brotherhood and Freedom," but rather used their position to enhance local and tribal satrapy. More than one of the "League of Communist" bureaucrats was to emerge as a spitting, snarling xenophobe when the time came. And more than one heroic "dissident" of the bad old days was to remake himself as a wooden spokesman of a new political or national orthodoxy. These are the ironies of history, or at least they are included among the ironies of history, and they are exactly the sort of phenomenon that flourishes in the absence of a free and caustic press.

The Sarajevo daily *Oslobodjenje* (in Serbo-Croat *Liberation*) cannot always be held to have been free and caustic, and it is not entirely free or entirely caustic now. But it, and its mixed staff of Muslims, Serbs, Croats, Jews, and—an essential minority—unbelievers did find an approximate collective voice. The ancient Greeks held that courage was not a virtue in itself, but that it was a quality that made all the virtues possible. By its demonstration of fortitude under fire, and under worse than fire, *Oslobodjenje* set an example of courage which the profession might well want to emulate. (In the following pages, Mr. Kurspahić is rather too generous to the international fraternity of editors and journalists. They may have given some awards and some recognition to his newspaper, but their general record of defending the free press in former Yugoslavia is one of lamentable inattention. Imagine if a tithe of the attention once given to *La Prensa* in Nicaragua had been given to *Borba* or *Novi Danas* or *Slobodna Dalmacija* . . .)

I was never as brave or assiduous as Susan Sontag for example, who spent some nights sleeping on the floor of the *Oslobodjenje* office when the bombardment was so ghastly that it was unsafe to go "home." But I did have a couple of moments with its reporters which made me proud to be in the same profession, and I did start an appeal fund for the paper, via my column in *The Nation,* which raised many thousands of dollars in a very few days—and which I only mention because it contradicts the widespread impression that the American reading public took the same cretinous, euphemistic, and morally null position that was played back to it by cowardly politicians annexing the rhetoric of a body-bag "peace" movement. And I did have a number of meetings with Kemal Kurspahić, which I set down here by way of introduction to the author as well as the book.

At Thanksgiving in 1993, I had Mr. Salman Rushdie to stay in my home in Washington. He was on his way to meet Bill Clinton. At a dinner in his honor (Mr. Rushdie's I mean, not Mr. Clinton's) I invited Kemal Kurspahić. Rushdie had been very forward in his rhetoric in defense of Bosnia-Hercegovina, and had appeared on Radio Zid and other outlets of the Sarajevo resistance. He had even tried to go to Sarajevo, not an especially easy voyage for a person in the position he then occupied, in order to register his solidarity. Like many people in the Muslim world and tradition, he identified Bosnia as a sort of "front line" in the argument between an inclusive and a literal Islam. He also quite properly saw it as a test case for the community that prides itself on commitment to "human rights." (He never got to make the trip, partly because of noncooperation from President Izetbegović which must remain another story.) When Mr. Kurspahić came, he was genuinely and generously warm. He recalled the day of the Ayatollah's lethal fatwah against Rushdie, and promised to send him the pages in which *Oslobodjenje* had discussed and criticized it. At the time, and since, Bosnia's need for relations with Iran and other Muslim states was well known. There would have been every reason to temporize or to split the difference or to be less than full-hearted, and in a Bosnian case there would have been (perhaps) more excuse or license for it than there was in the hesitations of other Western and secular "intellectuals." For Kemal, there was no issue that came before free speech and free expression and cultural liberty, and the two of them ended up making speeches to an assembly of guests who (while I won't name them) had some reason to be embarrassed about their previous prudence on both issues. Rushdie spoke about Bosnia rather than his own plight, and Kurspahić spoke about Rushdie's rather than his own. I almost felt that internationalism was still alive.

The second occasion is not so agreeable in the memory. Throughout the summer of 1995, one had watched in horror and revulsion and rage as the "safe havens" of Srebenica and Zepa had been surrendered to the Chetniks by NATO without a shot being fired. Why do I even employ the lazy phrase "without a shot being fired?" The evidence points to worse than that—to foreknowledge and even collusion. Then came the weeks during which, by dint of endless pressure on certain American officials, the satellite photographs of the scene had been released and a reconstruction of the atrocity permitted. What it must have been like to be Bosnian in that period I cannot surmise. I have now, though, a rough real-time idea of what it must have felt like to watch the hallucinatory, slow-motion surrender of the Rhineland, Austria, and Sudetenland, or the martyrdom of the Spanish Republic. Anyway, as the picture sharpened and became more graphic a delegation of Bosnians arrived in Washington. It included most of the leading Serb and Croat members of the Bosnian "rotating" government. Once again my wife and I hosted a dinner, at which General Jovan Divjak and others gave a toast or two. There was much hushed discussion of the news from Srebrenica. I distinctly and particularly recall Kemal Kurspahić, as he retailed the argument of an essay published in that morning's *Oslobodjenje.* The author had been enraged and had written, in effect, that "after Srebrenica, we are entitled to do anything."

At that time or near it, news was arriving of the persecution and murder of Serb civilians in the Krajina. Kemal argued softly but firmly that the essayist was quite wrong, and that he dreaded the idea of any sectarian revenge upon Serbs. I remember thinking that, if it was my own country under discussion, I might not have taken such a lenient tone. But few things are more tiring and inauthentic than a speaker who is a super-patriot for someone else's country (usually overcompensating for guilty and ambivalent feelings about his own) and I was impressed to see that anyway Kemal had the feeling of the meeting with him.

I can't be sure whether this conveys what I want it to convey, which is a version of grace under pressure. Many Western friends of Bosnia during this awful period used to say for themselves (or have sneered against them by intellectual thugs like *New York Post* columnist Hilton Kramer writing in the *Wall Street Journal*) that they had found their version of "Spain." Of course one must beware of intellectual and emotional transference, as also of historical analogies too hastily arrived at. I personally think that the Spanish example is a perfectly defensible one in two senses. First, Bosnia was a test case for the resistance to organized aggression and to recrudescent fascism. Second, it was a living demonstration of alternative ways of arranging society; in this case either as a version of the fantasy about ethnic and religious "purity" or as a democratic pluralism. The benchmark here is of course George Orwell's *Homage to Catalonia,* precisely because it reminds people that such a desperate and essential conflict is always fought within as well as without. Friends can be false, enemies can be genuine. Many struggles that extol the heroism of Prometheus end up as monuments to the Sisyphean style.

This means steady work for those of us who intend to outlast fascism and its descendants, and who believe that only a healthy society has a chance of succeeding in that task. Bosnia was—is—a warning. In future conflicts, and for the remainder of this one, we will be arguing about the lessons that were learned and ignored in Sarajevo and Gorazde and Srebenica and Mostar and Zvornik. In that necessary and painful process of education, we will be in some debt to the newspaper and the editor you are about to meet. And we will be grateful for ordinary citizens who met partycrats and flag-wavers and purists along the way, and who in spite of all temptation did not allow them to become their teachers.

The Miracle
of Sarajevo

Roy Gutman

*Recipient of the Pulitzer Prize
for International Reporting*

More than a year before the armed attack began against Bosnia, I toured what was then, in 1991, a fast-dissolving Yugoslav state. Serb nationalists had begun barricading roads in the Krajina region of Croatia and were openly organizing paramilitary formations in Belgrade, the capital of Serbia. In Zagreb, nationalists were selling Ustashe memorabilia, and elsewhere in Croatia, they were raising the checkerboard flag that Serbs denounced as a symbol of the World War II fascist regime. Local media, prodded by political leaders, throughout the region were fomenting ethnic hatred to prepare the populations for war. There was a notable exception.

"The air is freer in Sarajevo," a Serbian journalist in Belgrade told me. He recommended that I stop by the offices of *Oslobodjenje*, the principal daily. "In the last three years they took the drabbest paper in Yugoslavia and made a rather fine daily," added one of the leading foreign correspondents for *Politika*. His own paper, once serious and sober, was headed in the opposite direction.

In *Oslobodjenje*'s modern headquarters, editor-in-chief Kemal Kurspahić said he and his colleagues were determined not to become a tool of war in the multiethnic republic. They had to face down the entire government. The Bosnian parliament had recently passed legislation empowering it to appoint new editors according to ethnic origins. Radical Serb nationalists like Radovan Karadžić had initiated the idea, but President Alija Izetbegović's Muslim Party of Democratic Action went along. It would have spelled the end of the newspaper.

Information minister Velibor Ostojić, a Karadžić protégé whose journalistic training was as a proofreader at Sarajevo Television, complained that *Oslobodjenje* devoted too much space to criticizing the government, covering political scandals, and publicizing the political opposition. "We would like to choose top staff who are completely independent and cover the news objectively." Ostojić told me. "Why should we always be under critical observation? That creates a negative public opinion about the new government."

The newspaper challenged the constitutionality of the new press law. Its staff demanded full independence; and during my visit, thousands of Sarajevans demonstrated on their behalf.

A year later, in 1992, Bosnian Serbs took to the hills and with the weapons, logistics, officers, and strategy provided by the Yugoslav army and supplemented by "volunteers" from Serbia, attacked Bosnia along two fronts and set siege to the capital. They trained their artillery and their tanks on *Oslobodjenje,* and reduced its headquarters to a charred wreck. Ostojić became a minister in the Bosnian Serb government. In that capacity, he masterminded the brutal takeover of the eastern Bosnian town of Foca, where a "rape camp" was set up and operated in the center of the town.

War brought a bloodletting and destruction to Bosnia equal to anything in Europe during World War II, outside, perhaps, of Dresden. The major powers, after recognizing Bosnia, rendered no military aid and instead extended an arms embargo. Since the Serbs had a ten-to-one military advantage, by one conservative estimate, Bosnia was in effect abandoned to die. The Serbs had put out the word that they would take Sarajevo within ten days, and I personally think that had they moved as swiftly as they anticipated, no one in the West would have lifted a finger in protest.

It is a miracle that the city, the state, the newspaper, and the ideals they held in common, survived. *Oslobodjenje* made its contribution to this miracle, and at war's end remains what it had been at the start: the voice of multiethnic Bosnia.

Kemal Kurspahić's gripping, eloquent memoir makes clear that those responsible were individuals who risked their lives to safeguard their newspaper. They knew what was at stake. Preserving their free and independent voice against the *gleichschaltung* demanded by the Bosnian Serbs was only the most obvious of the survival struggles in which they had to engage.

Similar battles are being fought everywhere in the fledgling democracies of East Central Europe. At the political level, the struggle pitted two models for the post-Communist era—the militarist, nationalist, xenophobic state versus the state of laws with open borders and Western-style freedoms and institutions. At the strategic level, the major powers were engaged, however they tried to avoid it. They had to decide: Would the United States counter this new and dangerous outburst of violence? Would NATO venture "out of area" to stop a bloodbath? What is left of Europe if its citizens become spectators to genocide in their midst?

An independent publication such as *Oslobodjenje* cannot have a direct impact upon the strategic decisions made in foreign capitals during wartime, particularly if no foreign diplomat is present to read it. For foreign reporters, discovering this hallmark of professionalism and civility in the midst of shelling was not only a good story but in a personal sense a morale boost. Working conditions were far worse for Bosnians than for us, for we had flak jackets and helmets, secure communications, armored vehicles or hired taxis, hard currency, regular meals, occasional heat, running water, and electricity in our hotel, and most of all the freedom, if the humanitarian airlift was operating, to leave. They did not. They were working in the world's most adverse conditions, risking their lives to prepare and distribute the paper.

What we had in common was the existential challenge of telling the story. Today, with the country at an uneasy peace, tens of thousands of NATO troops in place, and the War Crimes Tribunal in the Hague holding its first trials, it is hard to believe the utter indifference major powers projected at that time to crimes without parallel in Europe since World War II. Snipers and artillerymen killed Sarajevans before the eyes of the world. Thousands of survivors of concentration camps in Serb- or Croat-held territory told credible accounts of systematic torture and execution. No outsider who spent time at the scene found it hard to differentiate victim from aggressor. Yet major western governments professed to be ignorant of every development. Repeatedly, they excused even an egregious crime such as a mortar attack against civilians queued for bread by asserting that all parties were equally to blame. Dismissing Milošević as a consummate liar, the Western powers nonetheless adopted his propaganda, a subtle signal he knew only too well how to read.

The distortions of fact by Western leaders made a complex situation even less comprehensible and undercut their own credibility; a strong case can be made that it also extended the war.

BOSNIA LIES IN A DANGEROUS and difficult neighborhood, surrounded by Christian Orthodox Serbia and Roman Catholic Croatia, two states with far greater military power and more homogeneous populations than Bosnia, and with sizable numbers of co-religionists in Bosnia. What makes Bosnia unique in Europe is its Muslim population, almost entirely converts from the centuries of Turkish occupation, and the tradition of tolerance toward all faiths that developed over the centuries. Western statesmen, who routinely asserted that all the "warring parties" were liars and killers, or would be if they had the same number of weapons, chose to ignore this entirely.

Early in August 1992 after the first news reports of a network of Serb concentration camps in north Bosnia where Muslims were routinely slaughtered, President George Bush said the atrocities illustrated "a blood feud" and "a complex, convoluted conflict that grows out of age-old animosities." Two months later, Colin Powell wrote in an op-ed that the conflict had "deep ethnic and religious roots that go back a thousand years." British Prime Minister John Major blamed the war on the removal of the "discipline" that the old Soviet Union had exerted "over the ancient hatreds" in Yugoslavia, overlooking Yugoslavia's status as an independent Communist state which Britain played an instrumental role in helping to achieve. Senator John Warner (R-Va.) topped them all when he told a Senate hearing: "My own research indicates that...these people have fought each other for not hundreds of years, but thousands of years for religious, ethnic, cultural differences." And even President Clinton the following year, as he looked for excuses not to lift the arms embargo, declared to his aides: "These people have been killing each other in tribal and religious wars for centuries."

They had all rewritten history. There was no way "these people" could have been warring since prehistory, since the Slavs arrived in the Balkans in the sixth and seventh centuries. And while Serbs had grievances against Croats dating back to the Ustashe fascist regime in Zagreb during World War II, they had no real quarrels against the Bosnian Muslims. Milošević made this clear to Warren Zimmerman, the U.S. Ambassador to Yugoslavia at the time the war began in April 1992. "Serbs in Bosnia are not threatened. . . . Repression against the Serbs in Bosnia is an impossibility," Zimmerman recalls him saying (see Zimmerman's memoir, *Origins of a Catastrophe*, New York: Times Books). As for the image of unending conflict, Bosnia experienced mass carnage only once before, during the Yugoslav civil war which coincided with World War II. And "age-old animosities" aptly describes relations between France and Germany in the past century.

The war that began in April 1992 was, in fact, a well planned landgrab. Using the army of rump Yugoslavia, Serbia conquered more than two thirds of Bosnia in a six week blitzkrieg. Federal army forces pounded Muslim and Croat villages with artillery, and using paramilitary forces formally under their command, "cleansed" the region of non-Serb inhabitants.

In their effort to ignore the real origins, Western leaders often referred to the Bosnia conflict as a civil war and blamed Germany for igniting it. The theory ran that Germany, which pushed the European Union to recognize Croatia and Slovenia, the first two breakaway states, in late 1991, had provoked Serbia into a policy of partitioning Bosnia. According to this theory, ethnic Serbs, who comprise about one third of Bosnia's population, and Croats, who comprised 17 percent, would not want to live in a state where Muslims, with 44 percent, formed the plurality. Bosnia would not have sought its independence had Germany not recognized Croatia, and Serbs would have seen no reason to attack it and secede from the multiethnic state. At the ground level, however, this thesis had no plausibility, because it was widely known, certainly through Western diplomats such as Zimmerman, that Serbs had no grievances against the Muslims.

The persistence of the theory revealed more about Western Europe in 1992 than about the Balkans. The English and French governments made no secret of their envy of the size of the newly united Germany and their fear that it would extend its power to southeastern

Europe. In fact, according to a yearlong study undertaken by the Carnegie Endowment for International Peace, the thesis that the Germans were to blame was a fallacy, as was calling it a civil war based on "ancient hatreds."

Principal responsibility "rests with those post-Communist politicians throughout Yugoslavia who have invoked the 'ancient hatreds' to pursue their respective nationalist agendas and deliberately used their propaganda machines to justify the unjustifiable: the use of violence for territorial conquest, the expulsion of 'other' peoples, and the perpetuation of authoritarian systems of power," the commission said in its study, titled "Unfinished Peace."

The charge that Germany had ambitions in the region was "patently absurd," it continued, noting that recognition had been approved by the European Community with the aim of isolating Serbia. "No other state upheld an alternative approach."

The real underlying factors in the conflict are in fact strategic, geographical, and historical.

East Central Europe has been the starting point of all three major wars in the 20th century and many lesser ones as well. Tensions among the small to midsize states sandwiched between Germany and Russia are endemic, due to the ethnic and territorial disputes that entangle them, the weakness of most armies, and the unreliability of outside allies. The vacuum tempts political or military intervention by stronger neighbors. When great powers relations are near explosion, East Central Europe is the tinderbox. A Bosnian Serb, backed by elements in the Serbian government, fired the bullet that fell Austrian Archduke Ferdinand in Sarajevo, triggering World War I. World War II began with the German march into Poland, after SS troops disguised as Polish home guard staged a phony assault on Sender Gleiwitz, the German-language Gliwice radio station. The Cold War began with the Red Army's march into East Central Europe and ended with its withdrawal.

In retrospect, the presence of the Red Army in the East and the United States army in the West kept a lid on the tensions of this region. Conversely the withdrawal of the Red Army and the reduced presence of the Americans lifted the lid. The problem was there for everyone to see, and just one year after the collapse of the Berlin Wall in 1989, Western statesmen spoke of developing a new security order to extend into the 21st century. But the politicians were too busy celebrating the end of Communism as their personal success to follow through on their rhetoric.

Withdrawing their attention, and to some extent their intelligence monitoring, Western states, led by the United States, effectively signaled disinterest as the anti-Communist revolution spread to Yugoslavia, which had fashioned its own independent style of Communism under its postwar strongman Josip Broz Tito. In East Central Europe, this was a formula for disaster, and nowhere more so than in Bosnia-Herzegovina, which has been at the center of great power politics more than once in modern history.

Bosnia first took shape within its currently recognized borders in the 14th century, and, like any multiethnic state, has had its share of tensions. To a large degree, they were generated by the territorial ambitions of outside powers and by Bosnia's location on the East-West fault line between the Roman and eastern rite Christian churches, and the north-south division between Christianity and Islam.

Under Turkish domination from 1463 until 1878, local Christians converted in numbers to Islam but lived alongside Roman Catholic and Orthodox. Bosnia developed into a haven of tolerance — Sarajevo in particular—in those four centuries, also acquiring a sizable Jewish population who fled the Spanish Inquisition, and scores of other minorities. The Ottoman Empire's slow death made Bosnia an object of competition between Serbs seeking a greater Serbia, and Roman Catholic Austria-Hungary, which already dominated neighboring Croatia. The rivals had allies. Russia, engulfed by pan-Slavic sentiment, backed Serbia, while the newly emerged German state gave tacit support to Austria. At the Congress of Berlin in 1878, Bismarck balanced off conflicting interests by placing Bosnia under Austrian occupation and administration, a step short of handing over sovereignty. In 1908, Austria peremptorily annexed Bosnia. Russia, alienated at the humiliation, began a major rearmament and military reform drive; and Serbia started down a path of revenge that culminated with Gavrilo Princip's slaying of Franz Ferdinand in 1914.

At Versailles, Bosnia became part of the Kingdom of Serbs, Croats, and Slovenes, with U.S. President Woodrow Wilson the chief outside sponsor. Its major ethnic groups went along, but Serbs dominated the Kingdom from the start, and the weak parliamentary structure collapsed in chaos in 1928.

World War II brought civil war to Yugoslavia, a war within a war that was fought mostly in Bosnia's hills and gorges. Croatia's Ustasha Fascists occupied the region and systematically murdered Serbs, Jews, and Gypsies there as in Croatia. That genocide, and a similar though smaller-scale brutality by the Serbian royalist Chetniks, generated recruits for Tito's Communist partisans, who fought both the Ustasha and the Chetniks under the banner of equality for all nationalities. After World War II Bosnia became an integral and peaceful part of Tito's independent Communist state, a Yugoslavia in miniature. Ethnic tensions existed but at a low level, evidenced by the intermarriage rate of up to 35 percent in the major cities.

The political context for the Bosnian bloodbath was the breakup of Yugoslavia after Tito's death in 1980. Elsewhere in Eastern Europe, wherever the Red Army had installed Communist regimes, the West throughout the Cold War encouraged liberal democratic alternatives. But in Yugoslavia, which Tito's forces liberated with minimal Soviet help, the West had seen a strategic interest in the survival of Communism. It backed Tito politically and financially and suppressed his émigré opposition. When Communist rule collapsed, the only political force in the wings was nationalism.

Nationalism has deep roots, especially in Serbia. Historically, Serbia saw itself as the Piedmont of the Balkans, the state around which a regional political entity would be established. The ambition to replace foreign dominating powers with a greater Serbia surfaced in the mid-19th century. It grew as Serbia, after centuries under Ottoman rule, was recognized in 1878 along with tiny Montenegro. But Serbs vastly overestimated their own skills in the contest with Austria over the destiny of Bosnia. While willing to use brute force or go to war, Serbs had failed to develop democratic or autocratic methods that would enable them to govern others, let alone themselves. Serbs were principal protagonists in the two Balkan wars of 1912-1913, hoping to carve out greater Serbia from the moribund Ottoman Empire, and the tensions accumulated during those conflicts ensured an all-Europe war after the assassination in Sarajevo. Heavy-handed treatment of Croats, Slovenes, and Muslims by the dominant Serbs was the major factor in the collapse into anarchy of the interwar Yugoslav state, aided and abetted by the erratic behavior of Croats.

Violence particularly against Muslims and Turks has been a central theme in Serbian literature and its oral tradition. In the greatest Serbian language epic poem of the 19th century, "the Mountain Wreath" written by Petar Njegoš in 1847, the Montenegrin Prince-Bishop, celebrates the "Christmas eve" massacre of Muslims by Montenegrin warriors a century and a half earlier.

"Not one witness was able to escape to tell his tale about what happened there. We put under our sharp sabers all those who did not want to be baptized by us," the warriors reported to the Vladika of the day, who like Njegoš headed both Church and State. "We set fire to all the Turkish houses that there might not be a single trace left of our faithless domestic enemy." The Vladika replied: "You have brought me great gladness, my falcons, great joy for me." Serb schoolboys learned the poem by heart, and Montenegrin villagers "found in it more than anywhere else the greatest expression of their way of thinking and feeling," wrote Djilas, the onetime close aide to Tito.

Violence against Muslims was usually justified in the context of revenge for Turkish victory at Kosovo in 1389, a heroic defeat celebrated in countless folk songs, novels, and films, and by Serbian clerics. A national church which has functioned as keeper of the cultural heritage and national idea, the Serbian Orthodox Church has backed the expansion of Serb lands from 19th century to this day. Church leaders stoked the nationalist revival by hosting a strange and ominous ritual in 1989, the 600th anniversary of Kosovo, when they circulated the reputed relics of Prince Lazar defeated in the battle to churches and monasteries in predominantly Serb regions of Bosnia and Croatia that later became the targets of armed conquest.

In the waning days of Communism, nationalist fervor pervaded every major institution in Serbian public life. Serbian university professors and writers played a critical role by giving their stamp of approval to the nationalist "big lie." In the 1986 memorandum of the Serbian Academy of Arts and Sciences, academics led by writer Dobrica Cosić complained that Serbs were being persecuted and expelled from Kosovo, the "cradle of Serb culture" now inhabited mainly by Muslim ethnic Albanians. The "scholars" alleged "physical, political, legal and cultural genocide." It was the big lie. To right the supposed injustice, they called for the "complete national and cultural integrity of the Serbian people...no matter in which republic or province they might find themselves living," and the incorporation of two autonomous provinces into Serbia proper—the overwhelmingly Albanian Kosovo, and the largely Hungarian Vojvodina.

The Serb proportion of the Kosovo population indeed had dropped from 23.5 percent in 1961 to 10 percent in 1991, while the Albanian share went from 67 to 90 percent. But the "genocide" claim had no factual basis: Serbs were not being expelled but emigrating from the poorest of the Yugoslav regions to elsewhere in Serbia. Moreover the Serb birthrate was falling as that of Muslims was rising or holding steady. Serbia proper registered only 1.4 live births per thousand in 1990, compared to 7.7 in Bosnia-Herzegovina, and 23.1 in Kosovo. Another motivating factor was that Serbs stood to lose the most in the transformation to a market economy and democratic political structure. Serbs dominated the army and secret police, and Serb intellectuals, who had faithfully served the Communist regime, feared the loss of privilege and wealth.

Milošević, a Communist apparatchik with an eye for the jugular, rode the nationalist wave to power by devising a concrete program and harnessing the machinery of the state including one of Europe's biggest land armies. He took up the "big lie" where the Academy of Arts and Sciences left off. Milošević seized center stage on April 24, 1987, in the town of Kosovo Polje. As he was attending an indoor rally of Kosovo Serbs, Serb militants outside began stoning the ethnic Albanian police guarding the hall. Milošević emerged and listened with sympathy to Serbs who claimed the police were beating them. "You will not be beaten again," he said in a filmed statement that led that evening's news in Belgrade.

Milošević had sent his own advance team to organize the violence and brought a Belgrade television camera team to film him. The film clip, constantly repeated on state television, became the basis for Milošević's political claim to lead Serbia: a Sender Gleiwitz in the video age.

In short order, he ousted the leadership of the Serbian Communist party, and those of the provinces of Kosovo, Vojvodina, and the republic of Montenegro. In May 1989, Milošević had won presidential elections giving him formal control of the Serbian state. Seizing four seats of the eight-member presidency gave him predominance in the cumbersome federal structure, but the constitutional crisis he thereby provoked proved terminal for the Yugoslav state.

By deliberately stirring nationalist passions for personal political gain in Yugoslavia's biggest republic, Milošević broke a central taboo of the Tito era. If Serbia, with a population of nine million out of the twenty-three million in all of Yugoslavia, could do this, so could everyone else. Nationalists in the advanced western republics of Slovenia and Croatia took their cue, founded their movements, laid their plans for a looser confederation, or failing that, secession. But Milošević was confident he could manipulate the Yugoslav army to Serb bidding. In early 1991 he announced that the Serbian people "want to live in one state." Dividing Yugoslavia and forcing the Serbian people to live in different states "is from our point of view, unacceptable, that is, let me emphasize, out of the question." The warning applied mainly to Croatia, which had a ten percent Serb population and Bosnia where it was one third. It was tantamount to a threat of war.

Milošević had nearly all the advantages in his preparations for war, but he overestimated the capabilities of the Yugoslav army. Preparation occurred in four stages: disarming the republic-level territorial defense forces starting in May 1990, arming the local Serbs starting later that year, organizing a political and constitutional process to set up Serbian states on Croatian and Bosnian territory, and then staging provocations to permit the federal army to intervene decisively on the Serb side.

War began in June 1991 with the decision by Slovenia and Croatia to quit the federation. The Slovenes had resisted disarming their territorial defense units, prepared their defenses, and won their war in 10 days. But in Croatia, which had been largely disarmed, the Yugoslav army had the advantages of vast military superiority, proximity to Serbia, the ability to infiltrate "volunteers," and the presence of armed ethnic Serbs. The use of armed gangs, some recruited from soccer fan clubs, some straight out of jail, gave Milošević deniability in the war's early stages. In fact from July, 1991, all paramilitary forces were placed by law directly under the Serbian territorial defense, a sort of home guard, which he controlled as Serbian president. In August, 1991, after observing Western disinterest in the assaults on Croatian cities by Serb "irregulars," Milošević ordered in the federal army. The army began bombarding the Croatian city of Vukovar from Serbian territory, and seized about a third of Croatian land before the "international community" called for a cease-fire. Due to desertions, the Army could not field the manpower to divide Croatia in three parts and obtain direct sea access for Serbs in Krajina as it had intended.

By the time Alija Izetbegović's Muslim Party of Democratic Action came came to power in Bosnia in December, 1990, nearly all arms had been collected in that republic. Some months later, the Bosnian government discovered while investigating a shooting incident in western Bosnia that arms had been distributed to twenty-two Serb-majority districts. "This was the crucial turning point," commented Vladimir Velebit, a retired Yugoslav ambassador to several countries, who is of Serbian origin. "No single event compares with the arming of the local Serbs."

Milošević's problem in Bosnia was the absence of a threat from Muslims. So Serb propagandists invented an enemy, namely an "Islamic fundamentalist" threat. The Orthodox Church joined in readily. In January, 1992, the Church's ruling synod stated that Serb citizens in Bosnia lived "under the threat that genocide will again be visited upon them." Once again, the underlying reality was demographic decline. In 1991, Serbs comprised only 31.4 per cent of the population and Muslims 43.7 percent, a reversal of 1961 when Serbs had 42.8 percent and Muslims 25.6 percent.

Throughout the slaughter in Bosnia, Milošević skillfully combined central control with plausible deniability for foreign consumption. To offset the shortage of Serb manpower, he expanded the use of "volunteers," or "paramilitaries." In December 1991, with the Croatian war winding down and Bosnia yet to come, the rump federal government under his control had ordered all paramilitary forces to come directly under the command of the regular army. Thus when Željko Ražnatović, the "commander" of "Arkan's Tigers," demanded the surrender of Zvornik, east Bosnia, at the start of the war in mid-April 1992, his force was fully integrated with the army of rump Yugoslavia and operating within its laws.

But in a conversation with Ralph Johnson, a senior U.S. official, a few weeks later, Milošević denied any responsibility. "If this sort of thing is going on, I'll try to stop them," Johnson recalled him saying. "It was a surrealistic conversation," Johnson added. "I never doubted personally he was behind or supportive of it."

Milošević still routinely denies any responsibility. "All these kinds of paramilitary formations were totally marginal in that war," he told

Time in July, 1995. He estimated there were only "a couple thousand." In fact, the "bandits and killers" were rallied by the state-controlled media in a major recruitment campaign. Arkan was a close ally of Milošević, operating out of a base in Serb-occupied eastern Slavonia. The UN's special Commission of Experts concluded, after a two-year study, that upwards of 20,000 "paramilitary" troops fought for Serbian interests in Bosnia.

Under Army supervision, a network of concentration camps was set up to which able-bodied Bosnian Muslim and Croat males were taken. The Army's classified 1987 Doctrine of Total National Defense permitted "political isolation" of domestic traitors "in combination with other measures and procedures, including physical liquidation." A secret 1989 decree permitted authorities in a state of emergency to "prohibit departure from certain places or order compulsory stay in a certain place for certain persons." On October 3, 1991, the federal government under his control announced a "threat of imminent war," which was reported in the domestic media as a state of emergency.

The creation of the Bosnian Serb army was another cynical ruse, devised to deflect a hostile Western reaction. "We knew that when Bosnia was recognized we'd be seen as the aggressors, because our Army was there," Borisav Jović, Serbia's representative on the collective presidency at the break-up of Yugoslavia, told the BBC in its series, *The Death of Yugoslavia.* "Only Milošević and I were thinking about it. We did not consult anybody else. We realized we had to act before the others did." Accordingly, Milošević transferred all Bosnian-Serb troops and officers back to Bosnia and withdrew some 13,000 non-Bosnians, leaving behind a trained and well-equipped army of 80,000, according to western military experts. Milošević stayed in control by providing supplies and paying their wages. "We promised to pay their costs," Jović said. "They couldn't manage even to pay their officers' wages." The officers stayed behind and the General Staff appointed General Ratko Mladić to lead them.

As reports multiplied of wide-scale atrocities and led to public demands for a response, Western powers undertook measures to address the symptoms but not the problem. They declared Bosnia a "humanitarian" disaster, classifying it with earthquakes and floods, and sent in food aid and UN troops to assist in the delivery. But there was another agenda at work. Britain and France led their own troops to Bosnia as the core of a UN peacekeeping presence. This gave them the major say in political developments and effectively excluded Germany, which was constrained by its history and constitution from following suit. But the troops, misnamed the UN Protection Force or UNPROFOR, were not sent in to protect victims, ensure that food aid was delivered, or even defend themselves. They quickly became hostages to the Bosnian Serbs and allowed Britain and France to block any more decisive response to the atrocities.

In parallel to this deployment, the major powers also launched a diplomatic process, which had the aim of partitioning the state and rewarding the aggression. Time and again, as Serb gunners stepped up the bombardment of Sarajevo, David Owen of Great Britain, Cyrus Vance of the United States, or Thorvald Stoltenberg of Norway summoned Izetbegović to Geneva to seek his assent to a plan which would split Bosnia into cantons, ethnic ministates, or some other form of partition. It was a classic example of negotiation under duress, with the Serbs acting as the diplomats' enforcer. The Bosnian leader usually accepted each proposal in the correct knowledge that the Serbs would reject it.

The negotiators developed an Orwellian newspeak to deflect public criticism. Thus the aggressor and the victims were called "warring parties," giving them moral equivalence. The stated aim was to bring "peace," but what that meant was the endorsement of a Serb military victory. They referred to a "political solution" but what they meant was a supervised surrender.

The charade had no impact on the fighting, and the war continued. A quarter million people, mostly civilians, were killed, and more than two million, or half the population of Bosnia-Herzegovina, were made homeless. Moreover, the crisis fractured and paralyzed the rest of Europe, divided NATO, and left the UN humiliated.

The public could scarcely grasp these developments, for the statements and actions of governments in no wise responded to the war. The sole action that did relate to events on the ground was that the UN Security Council, at American behest, set the wheels in motion for an international criminal tribunal to address the war crimes. But the tribunal quickly proved impotent, for even as it indicted Mladić and Karadžić, they committed more crimes.

While parliaments throughout Europe and North America debated the event, it was only in the United States Congress that demands to lift the arms embargo had impact. Using its own resources to determine the true facts, Congress began pressing in the summer of 1992. The percentage voting in favor rose after each successive atrocity until the summer of 1995, and the fall of Srebrenica, when Congress finally mustered a veto-proof two-thirds majority.

Srebrenica exposed the world's indifference to Bosnia as few other events did since the start of the war. By the summer of 1995, Bosnia had in fact become the number one focus of U.S. intelligence, according to top officials, but the Americans failed to see in the buildup an imminent attempt to capture the enclave, and failed to detect or report the atrocities that followed. Bosnian Army intelligence had intercepted radio transmissions indicating the atrocities as they occurred, but the United States showed no interest. Only after a State Department official went to Tuzla and interviewed several men who escaped the massacres did the CIA begin searching its aerial surveillance records. A full month after the killing, America's UN ambassador, Madeleine Albright, revealed photographic evidence of the murders to the UN.

The atrocities at Srebrenica, in which Bosnian Serbs killed as many as 8,000 fleeing refugees, also exposed the "international community" for what it really is. In the words of the Carnegie Commission, the "international community," symbolized by the United Nations and other institutions, "is a fictious entity, appealed to by those who feel wronged, called upon by others to sanctify their wrongdoing, and used as an excuse for inaction by all states unwilling to get involved—or as a pretext for action by those eager to enter the fray."

The entity is immune to accountability. There is compelling evidence that Srebrenica fell because the UN, which had the responsibility, chose not to defend it. Early in June 1995, the chief UN military officer, French General Bernard Janvier offered a deal to Mladić. Mladić's forces were holding hundreds of UN personnel hostage in response to two minor NATO airstrikes and humiliated them daily before the cameras. Janvier in a secret meeting offered to abandon all future air strikes if Mladić would release the UN personnel. Mladić released the UN officers, and Janvier kept his word. Despite repeated pleas for air support from Dutch UN troops stationed at Srebrenica, Janvier refused until minutes before the town actually fell.

The "community" doesn't want to be reminded of its failure. No UN investigation was launched on the procedures and personnel responsible for this worst atrocity in Europe since World War II, and when Dutch officials, prodded by the Dutch parliament, later inquired, they learned, not surprisingly, that none of the Security Council members had an appetite for an investigation.

With Srebrenica's atrocities before it and Congress preparing yet another rebuke, the Clinton administration had little choice as it headed, down in the polls, into an election year. Thus it launched an American initiative to end the war by intervening militarily with air attacks on Bosnian Serb targets, taking charge of the diplomacy, and committing ground troops to police the agreement.

In the run-up to the three-week marathon conference at Dayton, Ohio, some United States allies such as Britain still favored partition; Russia sided openly with Serbia. The new French President Jacques Chirac had shifted to a harder line, but his defense ministry, which had operational control over French military assets on the ground, stuck with the British position. Clinton took the path of least resistance, adopting as the goal a 50/50 split of the multiethnic state. The Bosnian Serbs were far more vulnerable than the Americans realized. Knocked off balance by Croatia's recapture of the Krajina, the liberation of Bihac in August, and NATO's bombing raids in September, they were on the run when the U.S. envoy Richard Holbrooke demanded that the Bosnians and Croats halt their offensive.

The result of U.S. diplomacy at Dayton conference was a diplomatic solution that left all the big questions open. The accord promised a unified Bosnian state but authorized two armies, two systems of justice, and two separate administrations of police within its borders. The accord demanded the return of refugees to their homes and the reform of the local police who had expelled them in the first place, but did not assure either outcome. Thus, it was anything but certain Dayton would usher in a lasting peace.

Yet, with the dispatch of 60,000 NATO troops, one third of them American, the first ever such deployment in NATO history, the Western alliance crossed a Rubicon, acknowledging Bosnia to be its inescapable responsibility. The conflict had not directly threatened the vital interests of any one NATO member, but, paradoxically, threatened all simultaneously. By shutting their eyes to the travesties in their midst and trading recriminations over their failure to act, the Western powers over three and a half years fractured their unity, paralyzed international security organizations, and damaged everyone's security.

OSOLOBODJENJE DID NOT BREAK all the news about the war as it was occurring, nor could it have. The paper's facilities were a prime targets for Serb artillerymen; its finances, except for foreign donations and prizes, were almost nonexistent; and its staff could not report outside the besieged capital, hardly even travel within it. Moreover *Oslobodjenje*, like most dailies in the Central Europe, was just discovering investigative reporting when it came under political attack in 1991.

What it did throughout the war was provide straightforward coverage and astute commentary. And while only a Bosnian can gauge how much the independent media helped sustain the victims in their hour of despair, my sense is its role is irreplaceable. Common people took life risks to obtain the newspaper, even as elsewhere in Bosnia, they devised extraordinary contraptions to generate power for the radio or television.

Just by reporting the news, *Oslobodjenje* provided a slim reed of hope, an intake valve for intellectual oxygen, in the besieged capital. Through its columns, it fostered debate and aired the choices Bosnians had to make at every stage as the process unfolded. The newspaper's continuing operation, and the loyalty of its multiethnic staff, made it a symbol for the outside world of the courage of Sarajevans and their thirst for the truth.

Its editors understood the big picture and knew what had to be done. Kurspahić describes a meeting with Clinton in the spring of 1993 when the president asked him to recommend a U.S. course of action. Kurspahić offered a five-point formula: air strikes against Serb artillery and strategic targets around Sarajevo and other cities; lifting the arms embargo; tightening economic sanctions against Serbia; a correction of the Vance-Owen plan so that it would not sanction a division on the principles of "apartheid," and holding war-crimes trials.

Events proved Kurspahić right; the problem was that the president lacked the will to act. The war continued for two and a half more years, during which the paper appeared daily. Its very existence was a statement of defiance: that this society was not going to be destroyed by weapons. And the pen proved mightier than the sword.

By late 1996, with NATO troops in control of overall security, the situation in Bosnia had changed, on the whole for the better. *Oslobodjenje* adapted readily to peacetime conditions, and its coverage of Bosnia broadened and deepened. It was doing what any independent publication must do: hold up a mirror to society. But its performance during the war, this defining event at the start of the new era, will go down in history. Its staff paid a high price, in lives lost or disrupted, to preserve freedom of the press. In their courage, they set the standard for the profession.

AS LONG AS SARAJEVO EXISTS

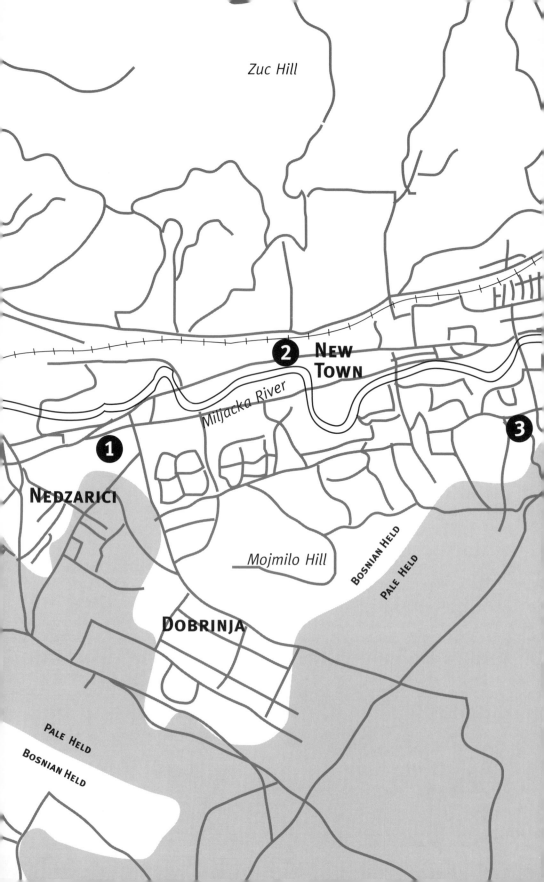

Zuc Hill

2 **NEW TOWN**

Miljacka River

3

1

NEDZARICI

Mojmilo Hill

BOSNIAN HELD

PALE HELD

DOBRINJA

PALE HELD

BOSNIAN HELD

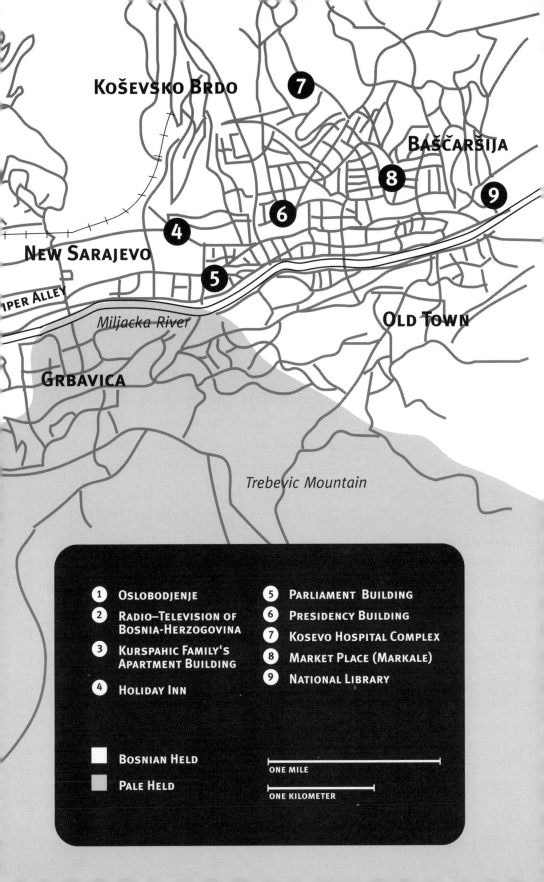

KOŠEVSKO BRDO

7

BAŠČARŠIJA

8

9

6

4

NEW SARAJEVO

5

SNIPER ALLEY

Miljacka River

OLD TOWN

GRBAVICA

Trebevic Mountain

1 OSLOBODJENJE

2 RADIO–TELEVISION OF BOSNIA-HERZOGOVINA

3 KURSPAHIC FAMILY'S APARTMENT BUILDING

4 HOLIDAY INN

5 PARLIAMENT BUILDING

6 PRESIDENCY BUILDING

7 KOSEVO HOSPITAL COMPLEX

8 MARKET PLACE (MARKALE)

9 NATIONAL LIBRARY

BOSNIAN HELD

PALE HELD

ONE MILE

ONE KILOMETER

D-DAY IN THE WARTIME of Sarajevo's daily paper, *Oslobodjenje,* arrived in late spring—May 14, 1992. It was the only day in the long siege of Sarajevo when the paper did not appear on the streets of Bosnia's capital. In their fiercest onslaught on the city, Serb paramilitary units, backed by the formidable arsenal of the Yugoslav National Army (JNA), had been attacking Sarajevo from all sides from the early morning hours. They hoped to conquer the city or cut it in half, so that they could lay claim to their exclusively "Serbian Sarajevo" which would be the entire left bank of the Miljacka River or the whole new section of town from Pofalići to the airport. From strategic locations in the hills encircling the city, every kind of artillery—mortars, tanks, cannons, anti-aircraft guns, rapid-firing multi-barrel rocket launchers—was targeting apartment buildings and residential areas, spreading terror and death.

For the first time since the early days of April 1992 when the siege of Sarajevo began, I was unable to leave my apartment in Hrasno. Together with my wife, Vesna, and our sons, Tarik, 18, and Mirza, 11, I had been forced to withdraw into the narrow hallway between the door into our apartment and the living room. The entire building shook with explosions. Deadly shrapnel was shattering every window in the apartment, bouncing directly into the cramped space where we had taken refuge. Shards of glass lay everywhere—in the kitchen, in the living room, in the bedrooms. We could hear the threatening whistle of mortar shells and the deafening detonations in the parking area in front of our building. At one point, I cautiously made my way over to the kitchen window to see what was happening in the neighborhood. Through the broken window, hiding behind the refrigerator, I could see a tank just a few meters to the right of a monument on the top of Vraca hill, the flash from its barrel and—in less than two seconds— a balcony on the neighboring Pere Kosorića Square disintegrating in a giant cloud of smoke and dust.

"They are aiming at people in their apartments!" I shouted.

Vesna and I watched that deadly ritual being repeated over and over again, unendingly: the flash of the tank's barrel, the crash of artillery as it ripped through concrete, the huge, dark hole in the neighboring high-rise where, until then, someone's home had been. We knew that each of those death-dealing shells could be aimed at our home, and that our lives, as well as the lives of all residents of Sarajevo on that day, and for hundreds of days that followed in the three-and-a-half years of the siege of Sarajevo, were simply mouthfuls for the insatiable appetite of these weapons. The merciless life-and-death game of "Serbian roulette" was only just beginning for the half million residents of the capital of Bosnia-Hercegovina.

When the artillery barrage let up a bit, either to let the barrels cool off or because those calling the shots thought that they had forced the defenders to take shelter and thus had "softened" the defense of Sarajevo, a fierce infantry attack began. At one point we could see the Serbian paramilitary "White Eagles," white ribbons tied around their heads or their sleeves, running through the children's playground in the midst of our buildings, crouching under the ground-floor balconies and shooting from there. It was the only time in many months of the Sarajevo siege that I seriously felt the danger that at any moment they might enter our building and pound on our doors, killing, raping, robbing, carting off to concentration camps those they encountered, as they had already done in their conduct of "ethnic cleansing" in the cities along the Drina river separating Bosnia from Serbia—in Zvornik, Bijeljina, Foča, Višegrad.

Without a word, I squeezed Vesna's hand, brushed my fingers through my sons' hair, and went to get the two pistols I had put away in a place out of the reach of the kids, hoping I would never have to use them. "You take the smaller one, the 7.65 mm; I'll take the 'Long Nine.' If they come, we'll shoot!" I told my older son, Tarik. We knew we did not stand a chance, that they would either kill us or take us prisoner, but we also knew that in the previous waves of "ethnic cleansing" those who were not willing or able to defend themselves had not been spared either. Fortunately, on that day we did not have to use the guns. Through our windows, we saw the reserve units of the Bosnian police from the neighboring police station arriving. They were taking positions behind the columns of the high-rise where the Nolitova bookstore was located. As they started shooting at the Eagles, the attackers let up on their firing, exchanged a few rounds, and then began to withdraw towards Hrasno Hill.

Over the following months of the siege, the Serbian forces attempted, often with tank reinforcement, to occupy the neighborhood. Almost every night I could hear the sounds of fierce infantry fighting and see the flashes of incendiary bullets and exploding shells aimed at the buildings, but I knew the young men from the neighborhood who had taken on the job of defending Hrasno, and was no longer worried. I knew that they were defending their own families and homes, and that they would fight to the death rather than yield. Therefore, even when worried friends and my own father urged me to move from Hrasno to a safer part of the city, I stayed on.

On that day, however, it appeared as though the world I knew would go up in flames—Vesna, my sons, the city I loved, and my newspaper to which I had come as a small-town cub reporter when I was a boy of sixteen.

Trapped by explosions all around us, for all practical purposes barricaded in our apartment, we heard the phone ring. It was my assistant, Zlatko Dizdarević, the editor on duty at *Oslobodjenje*. "Things are critical here!" Zlatko reported to me.

The building of *Oslobodjenje*, one of the most beautiful in prewar Sarajevo, was under relentless attack from Serbian artillery positions in Nedžarići, a settlement a bare 150 yards away. Only a flat area used for a basketball court and a few gardens that had just begun to turn green separated us from them. In spite of the firing coming from Nedžarići, the staff of *Oslobodjenje* carried on and had just finished their daily work on the newspaper when one of them shouted in disbelief: "Look, our guards are leaving!"

His eyes were not deceiving him. The guards there had met with their chief, Ilija Andrić, decided that with the few pistols, which was all they had, they would be unable to defend the building from the anticipated Serbian infantry attack, and had therefore prepared to withdraw. From the storeroom of the sales department, they had removed the big cardboard boxes packed with cigarettes, stuck them in the back of our Lada-Niva station wagon and, without any farewell, were taking off. They left the journalists and printing staff of *Oslobodjenje* in a completely undefended building located virtually on the front-line. Little did the Chetniks—the Serbian parmilitary forces—know that on that day they could have simply walked into the building they were so busy destroying! Unaware that it was completely unprotected, they continued to shoot at it from a "safe distance."

"The guards have run off, the printing staff also want to leave, and we can't finish the paper without them. So it seems that *Oslobod-jenje* won't be printed today," Zlatko said.

"Don't let them leave. Anyway, it's too dangerous to go out. I'll get in touch with Salko to make some emergency security arrange-ments. I am coming over and we'll get the paper out no matter what!" I said to Zlatko.

Salko Hasanefendić was *Oslobodjenje*'s general manager and also lived in my neighborhood of Hrasno, on the Pere Kosorića Square (now known by all Sarajevans as "Heroes' Square"). I called him and asked him to see if he could get the police, who were already defend-ing the Sarajevo Radio and Television station, to send a unit over to *Oslobodjenje*. Of course, we would pay them. We agreed that we would use his rented Volkswagen Golf (a few days later destroyed by a shell in front of his apartment building) and see if we could make it to *Oslobodjenje* without getting killed. We had also tracked down the manager of the printing section, Petar Skert, and his assistants, Rasim Rapa and Muamer Pašić, to figure out a way to continue to publish the paper. There were a number of ideas, including one of abandoning the front-line building and moving into the old printing offices in the center of the city, on Pavla Goranina Street.

"That wouldn't be good," I said. "If we abandon the building in Nedžarići, it will immediately be occupied, and then all our equipment will be stolen and carried off to Serbia or Montenegro. That's what happened with the printing plant in Cavtat (a town next to Dubrovnik) when the Yugoslav Army invaded." We agreed that instead of abandoning the building, we would get ourselves police protection and organize seven-day shifts for the journalists and printing staff. For the duration of their shift, they would stay at the offices and thus minimize the risk of getting killed coming to work and going home every day.

Within an hour or two of Zlatko's warning phone call, we had an editorial staff meeting in *Oslobodjenje*'s newsroom. I called together all the journalists who were still in the building and told them, "The city is having a horrible day. All of Sarajevo is under fire. We are in one of the most dangerous zones. But, as Editor-in-Chief, I want *Oslobodjenje* to continue to be published. I will stay here to work even if I have to do it alone, but the paper will come out. The manager and his deputy, Emir Hrustanović, and all the vital printing personnel will also stay. Those who want to leave, can leave. And for those who want to keep working, we have to finish today's paper."

No one wanted to leave. We finished the preparation of the paper, even though it was late, with reports from all the districts of the city where the Serbian offensive had run rampant. We decided not to print it that day, however, since—given the intensity of firing and shelling throughout Sarajevo—there was no way it could be sold on the deserted city streets. We would, instead, print it the next day with the double date of May 14 and 15, 1992.

Since then, we have not missed a single day, even when the entire *Oslobodjenje* building was set aflame and its destroyers—and most Sarajevans who still had electricity and could watch television—watched it burn through the night.

WHILE MAY 14 was the day the war, quite literally, came home to us, the paper had been confronted with many seemingly intractable problems much earlier. For instance, how does one get out a daily when for months not a single roll of newsprint had been allowed into the besieged city? The solution was to reduce the number of pages and number of copies, from the prewar 20 or 24 pages down to four or eight, and from the prewar circulation of 80,000 down to 12,000 copies. Later, as the quantity of paper began to run out, we were forced to print fewer and fewer copies: 7,000, then 5,000, then 3,500. At that point, the scarcity of the paper started to be a security problem in the city. People pushed and shoved, grabbed and sometimes even fought for their copy of the paper. For the citizens of Sarajevo, *Oslobodjenje* became a precious commodity. It was the only thing available for purchase every day, since the shelling of the bakery would often result in days going by with no bread. It was often the only source of news for weeks, because the city was without electricity, everyone's batteries were running low and there was no place to buy new ones; only a few could listen to the radio or watch the television by hooking up to automobile batteries. For some time, until it died, I was using the battery from my car, which itself had no other use since it had been irreparably damaged by shrapnel and bullets in the parking lot in front of my building. So *Oslobodjenje* remained for many long weeks and months the only source of news for the besieged capital. Sometimes the single copy of the paper was shared by five or ten or more families.

In Vratnik, a quarter of *Old Sarajevo,* the "real" value of wartime *Oslobodjenje* came to be established. A man set up business with a sign fastened to the fence behind him: "*Oslobodjenje* for rent. Price: one cigarette!" Beside him there stretched a line of people. They would make their payment, leaf through the paper, hand it back to him, and on it would go from one person to the next. "May I read today's paper tomorrow for one drag on a cigarette?" asked a passerby wanting to negotiate the price, presumably because his own supply of the "currency" was running low.

Because of the shortage of paper, by the end of 1992 we had changed the size of *Oslobodjenje* thirteen times, at times even printing on paper originally bought for textbooks. The paper also changed its color four times when we had to resort to paper originally bought for wall posters, so that we had editions in yellow, blue orange, and green tones. When the paper appeared with a greenish hue, Serbian-controlled media in Pale crowed in triumph: "*Oslobodjenje* has finally discovered its true color: that of Islamic fundamentalism!"

From the time the first shells exploded in Sarajevo we had not had any vehicles or drivers to distribute the paper through the town:

dozens of the vans and trucks with *Oslobodjenje*'s name on them were destroyed, burned or stolen. Besides, no driver was willing to risk his life to deliver the paper. There was not a single kiosk working. All of them were looted and burned. So the paper's journalists devised their own delivery system. They would arrive in two or three cars in the morning, load up with bundles of *Oslobodjenje,* and deliver them all over the city to colleagues who would sell the paper in the streets of their own neighborhoods.

Daily they would race through the increasingly dangerous intersections of Sarajevo. First they had to get past the notorious "Snipers' Nest" right next to *Oslobodjenje* in Nedžarići, then negotiate the perilous crossings at Dolac Malta and near Elektroprivreda, shooting galleries for Serbian snipers in high-rise buildings and Hrasno Hill who picked their targets at random. Countless cars were hit and had crashed and burned there. Beyond the snipers' intersections and into the center of town, the paper carriers would run into the ambush at Marshal Tito Barracks. The barracks were under the occupation of Yugoslav Army soldiers who would wage their war by shooting at passing cars. Nevertheless, our journalists took their chances. Fahro Memić was seriously injured on his delivery run. Dževad Tašić and Milan Borojević, on their "tour of duty" one day, saw the asphalt disintegrating behind their car on Kralja Tomislava Street, right in the middle of town—"ripped up like paper and rolled like a rug," they said—when it was hit by anti-aircraft guns. Thus was the paper distributed every day. All around the city, there was a network of reporters and editors of *Oslobodjenje* selling the paper in their neighborhoods: Dragan Stanojlović in Alipašino Polje, Slavko Šantić at Otoka, Zlatko Androk at Hrasno, Jovica Ajvazović at Marindvor, Ramo Kolar and Neven Kazazović from Baščaršija to the Cathedral, Duško Stajić along Marshal Tito Street, Miroslav Prstojević at Ciglane.

One morning I also took my turn selling *Oslobodjenje* in my neighborhood. The young fellow who normally sold the paper at the site of the burnt-out kiosk at Dolac Malta had not appeared that morning. From below my window I heard a car horn trying to get my attention.

"Chief, I don't know what to do. It's a nice day, people are gathered around to buy the paper, but the guy is not there today," Fahro shouted up to me when I looked out of the window.

"Don't worry. I'll come with you," I said, and headed downstairs.

He took me to the wrecked kiosk, left me with 800 copies of *Oslobodjenje* and headed off to continue the delivery of the paper to the others on his route who were waiting for him. Soon I was surrounded by a crowd of people. Many recognized me or knew who I was.

"Let me buy the paper from the Editor-in-Chief," said one of them, in great good humor. Soon I was joined by two editors from Television Sarajevo. Mladen Paunović and Konstantin Jovanović had come out for a walk, taking advantage of a brief respite in the shelling. Mladen, later wounded twice on the streets of Sarajevo, took to shouting, like some lively television advertisement, "O-slo-bo-dje-nje!," while Kosta was helping make change for the buyers.

"My dear comrades, I'd like all three of you to autograph my copy of the paper. It will be a document for the history of Bosnian journalism!" insisted our colleague from the neighborhood, the retired foreign news commentator from Television Sarajevo, Alija Nuhbegović.

I was giving autographs to some other "fans" when an Audi pulled up with a large "Press" sign on it. Michael Montgomery of the *Daily Telegraph* and Jonathan Landay of the *Christian Science Monitor* climbed out. "Congratulations," they said. "*Oslobodjenje* is a special war story and an inspiration to us all," added Jonathan. He had written a story for his paper with the title "Sarajevo Newspaper Keeps Presses Rolling Despite Sniper Fire." In less than an hour Mladen, Kosta, and I had sold all 800 copies and we headed off to a tiny bar at Dolac Malta. It was officially closed but, if one knocked, they would open the door. So we went in and had what was quite possibly the last cold beer of that spring in war-torn Sarajevo.

The next obstacle was the lack of communications. Sarajevo's main Post Office, one of the many impressive pieces of Austro-Hungarian heritage, was burned down at the beginning of May—together with most of the city's telephone lines—and by the summer of 1992 the entire city of Sarajevo had been cut off from telephone connections with the world. As a result our correspondents were no longer able to call us and file their stories. To keep the news flowing, we installed radio equipment both in our offices in Zagreb in Croatia, and in the basement of our building in Sarajevo. All our correspondents could send their reports to Zagreb, which would then be relayed with

the help of ham radio operators to Sarajevo. When there was no electricity, so that even the telephones within the city did not work, all the
reporters and photographers would bring their stories and pictures to
the rented offices of *Oslobodjenje* in the center of the city, and then one
of them, most often Vlado Mrkić, would take the copy and drive with
it through all the firing zones of Sarajevo to the beleaguered headquarters in Nedžarići.

Since May 14, when *Oslobodjenje* first came under Serbian fire,
the Nedžarići offices had been repeatedly attacked. On more than one
occasion, a tank had advanced across the intervening fields and fired
point-blank into our building; more than once the Chetniks set it on
fire. Finally, one, and later the other, of the ten-story-high twin towers
of *Oslobodjenje* collapsed into dust and ashes, leaving only the metal
elevator shaft as a monument to the barbaric nature of the Serb gunners. But we kept putting the paper out from our bomb shelter underground: instead of being stifled, *Oslobodjenje*'s voice became clearer
and louder and reached across greater and greater distances.

A question often asked by the foreign reporters who would come
to meet us and write about us was, why do the Serb forces so furiously
aim their guns at *Oslobodjenje?* "The Sarajevo Daily Miracle," announced
the front-page of the *Washington Post.* "Sarajevo Daily Defies the War"
reported the *New York Times.* "The Paper that Refused to Die" said the
European. "Blood in the Ink" was the headline in the *Guardian.*

The answer was fairly simple: *Oslobodjenje* was a symbol that
mocked the aims of the aggressors. In its pages and its editorial make-
up, it represented exactly that which they wished to destroy in Sarajevo:
the ideal of ethnic and religious tolerance and equality, the centuries-
old tradition and reality of a multicultural, cosmopolitan city where
Bosnians lived, loved, argued, and worked together as Bosnians. Muslims, Serbs, Croats, and Jews working on *Oslobodjenje*'s editorial staff
and writing in *Oslobodjenje*'s pages were the daily denial of the false
rationale behind the aggression: the impossibility of coexistence. *Oslobodjenje,* then, was anathema to the blood-and-soil Serb nationalists'
distorted vision of a world in which people were divided and set against
each other by their bloodlines.

For instance, I am a Bosnian who never felt comfortable being
squeezed into statistical census boxes, obliged by law to declare myself
first only as "Serb" or "Croat" or "undeclared," later as "Yugoslav," and,

THE TWIN TOWERS OF *OSLOBODJENJE* REMAINED STANDING DURING AN EARLIER ARTILLERY ATTACK. FOLLOWING THE USE OF INCENDIARY SHELLS, THE TOWERS BURNED AND THE BUILDING COLLAPSED.

since the constitutional change of 1971, as "Muslim." The latter category was no more satisfactory since many of us, our great respect and appreciation for the religion of our parents and our ancestors notwithstanding, considered ourselves secular and did not any more want to be defined by religion than by race. In the last few years as the old name "Bosniak" has been adopted as a category for the Muslims, I have come to wonder why we who do not have another country but Bosnia—whether we are Bosniaks, Croats, Serbs, or Jews—should not simply be identified as "Bosnians." My deputy editor, Gordana Knežević, was a Serb." Our columnist, Gojko Berić, also a Serb, has written perhaps the most subtle and insightful analyses of the roots and development of Serbian fascism. He was presented the Journalist of the Year in Bosnia-Hercegovina Award in 1993 and published a book, *Sarajevo at the End of the World,* which is a testimony to his own refusal to submit. What kept us together—"Bosniaks," "Serbs," "Croats"—in the midst of the life-threatening, soul-destroying horrors of the war was our sense of professionalism and a shared commitment to an open and pluralist society. "I'll keep on working at *Oslobodjenje* as long as I am free to write what I think and see, and you publish it!" was the straightforward statement made at an editorial board meeting by our best war reporter, Vlado Mrkić.

The majority of us never felt that what was coming down on our heads was a civil war between Muslims and Serbs. Rather it was a war against civilians, against all of our history, tradition, and culture in Sarajevo. When Serbian artillery from the surrounding hills targeted the apartment buildings and homes of Sarajevo, it was not merely killing the "Other" (the non-Serbs). Among the total of 10,609 citizens dead over the 43 months of the siege of Sarajevo, hundreds of those killed were Serb. Their crime, perhaps? That they were "disloyal" Serbs.

At *Oslobodjenje,* our greatest fear was that the Chetniks might make an infantry attack upon, and manage to occupy, the building. One day in the summer of 1992, during a Serbian offensive against the lines of defense at Stup, only a few hundred yards from our building, the on-duty editor, Midhat Plivčić, called me. "What do we do if they get into the building?" he asked. That prompted us to make further arrangements for the security of the building. The then commander of the First Corps of the Bosnian Army, Mustafa Hajrulahović Talijan, reassured me: "They cannot break through the line at Stup. We have got the best units positioned there."

Just in case, however, I asked Gordana Knežević to see if she could check with the commander of the French battalion at the Sarajevo Airport, Colonel Patrice Sartre, whether backup arrangements could be made for evacuation of our staff if a takeover by the Serbian forces became imminent. With his cooperation we planned that, in the event of a threatened invasion, the on-duty editor would call the colonel's office, which would then immediately dispatch an armored personnel carrier from the UNPROFOR headquarters in the former PTT Engineering building to evacuate *Oslobodjenje*'s staff. All of the editors for the seven-day rotations were made aware of this procedure, but, happily, we never had to make use of it. The city's defenders were always able to repulse Serbian attacks—and we continued publishing.

In those first months of the siege, my colleagues and I were so busy organizing the daily work of getting the next day's paper out that we could not afford to think about the dangers we faced at all times. Every day, usually accompanied by the newspaper's manager Salko Hasanefendić, I managed to go to our rented editorial offices in the center of town or to the already heavily damaged building in Nedžarići. At home, in the evenings, I would write a front-page summary of all the major events of the previous day to fax it across to the office before midnight. Nights, when the entire neighborhood shook from mortar-shell explosions, were also reserved for writing and for work on my *Letters from the War,* a series which ran in the pages of *Oslobodjenje.* I knew that my work at *Oslobodjenje* and what I wrote and said against the Serbian terror in the papers and on radio and television placed not only myself and my family in danger, but also made life more difficult for my mother and stepfather, Sena and Kemal Kolonić, who were living in Prijedor under Serbian occupation—and were eventually forced to leave and become refugees.

By then tens of thousands of innocent people had become the object of "ethnic cleansing" in the towns and countryside of Bosnia: they were being driven from their homes, tortured, and even liquidated. In the Prijedor region, my mother and the "Old Man" (as I call my stepfather), were among thousands of such victims. The entire Muslim intellectual elite of the town and hundreds of others were tortured and killed in the notorious Nazi-like concentration camps of Keraterm and Omarska. It was ironic that the chief of the Serbian police in Prijedor was Simo Drljača, my classmate in high school at Sanski Most. He was so proud of his accomplishments in the systematic "cleansing" of all non-Serbs from Prijedor that, in an interview with the local, Serbian-controlled paper *Kozarski vjesnik,* he took all the credit for atrocities committed there. "Serbian police acted according to my orders!" he said, and thus became well-known even to the UN's Commission of Experts on war crimes in former Yugoslavia. His statement was quoted in the Commission's final report which will be used by the War Crimes Tribunal in the Hague. In my book, *Letters from the War,* I addressed those former classmates of mine in Sanski Most and Prijedor, expressing my disbelief that they would be capable of approving, let alone participating in, such crimes. When I was writing *Letters* I could not yet know how horrible were the crimes they had already committed, but my worst fears were to be realized.

The battle to keep *Oslobodjenje* alive was thus fought at tremendous cost in pain, suffering, and lives. Five people from our staff were killed and more than 20 seriously wounded. Many lost their friends and loved ones but carried on. On the occasion of the first anniversary of the siege of Sarajevo, April 6, 1993, the French Rapporteurs sans Frontières organized the printing of a supplement of two pages of selected war stories from *Oslobodjenje* to appear in daily papers in thirty countries worldwide, with a total circulation of more than 17 million copies. And on September 16, on the occasion of the fiftieth anniversary of the first issue of *Oslobodjenje*, a similar insert was published in 82 daily papers, in a multitude of languages and alphabets, in all of the continents of the world, with a printing of 22.2 million copies. Thus for two days in 1993 *Oslobodjenje* had the signal honor of being the paper with the largest circulation in the world.*

The international weekly edition of *Oslobodjenje*—a selection of the most significant stories from our daily paper and published in Ljubljana, Slovenia—has been gaining an ever wider subscription list and circulation in cities around the world. I was pleasantly surprised when an old friend of mine, Hari Handanović, originally from Sanski Most, now an American citizen living in New York, asked me, "Shall we go and get the latest edition of *Oslobodjenje*?" He regularly picks it up on 42nd Street in Manhattan or in Astoria in Queens. Even greater was my surprise and pleasure when I discovered it among the foreign papers being sold at the Newsroom on Connecticut Avenue in Washington, D.C., and later at the "Out of Town Papers" kiosk in Harvard

---

* The international press that carried *Oslobodjenje* included the *Al-Ahram* in Egypt and the *Ha Aretz* in Israel, *Yomiuri Shimbun* in Japan and the *Guardian* in Great Britain, the *Dagens Nyheter* in Sweden and *Democrazia* in Bulgaria, *El Diario de Caracas* in Venezuela, *Frankfurter Rundschau* in Germany, *Gazeta Wyborcza* in Poland and *HetParool* in Holland, *La Libre Belgique* in Belgium and *Jornal de Brasil* in Brazil, *Le Parisien* and ten other papers in France, *Kinyamateka* in Rwanda, *La Nacion* in Chile, *L'Observateur* in Mali, *Milliyet* in Turkey, *Publico* in Portugal, *Times* of India and *The Jordan Times, To Vima* in Greece and *Zeri i Rimine* in Albania, *Lidove Noviny* in the Czech Republic and *Za Rubezhom* in Russia, as well as many others. Also included in this number were a few independent papers in the countries of the former Yugoslavia—among others, the weekly *Vreme* in Belgrade and *Monitor* in Podgorica, the capital of Montenegro, and *Feral Tribune* and *Novi list* in Croatia.

Square in Cambridge, Massachusetts. "We have won," I thought to myself upon finding the paper, which had been condemned to die, available for sale on newsstands so far from besieged Sarajevo.

By keeping *Oslobodjenje* alive in the years of the Serbian terror against Sarajevo, where our journalists, like everyone else, were being wounded and killed and the places where we lived were being destroyed and where death awaited us at every corner, I believe that we managed to demonstrate two things: first, that freedom of expression cannot be silenced by cannons and tanks; and second, that a centuries-old tradition and culture of tolerance in a multiethnic Bosnia cannot be erased even by a genocidal war.

And *Oslobodjenje* continues to prove this. Departing in March of 1994 on my new assignment as the paper's editor-correspondent for the United States, I did so with a feeling of pride for all the people with whom I had worked. I was honored to be a part of the group that gathered together on February 27, 1994, to vote in the selection of the new Editor-in-Chief, Mehmed Halilović. It was only then, as I said farewell to my dear and brave friends, that I took time to reflect on the years that we had lived through together. For me, the terrible period of the siege and destruction of Sarajevo and our joint battle to keep *Oslobodjenje* alive were only the finale of a hard, protracted battle as editor (1988–1994) to liberate a paper called the "Liberation."

The years at the turn of the decade, 1989–1990, had marked the struggle to wrest the paper from the control of the League of Communists and to make it into one which would express and cultivate political pluralism. In recognition of this transformation, *Oslobodjenje* was proclaimed "Newspaper of the Year" in the former Yugoslavia in 1989. Then followed the battle to defend this newly acquired independence against the ambitions and demands of the nationalist parties that came to power in 1991. And, finally, in the brutal war waged against Bosnia, we had to fight as never before to keep the presses rolling every day. These three battles—fought to take *Oslobodjenje* from the promises of communism to the reality of pluralism, to defend it against the threat of rising nationalism, and to secure its survival under the onslaught of Serbian fascism—are the subject of this book.

The story of *Oslobodjenje* is, above all, the story about the journalists and editors of the paper—Muslims, Serbs, Croats, and Jews—

who remained faithful to their profession and whose commitment to the tradition, culture, and ideals of a multiethnic and pluralist Bosnia-Hercegovina did not waver through the long years of terror and the destruction of their city and their country. Thus at one level, it is a painfully human story. A group of people in one of the most visible professions of all had to take positions on a daily basis on the issues of life and death affecting not only their readers, but their own families and neighbors, friends, and colleagues. Could you publicly denounce Serb or Croat terror while your wife or husband, parent or child, were in "enemy territory" controlled by those who had already tortured, raped, killed thousands of innocent people? If you were a Serb or a Croat denouncing your "own" people, were you prepared for the consequences? Or, if as a Muslim, you condemned acts of violence or revenge against innocent Serb and Croat civilians, could you contend with being branded a "traitor," recognizing that such a judgment might well equal a death sentence? The journalists of *Oslobodjenje* dealt with these very human dilemmas by defending Bosnia's tradition of tolerance no matter who threatened them: Serbian ultranationalists in their genocidal "ethnic cleansing" of territories for their "Greater Serbia," Croat ultranationalists in their equally vicious drive to create "Greater Croatia," or Muslim extremists trying to use the destruction of Bosnia as an excuse to create a smaller, Muslim, para-state of their own.

On another level, their story is purely professional: there is a war in your city, in your country, and what is a reporter to do but to report what he sees and experiences? Our journalists did exactly that, witnessing and reporting, distributing and selling their paper, even when the editorial offices were bombed and burned down, when they had to continue working from an underground atomic bomb shelter, producing the paper under artillery and sniper fire for three and a half years.

And, finally, this is also a story about the institution. *Oslobodjenje* started as the paper of the antifascist movement that fought the Nazis, the Croatian Ustashas, and the Serb Chetniks from the mountains of Bosnia in the Second World War. It was this liberation struggle in the forties which gave the paper its name—*Oslobodjenje* means "liberation." After the birth of modern Yugoslavia under the leadership of Josip Broz Tito, it became the leading Bosnian publishing house for more than five decades but also came under strict Communist control as did the rest of the media in the years of one-party rule. In a struggle for political pluralism and democracy in the late eighties, like all else in a society in transition, *Oslobodjenje* changed its ideological allegiances and its nature, but through all the years it remained true to the ideals of coexistence and equality among all the peoples of Bosnia-Hercegovina, their culture, traditions, and religions.

Three and a half years of war have changed a great deal. In Sarajevo alone, 10,609 people were killed under the Serbian siege. The Dayton peace agreement, based on the recognition of realities created by genocidal crimes through the ethnic partition of Bosnia into a Serbian "Republika Srpska" and a "Bosnian-Croat Federation" has rewarded the perpetrators of "ethnic cleansing" with territories and legitimacy. Even most of the staff of *Oslobodjenje* has changed, some of them escaping the terror or joining their families as refugees scattered across the world. But *Oslobodjenje*, as the title of this book—*As Long As Sarajevo Exists*—attests, continues to guard the flame for the united, multiethnic Bosnia which has been destroyed. It does so not in stubborn refusal to see the realities of partition but in deep understanding that for long-lasting peace and reconciliation in the country there has to be some justice. Dayton is not the road to justice, and therefore not the road to peace. The foundations of real peace will be established when the people of Bosnia, Muslims and Serbs and Croats, secure their freedom of movement and their right to return to the homes, villages, and towns from which they were expelled or compelled to leave. And justice will be seen to be done when those directly responsible for the genocide in Bosnia (such as the Serb political and military leaders Radovan Karadžić and Ratko Mladić and the Croat political leader Dario Kordić) are brought to trial, and when there is no amnesty for those who were equally, if not more, responsible in the higher reaches of Belgrade, Zagreb, and elsewhere.

In sum, here are the recollections of six years in the life of a journalist who happened to be the editor of a newspaper at the center of a whirlwind of historic changes, indescribable tragedies, and unique challenges.

CHAPTER ONE

Oslobodjenje's Liberation

I N THE SUMMER OF 1988 the winds of change blowing across Eastern Europe and post-Tito Yugoslavia had reached *Oslobodjenje*. The major daily newspaper of Bosnia-Hercegovina was to have a new editor-in-chief, and for the first time in its history, the Socialist Alliance, the "founder" of all the media in the country, had agreed that the appointment would be made on the basis of the democratically expressed choice of *Oslobodjenje*'s own journalists. Before then, the editor had always been appointed by the Party (the League of Communists) and was accountable to it. But that summer, as the term of the incumbent editor-in-chief, Ivica Mišić, neared its end, the paper's journalists held an editorial staff meeting at which they decided to inform the Presidency of the Socialist Alliance of Bosnia-Hercegovina that they themselves would choose their next editor and the choice of the candidates would be determined solely on the basis of clear professional criteria. The fact that the Socialist Alliance accepted the journalists' demand was a visible sign of the weakening of one-party rule in Bosnia and a rising respect for democratic public opinion among the largely reformed leadership of the Republic.

After a series of meetings in all departments of the paper at which journalists debated the criteria for the selection of a new editor and discussed the merits of the candidates suitable for the post, the editorial staff voted for two candidates—our correspondent in New York, Zoran Kurtović, and me. Both names were then sent up to the Presidency of the Socialist Alliance as "equally acceptable candidates." On the evening of December 12, 1988, the phone rang. It was Snežana Rakočevic-Novaković, a colleague at the paper. "Congratulations!" she said. "You've been chosen as the editor-in-chief." The Presidency had voted 21 to 4 to give me the job. I certainly would have been happier if the final decision had also been made by *Oslobodjenje*'s staff, but it was a beginning: no editor of the paper—or any other paper in communist Yugoslavia—had ever been appointed through a more democratic procedure. The news that *Oslobodjenje*'s editor had been chosen by secret ballot from the two candidates proposed by the paper's own journalists was announced that evening on radio and television and created quite a stir among the general public. This was an unprecedented development and, as telegrams hailing the "liberation of *Oslobodjenje*" poured in, it was clear that the prevailing perception was that the country and its media were moving towards greater political freedom.

ALL THE PARTY'S MEN

UNTIL YUGOSLAVIA ENTERED its period of political upheaval in the late eighties, the Socialist Alliance was a monolith that encompassed almost all of civil society. It served as a political umbrella for all other political groups in the one-party state: trade unions, youth organizations, World War II veterans, women's organizations and so forth. It was through the Socialist Alliance that the League of Communists maintained control and determined who would be in charge of all significant institutions in the economy, in politics, in education and health, and—especially—in the press. There it was essential that only "people who could be trusted" be placed in positions of power as directors and editors-in-chief and the job of these appointees was to ensure that no opinion that had not first been put on the agenda and filtered through the "front of organized socialist forces" (the Socialist Alliance) would appear in the media.

Within this overarching control of the Socialist Alliance, however, there was still some room for interesting and unpredictable developments. Tito's refusal to accept the dictates of Moscow and Stalin in 1948 made Yugoslavia a more liberal place than the Eastern European countries that were under the direct influence of the Soviet empire. As a result there were waves of reformist and hard-line communist tendencies which also were reflected in the ways in which the Socialist Alliance defined its criteria for the selection of the editors-in-chief. Once in a while it would appoint actual professionals to the position. But it was taken for granted that once appointed by the Socialist Alliance, the editor was responsible only to the Alliance and he was readily replaced if he showed the slightest bit of independence or if his decisions were ever defined more by his knowledge of the news and the interest and right of the public to know than by the expectations and orders of those who had appointed him. For this reason it was often the case that the turnover of the editors would be a direct expression of the struggle for power within the ruling party itself: the people at the top of the hierarchy would routinely replace the top editors appointed by others with their own men. We, the ordinary journalists, would usually learn about the change by reading our own newspaper. Apart from the utterly undemocratic nature of these appointments, what disturbed us most was the fact that virtually all the editors-in-chief appointed to our paper were brought in from the outside.

The last editor of *Oslobodjenje* chosen by the Socialist Alliance was Ivica Mišić, a former Radio Sarajevo journalist. I got the news of his appointment from the paper's stenographer while I was in Los Angeles covering the 1984 Olympic Games with my friend and colleague Branko Tomić. "Guess what?" the stenographer told us, "We have a new editor-in-chief and a new director!" From her we had learned that the Socialist Alliance had announced the appointment of Ivica and the League of Communists press officer Petar Jović, respectively, to the two positions. The news that the appointments had been dispensed from above was hardly surprising but even so we could not help feeling greatly dispirited. Not because of Ivica or Petar, whom we knew well—and Ivica was one of the best radio reporters and a friend of ours—but because we felt that *Oslobodjenje* was fated always to take its top people from outside.

The fact was that the government wanted the editor-in-chief and the director to be people who would be more concerned about the party line than about professionalism. All that mattered was that every day the paper report everything that had been said the previous day at important Party and state meetings—"even at greater length," as we wise-cracked in the editorial offices. I remember the many problems we had with Ivica Lovrić, the director of *Oslobodjenje* in the 1970s, who would go to various Party meetings in the Bosnian provinces and promise the local functionaries that *Oslobodjenje* would run their speeches in their entirety. Once our correspondent from Trebinje, Mustafa Arnautović, sent twenty pages of a speech by the mayor of that town with the message: "Director Lovrić was at this meeting and sends you instructions that this speech must be printed in full." At the time, I was the newsroom editor and decided that only a few lines from the speech merited any space. Lovrić let that demonstration of insubordination pass without comment. Next time, however, he was more adamant because the speech in question, delivered at yet another "historic meeting," belonged to a crony from his hometown in western Hercegovina, Ante Budimir, who was president of the Syndicate of Bosnia-Hercegovina.

"Comrade Kurspahić, I am sending you twenty-eight pages of Comrade Budimir's speech. Comrade Lovrić said that you will publish it in full," Budimir's chief of staff informed me over the phone.

"You send it and I will see how much of it we can use," I answered.

"But, I already told you, it has been agreed that it will be published in its entirety," she insisted.

"That would come to two full pages of the paper. I don't know what your president has said in that speech, but I do know that the entire thing cannot be printed," I said.

"Do you want me to tell Comrade Budimir that you said that you won't publish it?" she continued in a threatening tone.

"You tell him what I told you: you go ahead and send it and I will see what can be published."

Half an hour later, Lovrić called me into his office. "They tell me that you refuse to publish Budimir?" he said, as soon as I opened the door.

"I said that I would decide when I see the text," I answered.

"But," said Lovrić, "I told him that it would be published and there is a reason for that."

"Then find an editor who will do it for you," I replied and walked out of his office.

He did not call me again, probably because he was worried that if he did dismiss me, he would find himself in the awkward position of having to explain to his superiors in the Party why his hometown friend merited the privilege of such exclusive coverage in *Oslobodjenje*. I included as much as I felt compelled to in the light of the quantity of other news that day and took my chances.

Over the entire period of his tenure, Lovrić's primary concern was to get the political upper echelons of Bosnia-Hercegovina—their faces, their activities, and their pronouncements—prominent coverage on the front page. And he saw to it that they knew that he had personally arranged it all. In the end, unable to accept Lovrić's constant interference in editorial decisions, I left the position as newsroom editor. Later I learned from Bahrudin Bijedić, a cousin who worked with the police, that Lovrić had prepared and sent to the police an entire dossier about my impertinence. For the preparation of this dossier he had employed a few stool pigeons among the editorial staff who sent him slips of paper with reports of this nature: "Kemal Kurspahić said on Friday at 5:30 P.M. in the newsroom that *Oslobodjenje* cannot have either a high circulation or a decent reputation as long as the director continues to edit it along party lines."

When Lovrić was leaving the *Oslobodjenje* publishing house, Ljubiša Jakšić was appointed to the position of editor-in-chief. Lovrić's parting instructions to the new appointee, handed down as an order from the "higher offices" were as follows: "Replace all editors; all of them must be removed. They do not respect the Party!" And, indeed, Jakšić followed that advice to the letter. In 1978, he relieved all the editors of all the departments from their positions, replacing them with new people, many of whom had never had a single day's experience in a newspaper. A typical case was that of Ivica Češkić. Until then, that quiet and honest man was secretary in a Party commission for Bosnians and Hercegovinians working abroad which had been headed by Lovrić. He was now appointed editor for the international weekly edition of *Oslobodjenje*. For a few days he came to the offices, watched the staff at work, attentively observed the process of a mass of text and photographs from the newsroom being turned into a newspaper, and, respectfully, turned in his resignation. "I'm not cut out for this kind of work," he said, and left.

As editors came and went, the paper alternated between periods of dull obscurity and periods of liveliness, times of narrow limitations and times of greater freedom, phases of submissiveness and cynicism and phases of guarded optimism. During the years of complete Party control, editors would insist on optimistic titles and sunshine stories. Attending an editorial board meeting grappling with the next day's stories, *Oslobodjenje*'s highly respected film critic Aco Štaka was not able to contain his exasperation. "I wouldn't be surprised some day," he had said with biting sarcasm, "to see a banner headline in *Oslobodjenje*: 'A Great Fire Succeeds in Brčko!'" It was a telling commentary on the state of politics and journalism in the country. One after another, however, the other editors who had been brought in by Jakšić at the Party's behest also left, and *Oslobodjenje* eventually was to regain its professional climate.

From the time I was hired by *Oslobodjenje* on November 20, 1969, I had worked in various positions. As a small-town correspondent in Jajce, where I knew everyone and everyone knew me, the experience of reporting was an especially instructive one. The response from the readers—their reactions, comments, and criticism in our daily small-town encounters—was immediate and helped formulate a perspective very different from the one that is available in distant newsrooms. I also did my time as the sports correspondent in Belgrade, then the editor of the sports section, and, briefly, of the political section and the newsroom. My final two assignments, before assuming the position of editor-in-chief, were as *Oslobodjenje*'s correspondent in New York and then as deputy editor-in-chief. In all these years, I often found myself in the thankless position of a professional who had to do battle with one's own director and editor-in-chief on behalf of journalistic standards in the paper. It was not easy, for example, to convince Zdravko Ostojić, a former Party secretary from Mostar and director of *Oslobodjenje* from 1978 to 1982, that he could not suspend our longtime editor in Hercegovina, Mugdim Karabeg, simply because the powers-that-be at that time did not like his article on the electrical power industry in Ostojić's hometown. With deep sympathy I watched Ivica Mišić, appointed editor-in-chief in 1984, caught in his dilemma between his own professional instincts as an experienced and dedicated newsman of Radio Sarajevo and the demands and obligations placed upon him by the Party—which included his mandatory attendance at all Party meetings, from the district committee to the city committee, right up to the Central Committee of the League of Communists of Bosnia-Hercegovina!

The life of journalism was played out on two levels. The reporters attempted to adapt their talents and energies to the limitations of what was allowed, trying to cover Party and government actions and events as blandly and factually as possible. They sought refuge in some form of semiliterary reporting, the so-called "stories of everyday life," or in the coverage of news from abroad or working on the metropolitan, cultural, and sports sections, where one could write more freely than on the political pages. The editors, meanwhile, either blindly obeyed the orders of those who had appointed them or they attempted to define their job by the principles of their profession. The latter course was, needless to say, more hazardous, for while its pursuit gained them the sympathy and respect of the editorial staff, it also provoked more often than not the wrath of their superiors. Some of the "imported" editors and directors demonstrated a degree of respect for the profession. Some of them, like Mišić, even earned the trust and respect of their colleagues because of their honest human attitude and willingness to stand up for the journalists whenever they were confronted with problems from the local or even the state government. Others readily followed instructions from above and were ready to sacrifice to the last man every one of their staff writers in order to remain in the good graces of the Party. Still others preferred to leave rather than compromise their principles.

But for those of us who had risen through the ranks and spent our entire professional lives in *Oslobodjenje*, there came a point when Party dictates and its control of the paper had become utterly intolerable. Towards the end of the eighties, the dominant feeling among the journalists was that they could no longer continue to defend the paper against the actions of its own directors and editors-in-chief. There was a restlessness on the streets and in the newsrooms of Bosnia-Hercegovina, and, in defiance of the party line, the expression of a new political and critical awareness on the pages of *Oslobodjenje*.

POWER TO THE PAPER

IN THE LATE 1980s, politics in Bosnia-Hercegovina were in a state of tumult. The political leadership of the Republic was reeling from the impact of the Agrokomerc affair which erupted in the summer of 1987. In brief, it was revealed that the economic wonder of Velika Kladuša, a huge marketplace expansion of the agricultural industrial giant, Agrokomerc, had been founded upon unsupported promissory notes worth $865 million issued to 57 banks in four Yugoslav republics, which was an economic and political crime. The vice-president of the Presidency of Yugoslavia, Hamdija Pozderac, was forced to resign and soon thereafter died. It was claimed that he had used his high office to enable and cover up an illegal intrusion into the system of payments within the country by the biggest firm in his own region of Cazin Krajina. The director of Agrokomerc, the Party strong-man of the area, Fikret Abdić, was arrested and sentenced.* In the battles behind closed doors within the Party, a number of Party and state functionaries in Bosnia-Hercegovina were replaced.

According to some, the entire Agrokomerc affair was nothing more than a ruse on the part of the federal government—increasingly dominated by the the Serbs—to overthrow Pozderac, who, in the following year, would have assumed the office of the president of Yugoslavia's Presidency which was held by each of the republics in rotation. Pozderac had played a major role in writing the new federal constitution which was expected to determine the course the country

---

* Abdić, who for many years used to be the member of the Central Committee of the League of Communists and was the Party dictator in the region—deciding who would get the jobs, promotions and benefits—managed to make headlines on another three occasions in his quest for power. First, in the summer of 1990 when, returning from jail as a "victim of the previous regime" and thus a popular hero, he accepted Alija Izetbegović's invitation to join the Muslim political Party, SDA, and helped them to win in the elections. Abdić won more votes for the membership in the Republic's Presidency than Izetbegović but the latter became the president in accordance with agreements worked out within the SDA. Then, in the summer of 1993, when, encouraged by the European mediator in Bosnia, Lord Owen, Abdić proclaimed his own "West Bosnia Autonomous Province" in the Bihać region caus-ing the bloody fighting between Muslims loyal to their government in Sarajevo and those loyal to him. And finally, in the summer of 1994, when his forces were defeated and he escaped, as a traitor, to Serbian-controlled areas in neighboring Croatia.

would follow: along the totalitarian Communist-Nationalist route of Milošević and Belgrade or the democratic tendency which was especially evident in Slovenia but which was beginning to surface in the other republics as well. According to others, this was a scandal put out to settle intraparty accounts, such as could happen in any region or any of the republics. Still others claimed that it was indeed a great plundering of the coffers which put a serious and heavy burden upon Bosnia-Hercegovina and the entire country. Agrokomerc's actions, in their effect on the economy, were not very different from those of Serbia when it spent an enormous sum of money out of federal coffers. The major difference was that in the little town of Velika Kladuša, the theft was prosecuted, whereas in the case of Belgrade, no one was accused or removed from office.

Regardless of the factors behind it, the Agrokomerc affair spun out of the control of those who had set it in motion. In the process, not only was the vice-president of Yugoslavia deposed, but the Party itself was weakened as a consequence of the merciless infighting that erupted among and within the personalities and factions at the top in Bosnia-Hercegovina. In the exchange of accusations and counter-accusations and the settling of scores among those who had until then constituted the untouchable power structure, all of the dirty laundry of the system of government was brought out for all to see: the corruption and privileges of family members in the highest parts of the government; the misuse and misappropriation of government funds for purchase and upkeep of property and the construction of luxurious villas for Party officials at Neum, the only Bosnian town on the Adriatic coast; the use of cheap credit and other perks unavailable to ordinary mortals. With the fall of the powerful there ensued the collapse of entire sets of family members, favored friends, and charges promoted to various diplomatic, public, and official government positions. The strictly controlled pristine image of the faultless Party and its elect was tarnished beyond redemption.

The Agrocomerc affair acted as a catalyst, opening up fissures in the body politic of Bosnia-Hercegovina through which popular discontent, long suppressed, began to surface. On the ruins of the once powerful Party pyramid a new and different critical public opinion began to speak out. At first, simply following and reporting on the debate and the fighting within the ruling elite and then, step-by-step, encouraging open public discussion and conducting its own investigations, the Bosnian media had helped to weaken the Party's control. The lead was taken, interestingly but not surprisingly, by the youth of Bosnia. In their media, especially in the magazine *Naši dani,* and then in Valter and on their radio programs, discussions on the misuse of power by the apparatchiks in the Party and government became a regular feature. Shortly thereafter, the journalists of the strictly controlled daily media moved to extend the boundaries of freedom, converting *Oslobodjenje* as well as Radio and Television Sarajevo into organs of more authentic journalism, serving the interests of the public rather than its political elite.

Suddenly there was also a settling of accounts with those who had given journalism a bad name, who had sold their soul to the Party in exchange for sundry privileges. A typical and most obvious, although far from the only, example was the editor of Television Sarajevo, Smiljko Šagolj. Consistent and even enthusiastic in his service to the government, he had once announced: "I am proud that I got my apartment from my Party!" Šagolj never managed to move into that apartment in the elite Sarajevo residential area of Ciglane. He was removed from his editorial post in Television Sarajevo. And, subsequently, when it was announced that at one time he had used a picture of himself taken in front of a Sarajevo wall as the backdrop for his supposed report from the Berlin Wall, he was also removed from his position as the president of the Association of Journalists of Bosnia-Hercegovina. Šagolj later proved that he could be equally enthusiastic in his service to the nationalists as he was to the communists. After the three nationalistic parties won elections in 1990, he was considered the leading candidate of the Croatian Democratic Union to become the editor-in-chief or the general manager of Television Sarajevo. And when the war broke out he joined the television station at Široki Brijeg, run by Croatian extremists, spreading hatred among Bosnian Croats and Muslims.

When Šagolj resigned in 1987, the journalists of Bosnia-Hercegovina voted to elect me as the president of the Association. I was assuming my new responsibilities at a propitious time. With the Republic's power structure in crisis, and the Party's dominance challenged every day in the media, there were greater possibilities for the Association to change the crippling conditions under which Bosnia's journalists had been compelled to practice their profession. As the president of the Association, I was invited to attend the regular briefings for the editors and directors of the principal media which took place every Wednesday morning at the Socialist Alliance's building. With the collaboration of several colleagues, I worked to change the character of these meetings. Rather than silently suffer the weekly proclamation of advice or even orders, as to how we were to report the major political events of the week in the Republic, we began increasingly to speak up, asking difficult questions about the important issues of the day, seeking answers from the highest reaches of the Party hierarchy. Furthermore we asked that the Socialist Alliance meet its responsibilities as the official "founder" of most of the media and defend the professional rights of journalists wherever they were threatened. By taking the offensive at that critical juncture we succeeded in converting these briefings from just one more method of media control into a channel of communication which would, if anything, serve the interests of journalism and the public. Our efforts were helped by the support we received from the Republic government's Minister of Information, Mihajlo Djonović, and his assistant, Luka Popović. It was through them that we secured the right of the editorial staff to establish on its own terms the professional criteria for the selection of the editor-in-chief. This right was incorporated into the new law on the media adopted by the Bosnian parliament in the last years of one-party rule.

I recall, nonetheless, two attempts to put the newly and increasingly liberated press on political trial. The first was the attempt to silence *Naši dani*, the student magazine which had published a series of articles attacking corruption in high places in the Party. A meeting was called of the Advisory Board of the magazine. One of the Party's executive secretaries, Goran Kosorić, was sent with the Party's indictment—a long list of "mistakes" and "editorial blunders" committed by the paper. The Party wanted the editor, Zoran Milanović, replaced. As the president of the Association of Journalists, I was the first to take the floor, and on behalf of our organization, proceeded expansively to acknowledge the great debt of gratitude that was owed to the editors of *Naši dani*. They had set standards which we in the big media would do well to emulate: "We can learn from our young colleagues about the openness with which one can approach even the most sensitive of subjects." I was supported by the university professor, Dr. Zdravko Grebo.

He spoke of the significance of the student press in the awakening of critical public opinion in Bosnia-Hercegovina. The Party representative—when finally given the opportunity to speak—was almost apologetic as he urged that, "along with all the well-deserved praise" the editorial board also deserved "certain criticism." Of course, the Advisory Board supported the editor and that particular skirmish for freedom of the press was won.

The next attempt was to be directed at us at *Oslobodjenje*. In a last-ditch action to silence criticism and to contain the growing challenge to its own power, the Party dispatched a high-powered delegation to pay visits to the editorial boards of the Republic's media. This delegation included Gojko Ubiparip, a member of the Bosnian Presidency and the president of the Council for Protection of Constitutional Law and Order, Edina Rešidović, the president of the Socialist Alliance, and Zoran Udovičić, the Party Central Committee executive secretary in charge of the press. We were prepared in advance for the visit, having already heard that, the day before, Ubiparip had practically dictated to the editors at Radio and Television Sarajevo the rules of behavior "in a complex situation" in which "irresponsibility in the media" was the "threat to the foundations of the system." At *Oslobodjenje* we had deciphered those ponderous phrases as an announcement of the renewal of the Party's strict control over the media. In order to put the delegation on the defensive and preempt the issuance of Party diktat, we planned to seize the initiative from the beginning and define the terms of the discussion. We spoke of the role of the press in the democratic control of the government; of the right of the public to be informed about the government's actions; of the obligation of the holders of public office to be accountable to the public in whose name they professed to act. In the end, instead of giving a lecture on the "responsibilities of the press," our guests found themselves at the receiving end. It became abundantly clear to them that *Oslobodjenje* was no longer the paper whose abject loyalty they had taken for granted (lampooned and renamed in the past by critics as *MIM—Med i mlijeko* or "Milk and Honey"—for the rosy picture of the country it always painted). The Party could no longer depend on remote-controlled editors: its representatives had had to contend with an editorial staff of autonomous individuals who would not accept anyone lecturing them on how to do their job.

In sum, by challenging the power of the Party, Bosnia was joining Slovenia in setting a precedent for Yugoslavia in the media as in
other arenas of politics and culture. In those twilight years of the
League of Communists' power in post-Tito Yugoslavia, a fascinating
and ominous process was taking place. While in Sarajevo, for a long
time the stronghold of Party discipline, the Party was steadily losing
ground to a popular upsurge, in Belgrade—the country's capital—a
darker and more totalitarian phase was beginning. With the rise to
power of Slobodan Milošević in the League of Communists of Serbia,
Party control of the press in Belgrade became total. New editors were
appointed whose only responsibility was to promote "Serb unity" in
the face of the "Anti-Serb conspiracy" led by the Vatican (Catholicism),
Teheran (Islamic fundamentalism), Bonn and Washington (Western
imperialism). While in Belgrade the crackdown on dissent was harsh
and unyielding, and the space for any challenge to the reigning orthodoxy shrank daily, in Sarajevo the streets and public places were filled
with political and intellectual ferment, and the air was heady with the
promise of liberation. The city had become an arena for popular self-
expression. There was a blossoming of alternative music, theater, and
film; and there were open forums at which "forbidden" writers and
intellectuals from the other republics appeared and spoke freely. We
talked, argued, debated and, above all, held on to our gift of laughter.
In short, we celebrated the coming pluralism.

And thus it was at the end of 1988, on the expiration of
the four-year mandate of Ivica Mišić as editor-in-chief, that we at *Oslobodjenje* informed the Socialist Alliance that our editorial staff had
nominated candidates for the post based on the polling conducted at
candidate selection meetings held in all the departments and correspondents offices of the paper. Gone were the days when the journalists of *Oslobodjenje* waited with bated breath for the plume of white
smoke to lift from the building of the Socialist Alliance, as if from the
Vatican, to learn who in the Party's superior wisdom had been chosen
to run the paper. The new editor-in-chief would be someone who had
risen from the ranks within *Oslobodjenje* and who was the choice of its
own journalists.

Taking on the responsibilities of the editorship, I could not but
be cognizant of the burden placed upon my shoulders. To transform
Oslobodjenje into a paper that would be worthy of the respect of those

who worked for it and wrote for it and the public that read it was not a small undertaking. The knowledge, however, that I was accountable to no authorities outside but only to the readers and the journalists of the paper was the driving force behind all the later changes in *Oslobodjenje* and the prestige it came to acquire in Bosnia-Hercegovina and in the former Yugoslavia.

KEMAL'S WISH

THE DAY AFTER MY ELECTION, the editor of *Male novine*, Svetozar Malesev, came to visit. *Male novine* (Little Newspaper) was a magazine for children published by *Oslobodjenje* and was vastly popular all across Yugoslavia. Malesev had brought me an unusual gift: a yellowed clipping from a 1965 issue of the magazine with my picture taken at that time and the heading: "Kemal's Wish." "Do you remember this?" he asked me.

In the sixties he was a reporter for *Male novine* and, making the rounds of elementary schools in the little towns of Bosnia, writing about the promising young students he had met, he had run into me. I was fifteen years old, in the eighth grade at the Hasan Kikić School in Ljubija, near Prijedor, and had started the school newspaper *Odjek* (The Echo). Sveto asked me the usual question adults ask children: "What do you want to be when you grow up?" "A journalist," was my answer.

"Well now, you see, you are the editor-in-chief and I am very happy that your wish has come true," he said.

I had, in fact, chosen journalism as my vocation much earlier, and all because of a horseback riding accident. In Sanski Most, as a boy of six or seven, I had gone riding without permission and fell and injured my right hip. When I got home I said nothing about it because I was afraid that I would never be allowed to go riding again. As a consequence, my hip developed a severe infection which eventually led to tuberculosis of the bone, and my mother and I went from hospital to hospital until we finally ended up at Rovinj, on the beautiful Istrian Peninsula on Croatia's Adriatic coast. There I remained in the hospital, most of the time immobilized in a cast, for a full five years. My mother was a school teacher, and she worked with other parents of the children at the hospital to organize a school. Thus, confined to a hospital bed, I got my first five years of elementary school education. At the same time I fell in love with two things: soccer and journalism. For a child who thought he would be forever bedridden with a cast on his leg, soccer was magical, a feast of unimpeded movement so far removed from his own cramped, immobilized world. I especially loved to listen to the radio broadcasts of the soccer matches, and imagined how wonderful life must be for a sports announcer like Mladen Delić of Radio Zagreb, constantly on the move, reporting one week from one city and the next week from another, describing the atmosphere and excitement of such events as the soccer match between Yugoslavia and Italy in 1956, where my team won by a score of 6 to 1, and my favorite player, Miloš Milutinović of the Belgrade Partizan, scored two goals. It was sometime just after that game that Delić visited our school at the hospital at the invitation of the principal, who happened to be my mother. Awestruck, I listened to his stories of the great sports events which he had attended, and after that I read and reread the book he gave me, entitled *The Unbeatable Smilies,* and decided that I would "be a reporter, like Mladen Delić."

After I left the hospital I went to visit my father Sulejman in Sarajevo. He and my mother had divorced when I was three. My father showed me around Sarajevo. After five years in a hospital room, experiencing Sarajevo was like moving through a dream. The enchantment stayed with me as we went on an outing to Vrelo Bosne, the source of the river Bosnia, at Ilidža on the outskirts of the city, and led to my first piece of writing. I wrote about the beauty of the streams of water welling up from under the mountain, and sent it to the editor of the Radio Zagreb program, "Good Morning, Children." I can still remember the wonder and excitement of hearing my name and listening to the reading of my story on the radio.

After that brief sojourn with my father, I returned to live with my mother and my stepfather, Kemal Kolonić, in Ljubija, and began writing for the regional and children's newspapers, and was the happy recipient of a prize for my editing of the school newspaper, *Odjek*. In the fall of 1962, at high school in Sanski Most, and not quite sixteen, I became a stringer correspondent for *Oslobodjenje*. In a hurry and anxious to become a professional journalist, especially since I was already supporting myself on the income from my reporting, I completed the final two grades of high school in one year. Moving to study law at

Belgrade University, I was constantly looking for reporting assignments. And so it happened, one day, sitting in my dormitory working
on a piece on my old typewriter, I caught the attention of my older
roommate, Djordjije Vuković.

"What are you doing, freshman?" he asked me.

"Writing," I said.

"I mean, what are you writing?"

"An article for Borba," I answered. I was really writing for the
sports pages of that daily and Djordjije was curious to read my piece.

"It's good. You could even join us at The Student," he told me,
explaining that he and our other roommate, Rade Kuzmanović, were
the editors of the university's weekly magazine.

"I would, but only if you pay for what I write," I answered,
explaining that for me writing was the way to support my studies. Not
long after that I became one of The Student's editors. It was the late sixties and a time of great political ferment in European universities and
in Yugoslavia. The Student was a paper of left politics at the University
and a central player in the student uprisings of 1968. As a member of
the editorial board, I lived through that dramatic summer of student
demonstrations against the "red bourgeoisie" and the privileges of
those in power; the state's brutal response; the seizure of two issues of
The Student that had criticized police brutality; and our continued
defiance (we had proceeded to publish a report—which I wrote—on
the assault on The Student).

But the sixties passed and the world remained essentially the
same. In November 1969 I got the job of sports correspondent for
Oslobodjenje in Belgrade, doing what I had once dreamed about as a
child in Rovinj hospital: reporting on sports events in Yugoslavia and
covering international events such as the Olympic Games and the Soccer World Cup in Germany. On one occasion, at a dinner attended by
reporters covering the Winter Olympics at Lake Placid in 1980, I found
myself sitting next to my childhood hero, Mladen Delić. "You should
know that it's all your fault that I am here now," I told him and went
on to explain how his hospital visit more than a quarter of a century
earlier had been decisive in making me who I was—a reporter. That
long trajectory had brought me in 1988—when the country stood at
the threshold or precipice of convulsive change—to the post of the
editor-in-chief of the leading daily in Bosnia-Hercegovina.

CHANGE AT *OSLOBODJENJE*

ON MY FIRST DAY AS EDITOR-in-chief in late December we got down to work, introducing changes to the paper. I did not have my predecessors' problem for they had usually come with instructions to replace or appoint particular individuals favored by the Socialist Alliance. I knew everyone and I knew their abilities.

"Starting tomorrow," I said, "on the front-page of every issue, in the lower left hand corner, we will have a column entitled: 'In Focus', with commentary on the major event of the day."

Ivica Mišić, who had turned the job over to me that day, was a bit apprehensive:

"Do you think you'll be able to do it every day?" he asked, reminding me that the folks at *Oslobodjenje* had not developed the reflex of reacting and commenting upon events within a day of their occurrence, and that those who had demonstrated the ability were often pushed aside.

I knew that there were a number of journalists with great professional skills on the editorial board, and the fact that *Oslobodjenje* did not carry their opinion was not their fault. The absence of any commentary was a subtle form of Party censorship. In newspapers in Yugoslavia there were no regular op-ed pages, nor space for the exchange of opinions or any genuine debate on important issues. "Don't make waves," was the rule which journalists had to follow both in the press and on radio and television. Silent self-censorship was the norm. They did not write opinion pieces because they knew there was no space for them, and editors did not ask for them. There was greater freedom and display of creativity in the departments which were not under the direct supervision of the government: news from the outside world, arts, music and culture, sports, and metro pages—yet even then, there were limits. One could not, for example, criticize the local soccer club if there were powerful Party members who were on the presidency. The director or the editor-in-chief, overwhelmed with worry about his Party mandate, would begin to ask whether a particular journalist who had taken liberties might possibly be "influenced," what the "forces" were which were standing behind him, and why he was provoking "discontent among the people."

The purpose of the "In Focus" column, therefore, was to break the silence. It was authored not only by writers on the editorial board but, depending upon the events of the day, the column represented some of the most respected, independent voices in politics and among intellectuals, artists, and scientists. Thus, on the day of the premiere of the film, *The Time of the Gypsies,* the author of the column was the director, Emir Kusturica. And when the Central Committee of the League of Communists of Yugoslavia convened yet another of its many "historic meetings," the president of the Bosnia-Hercegovina's reform-oriented Party of Democratic Change, Nijaz Duraković, wrote the column presenting his own critical and independent left perspective. From the editorial board the most frequent contributors to the column included: Zlatko Dizdarević, Ljiljana Smajlović, Miroslav Janković, Hamza Bakšić, Slavko Šantić, Branislav Boškov and myself. The team was noticeably strengthened with the arrival of Vlastimir Mijović, formerly the editor of the Belgrade youth paper, *Mladost.* His reputation as an "inconvenience" in the political circles of Belgrade because of his opposition to Serbian nationalism had preceded him. In Sarajevo, too, he had earned the displeasure of the powerful because of his critical writings. As one of the best editorial commentators, Mijović was an invaluable asset to our paper.

In opening its pages to a diversity of opinion, *Oslobodjenje* was becoming an active participant in the struggle for democratic, pluralist politics, and it had an editorial team able to meet the challenge. Most of my closest associates had extensive international experience. Our first deputy editor, Drago Soldo, had worked for eight years as the correspondent in Moscow; the second deputy editor, Zoran Kurtović, had just returned from a four-year stint as the correspondent in New York; the editor of the political section, Ljiljana Smajlović, had spent several months working for the *Plain Dealer* in Cleveland and was fluent in English and French; the editors of the foreign affairs section, Mehmed Halilović and then Mile Duvnjak, had been correspondents in Cairo and in Bonn; the editor of *Nedjelja,* Zlatko Dizdarević, had been a correspondent in Cairo; and I had, among other assignments, spent four years as correspondent in New York. The contributions of this team were very significant in the development of liberal, independent, non-partisan positions at the paper.

"I would not exchange the top ten writers at *Oslobodjenje* for the top ten at any other newspaper in Yugoslavia," I had said repeatedly when asked about the changes that we were introducing to the paper. Quite apart from the regular writers for the "In Focus" column, there was Gojko Berić, a top-notch professional, who wrote some of the best pieces in *Oslobodjenje*. His work included several in-depth interviews recording the testimony of people who were important witnesses of Yugoslavia's history, as well as a series of portraits of ordinary men and women talking about their world as they had experienced it. In addition, he was a skilled commentator whose pieces, while taking up little space, contained the complexity of thought of a great essayist. He had never had the good fortune of working with editors who respected his perfectionism and recognized his value as the leading writer in the paper. Then there were a number of younger writers who had already developed a recognizable style. Furthermore, *Oslobodjenje* was in the enviable position of boasting of the best team of cartoonists in all of the Yugoslav press.

In addition to the commentary on the front page, we also decided to introduce regular columns on the second page. Thus Hamza Bakšić wrote "The End of the Century," Gojko Berić, "Here and Now," Slavko Šantić, "Controversial Things," and Slobodan Lovrenović, "For and Against." Periodically, we would have guest columnists contributing to the page, such as Goran Milić, the most prominent television journalist in Yugoslavia, writing "The Journal" and Aleksandar Tijanić, a highly controversial Belgrade columnist, writing his "Political Zoology." There were other guest authors whose writings appeared in *Oslobodjenje*'s political weekly, *Nedjelja*, edited by Zlatko Dizdarević. When *Nedjelja* became a separate publication, it was replaced in *Oslobodjenje* by the Sunday supplement *7 Days* which was edited by Rasim Ćerimagić. That addition to the paper, containing regular contributions by some of the best journalists, scholars, and writers in Yugoslavia—Goran Milić, Bogdan Tirnanić, Vladimir Gligorov, Vlado Goati, Žarko Puhovski, and Abdulah Sidran—and was given the highest rating in the first annual survey of *Oslobodjenje*'s readers.

There were, of course, changes not only on other pages of the paper but in the paper's perspective on news and opinion. I was determined that *Oslobodjenje* would have a genuinely "Yugoslav" orientation.

I use the term advisedly, knowing full well that those who are allergic to every mention of the word "Yugoslav," especially after the bloody collapse of Yugoslavia, will immediately seize upon it: "Yes, it's just as we thought! *Oslobodjenje* was always the nest of Yugo-unitarism." However, that is not what I am talking about. The "Yugoslav" orientation in the meaning of the expression that I was giving to it, and how it was shaped and presented on the pages of *Oslobodjenje*, meant something altogether different. It was a concept, until then, almost entirely foreign to a media which was rapidly succumbing to nationalist euphoria and, without exception, uncritically supporting everything that "their" party or political leaders did or said and equally unreservedly attacking everyone else. My objective was to distance *Oslobodjenje* from this "new" breed of journalism and insist on as cold, objective, and professional a presentation of information as possible about everything that was happening in whatever part of the still-existing federation. In *Oslobodjenje*, I wanted the reader to be able to find out what was actually taking place and what those "others" were thinking and saying, separate from our commentary and various opinions on the subject, appearing in our op-ed columns. This meant the free flow of news, ideas, arguments, and even polemics.

Oslobodjenje's new editorial policy meant a reprieve, for instance, for someone like Zoran Odić, our correspondent in Slovenia. In the times of strict Party discipline, he was expected to present more commentary and judgment than facts about "that Slovenian liberalism" which was anathema to the Party. Now he was able simply to report on what was going on in Slovenia without having to lace his stories with attacks on the political events he was reporting. Unlike most of the other daily papers, *Oslobodjenje* no longer considered it to be the responsibility of the paper to represent, defend, or promote any particular republic or its politics, nor to represent any individual, but rather it was our job, just as it was the job of any sufficiently free newspaper anywhere in the world, simply to report. And of course, it was also perfectly within our rights to present our own position in commentary.

The change at *Oslobodjenje* was especially difficult to come to terms with for the politicians of Bosnia-Hercegovina who had taken it for granted that they would be beyond criticism, at least, in "their own" newspapers. When, for instance, the Party's Central Committee for the Republic presented its list of candidates for the highest positions in the government, *Oslobodjenje* promptly printed a commentary calling it one more step along the way to political suicide for the Party, because—instead of proposing new, educated, reform-minded, and respected persons—the Party's list had been drawn from the dregs of the same barrel of political thinking. Similarly, now it was no longer unusual to read, in the same issue of the paper, the news that the Committee had taken "ideological-political measures" in the form of various reprimands for the misuse of the state's funds and property, and an accompanying commentary stating that these measures were not appropriate punishment for being caught in the act of theft and that the top Party members were out of touch with public opinion on this matter. In addition, high officials of the Republic could read in *Oslobodjenje* the complete account of the privileges they had abused in the construction of vacation homes on the Adriatic coast. While former editors of *Oslobodjenje* always feared calls by the high officials, knowing that they would be taken to task for omitting "the most crucial" part of their speeches or because their pronouncements were not given "the proper space and place" (meaning that they were not published verbatim, and on the front page), my conversations with them were of a different nature. They would now ask to meet the journalist who had written a particular story and would offer files with the documents and receipts which were supposed to prove that we had gotten it wrong. But, most often, we proved to be right.

A change especially popular among the readers was the "Tribunal"—an entire page devoted to their letters. In the past, "letters from our readers," had never been anything more significant, interesting, or controversial than remarks about community services or the conduct of the streetcar conductors. The "Tribunal" opened up space for dialogue and debate on the most significant topics of the time: the readers freely voiced their opinions on politicians and their privileges, disputed the views expressed in the Central Committee and the Assembly, often criticized the views of the journalists of the paper, and wrote about the most sensitive political issues. Often discussions which unfolded on the pages of the "Tribunal" would stretch out into long and fascinating debates, leading to the inclusion of explanations by those holding political office of their own involvement in such affairs as Agrokomerc, Neum, or other areas of the Party or government's misconduct or misrule. On some occasions, even the presidents of the Presidency of Yugoslavia—first, Janez Drnovšek from Slovenia, and later Raif Dizdarević from Bosnia-Hercegovina as well as federal Prime Minister Branko Mikulić—wrote in response to a reader's letters and were published on *Oslobodjenje*'s "Tribunal" page like any other citizen. In other words, this became one of the most well-read pages of the newspaper, open to everyone and to all sorts of views. Open social criticism was limited only by one condition: that the identity of the author of the letter could be confirmed and that his name and address were known to the editorial board.

The liberal editorial concept of *Oslobodjenje* was also evident at the time in the space the paper reserved for views from other parts of Yugoslavia. We introduced a daily column entitled "YU-PRESS," in which we carried the most interesting stories and commentaries from other papers, and the "YU-Journal," which appeared every Monday on page two and which was written for *Oslobodjenje* by some of the best known television journalists from all republics and provinces. Although the readers often complained of individual controversial pieces by certain authors, that page was an authentic reflection of the country as it was confronting its disintegration. It expressed all the deep differences and political faultlines in Yugoslavia. Essentially, it enabled the reader of *Oslobodjenje* to get a realistic picture of the events of the week around the entire country, each from an individual point of view.

The readers readily welcomed the changes at *Oslobodjenje* and gladly accepted its openness to the expression of various and often opposing opinions and points of view. I knew this not only from their numerous letters of support for the new liberal concept of the paper but also from many comments expressed in person by people I ran into on the streets. We promoted and verified the acceptance and awareness of these innovations by organizing forums entitled "Speaking Openly about *Oslobodjenje*" in many of the cities and towns around Bosnia-Hercegovina. Together with several of our best known authors and well respected guests and editors, I visited Tuzla, Banja Luka, Mostar, Čapljina, Zenica, Travnik, and, of course, we also held meetings with the public in Sarajevo. These appearances were an opportunity for long, open, often lively and heated discussions on *Oslobodjenje* and on individual authors or stories published in *Oslobodjenje,* as well as on a wide range of political and economic topics. Such direct exchanges with the readers who always showed up in large numbers were an invaluable source of inspiration for us. Not only did these meetings encourage us to stay the course, but also provided ideas for new subjects, articles or columns. They helped us to focus on the central issues in the towns and regions we visited away from Sarajevo. In addition, they contributed to the popularity of *Oslobodjenje*. In my view so important were these public discussions to the growth and continued progress of the paper that I found myself working almost round-the-clock. Very often, I would finish the front page at the newsroom at five or six in the evening, then drive to a gathering one, two, or even three hours from Sarajevo, spend the evening meeting and talking with our readers and our correspondents, return home well after midnight, and be back in the office in the morning—and so it went, for a whole year.

A very significant event publicly affirming the new independence of the paper came in the form of the "Kecmanović Affair" in the spring of 1989. This was in connection with the election in Bosnia-Hercegovina of the Republic's member in the Presidency of Yugoslavia, the highest representative of the Republic in the federal government in Belgrade. To the great consternation of the Party which usually decided on suitable candidates for the office, a university professor, the Dean of the School of Political Science in Sarajevo, Dr. Nenad Kecmanović, emerged as a serious contender. Coming as an "outsider," and therefore not compromised by membership in the "insider" group, he received the largest show of support from various regional "consultative assemblies." Then, as a complete surprise, immediately prior to the elections, there came the brief announcement from the closed session of the Republic's Conference of the Socialist Alliance: "Kecmanović is dropping out of the race because he has made a political evaluation that there are good reasons for doing so." And that was all!

The media were asked not to probe any further into the matter, the strictly confidential "state secret" stamp was slapped onto the Kecmanović dossier, and the entire city of Sarajevo was abuzz with the rumor that the professor had been accused of spying. We, of course, were not willing to accept that the withdrawal of a major candidate for the Presidency could be explained away just by a single vacuous sentence and therefore I called Kecmanović and offered to publish his reasons in *Oslobodjenje*. He declined, however, partly because he could not believe that we would be able to print his statement in *Oslobodjenje*, and also because he was scared by the charges of spying that had been leveled against him. Instead, he decided to publish his explanation in *Borba* in Belgrade stating that he had withdrawn his candidacy because of the false accusations made against him and under pressure from the people in power. In his statement, Kecmanović also expressed his gratitude for my interest and readiness to publish his version in spite of the "state secret" label.

At the conference of the Socialist Alliance which was held to discuss the affair, and which was broadcast on television, Muhamed Berberović, a member of the Republic Presidency and president of the Council for the Protection of Constitutional Law and Order, criticized the press for having placed itself "on the side of Nenad Kecmanović." As president of the Association of Journalists, I stood up to confront him publicly. "The press did not put itself on the side of Kecmanović," I replied, "but rather on the side of democratic public opinion and the public's right to know why the leading candidate for the country's Presidency is withdrawing his candidacy. Such matters cannot be conducted behind the backs of the public, and it is our professional responsibility, on behalf of the public, to put forward all the questions they have."

During the recess, Berberović came up to me and, as if he was delivering some serious accusation or incontrovertible proof of our "agitation on behalf of Kecmanović," stated in the presence of several other members of the political leadership, "We know more. We know that you personally sent a message behind our back to Stane Dolanc requesting that he give you his explanation of the situation."

"Well, that again is the perfectly natural thing for an editor-in-chief confronted with the 'state secret' label to do," I responded. "You have claimed that this secret may not be revealed in Bosnia-Hercegovina without the consent of the highest Yugoslav government authorities, and since Dolanc is the president of the federal Council for the Protection of Constitutional Law and Order, what could be more normal than to ask him for confirmation as to whether the highest government authorities are aware of what Kecmanović has done, and what kind of violation it might be?"

It is important to realize, as I pointed out in my "In Focus" comment on this matter, that Kecmanović as an individual was almost irrelevant. What was at stake was the defense of the right of the public to know what the government was doing by taking refuge behind this "state secret" stamp. The entire incident, thanks to the decisive stand taken by the press, contributed to ensuring that the final appointment to the position would be made through a procedure hitherto unknown in Yugoslavia: by the general secret ballot among a choice of five candidates—all of them Serb since, according to the "ethnic key," Bosnia's next representative on the Presidency had to be a Serb—and the winner was a politician from the younger generation, Bogić Bogićević.

It needs to be said that Bogićević happened to be much better choice for Bosnia than Kecmanović. As a Bosnian Serb, he was the key factor in preventing Serbian nationalists from putting the stamp of the federal Presidency and, hence, the stamp of legality, on their attempts to impose military rule across the whole country and thus to suppress the movement for autonomy in different republics. With the appointment of loyal "representatives" from Serbia, Montenegro, Kosovo, and Vojvodina to the Presidency, Milošević had automatically four votes for any decision and he needed just one more for a majority. Bogićević proved to be more loyal to his Bosnian voters, citizens of the Republic who elected him to the Presidency, than to the war cries for "Serbian unity." On the other hand, Kecmanović, even after having accepted a place on the new Bosnian Presidency in the spring of 1992, decided to leave the country in the first summer of Serbian aggression.

In 1989, within a year of assuming my new responsibilities at *Oslobodjenje*, we had covered a great distance. There could not be a more fitting tribute to our journey towards independence than the one paid to us by the professional journalists of Yugoslavia who, in an annual poll organized by the daily *Slobodna Dalmacjia*, voted to proclaim "the paper of the Socialist Alliance of Bosnia-Hercegovina," *Oslobodjenje*, the "Newspaper of the Year." In explaining the reasons for honoring us thus, *Slobodna Dalmacjia*—itself an independent iconoclastic daily from Split, Croatia—cited *Oslobodjenje*'s "exceptional effort to change and to overcome its own nature (which is, for newspapers, as it is for people, a most difficult thing to do)." It continued:

> Today, without any doubt, *Oslobodjenje* is a newspaper in the real sense of the word, and even—according to the poll taken by *Slobodna Dalmacija*—in the year of 1989 the best one in Yugoslavia! . . .

In this last year *Oslobodjenje* has been the one newspaper which, in the face of multiple and conflicting interests and attitudes (including extremely bureaucratic and undemocratic ones), has suffered least from the uncritical love of "its own" and rejection of "outsiders" or "others"; it honestly informed its readers of what was happening and then gave its commentary. Conscientiously, professionally, and politically it stood its ground and took the risk of being accused, both "outside" and "within" its own territory, of serving as "the blind instrument and weapon of enemy forces," precisely because it has made room for democracy, not mincing words in its pronunciation of the truth and the drawing of conclusions. . . .

The pages of *Oslobodjenje*, and especially the weekly supplement, *Nedjelja*, from one issue to the next, have appeared as an exceptional journalistic phenomenon, in which authors from their own team and from throughout Yugoslavia, with a tone of unusual and unreserved editorial openness, have affirmed their professional . . . and analytical qualities.

Therefore, for those of us evaluating and choosing the best, our task was perhaps quite simple. It was simply a matter of recognizing which newspaper . . . successfully attained the essence of its name. In other words: *Oslobodjenje*—Liberation.

This recognition was all the more significant in that *Slobodna Dalmacija* did not hand out the title easily. In 1987 it had been awarded to *Borba* at the time when it was under the editorship of Stanislav Staša Marinković. In its opposition to the ideological totalitarianism which had come to dominate the Belgrade media following the ascent of Milošević, *Borba* was a lonely oasis of dissent. In 1988, no paper was found deserving of the award. In 1989, it was awarded to *Oslobodjenje*. In 1990, again, none passed the test.

My favorite compliment for our work at *Oslobodjenje*, however, came from the author, Abdulah Sidran. At the end of 1989, he was speaking at a ceremony at which Emir Kusturica was being presented the award for the best film of the year (for whom Sidran had written his finest screenplays). "Joking with Adil Hajrić, my childhood friend who is now an editor at *Oslobodjenje*," he recalled, "I used to say, 'Adil, somehow *Oslobodjenje* looks worse to me.' And he would ask, 'Since when?' And I would say, 'Oh, for the last forty years or so.' Now, I'm glad to say that *Oslobodjenje* has begun to live up to its name."

COMRADE TITO, (WITH RESPECT)
FAREWELL

AT THE BEGINNING OF THE NEW YEAR, I had made up my mind: it was time for *Oslobodjenje* to signal its decisive break with the past. The highest professional recognition that had been conferred on the paper at year's end, no doubt, contributed to the decision. Starting with its first issue of 1990, *Oslobodjenje* would dispense with the ubiquitous oath of loyalty to Tito that appeared daily at the top of the front page. It was a symbolic gesture, but symbols, as we know, can be invested with a great deal of power and meaning.

The oath—"Comrade Tito, we pledge ourselves to you"—was taken from a song-poem that had had tremendous resonance in Yugoslavia—a promise to Tito, after his death in 1980, that his people would continue to follow his path. Even in Belgrade, (where a few years later Serbian ultranationalist Vojislav Šešelj and his followers would threaten to dig up Tito from his grave and carve him up into eight pieces "so that every republic and province can have their part") tens of thousands of people had waited in lines to visit his grave and pay their respect to the late Marshal. It was at the time of Tito's death that someone decided to put that slogan on the header of the front page of *Oslobodjenje*. After I became editor-in-chief I still had Tito's picture in my office and I would explain to curious foreign journalists and visitors who commented on it: "It was here when I entered the office and I see no reason to remove it. Tito is part of our history."

But I did not like the slogan. Even liberated *Oslobodjenje* with that ideological symbol looked more like Moscow's *Pravda* from the time of strict Party control than a paper that stood for political pluralism. "Today I'm going to get rid of that oath," I told Vesna as I was getting ready to leave for work. Vesna was alarmed. "I don't know if you should do that. You'll have problems. They will attack you from all sides. Is it wise to expose yourself to all that when you've already been voted the best paper in the country? Perhaps it should wait for a more appropriate moment," she argued, knowing that this would not change my mind. I sat down at the typewriter and wrote a piece entitled, "Loyalty and Life," for the "In Focus" column in which, while expressing appreciation for Tito's role in the past, I explained the reasons for removing the oath of allegiance:

In the public forums called, "Speaking Openly about *Oslobod-jenje*," held in 1989 in a number of cities of Bosnia-Hercegovina, and even earlier in similar open discussions with students of journalism in Sarajevo, there was always one simple and inevitable question: "Why does your paper maintain, as the only one in the entire country, the dedication, 'Comrade Tito, we promise you ...' Is that some kind of avant-garde expression, an alibi for possible mistakes, an oath of loyalty...?"

Whatever it was, judging from the comments of our readers, it sounded banal, "bolshevik," and inappropriate for serious journalism.

Although it never occurred to any of us at *Oslobodjenje* to doubt the sincerity of those who, grieving for Tito at his passing, were moved to place the verse at the head of the newspaper, there were many of us who had to agree that these slogans, no matter how noble their commitment, were more appropriate at Party meetings than they were in a daily newspaper.

For this reason, in this first issue of the new year, we have removed the dedication from our header.

To all those who might honestly or falsely be concerned about this change and worry that we might wander from the course set for us by Tito, we say this: Tito's achievements stand above all political mystification and petty scandal and cannot be obscured by any anti-Tito nationalistic hysteria and confrontation. The struggle for our liberation from fascism and the unification of the country; the courageous "no" to Stalin in 1948; self-management as a vision of liberated man which generated the momentum for the annual improvement in our quality of life; non-alignment as a guarantee of independence and respect in international affairs, and so on and so forth—these must stand the test of time and the judgment of history. It is our view that Tito belongs to our past, and his historic legacy is such that, in the inevitable evaluations of history and scholarly scrutiny, it will continue to garner additional reasons for respect.

This was not, even in the past, and still less will it be in the future, dependent upon how often, in special celebrations or in the headers of newspapers, we avow our allegiance even to the most noble of paths; instead, of much greater significance will be how sincere our dedication is to this path in actual life. And all of us who live in this country, in this decade after the passing of Tito, in everything that is connected with ordinary life, in our dismal day-to-day existence and the fearful uncertainty about what tomorrow may bring, have already so thoroughly strayed from that path that we have nothing left but to hope that perhaps we can, one day, turn around.

And that was it. That was the comment which terminated the decades of ideological loyalty of the paper to the Party still in power. Not that I did not appreciate Tito's legacy: Yugoslavia with its independence from Moscow and its promise of "socialism with a human face" was a much better place to be in than any other Eastern European country. It was well ahead of Poland, Hungary, Bulgaria, or Romania. Self-management, free health care and education, and freedom to travel with a Yugoslav passport—which made it possible for hundreds of thousands of people to work abroad and invest their savings in comfortable homes and small businesses in Yugoslavia—had provided for decades of a steady rise in living standards in the country. Special attention was paid to equality among the different ethnic groups and to promotion of minorities. Clearly, Communist authorities were sometimes too restrictive in their interpretation of what constituted propagation of ethnic or religious hatred—and that led to restrictions of freedom of speech—but developments in the nineties have proved that there was a need to keep an eye on ultranationalist extremists, many of whom became the leaders and war criminals in a genocidal drive for domination over others. An old Bosnian woman, attending a protest rally in Boston against the crimes committed in the "safe zone" of Srebrenica in the summer of 1995, was to express her nostalgia for those decades of peace in Yugoslavia in a very emotional way: "You know, Mr. Kurspahić, my dream in childhood was to come to America. Now, from here, I see that we had our America—at home."

My decision to remove the slogan from the top of the front page was not my judgment against Tito's years. It was more a move aimed at further opening up the paper in support of democratic, economic, and social reforms initiated at that time by the reformist forces and voices within society. But Vesna was right to be concerned about the attacks that I would invite as a consequence of that decision. The very next morning, Branko Tomić, at that time my assistant editor for the correspondents' network, was the first to arrive in the editorial offices, and he greeted me with fury: "You should have been the first one here, so you could take all the phone calls."

"What are they saying," I asked.

"They're all swearing at you, every last one of them."

The telephone rang again and it was "a Bosnian from Vojvodina" who heard on the radio the Tanjug wire service announcement that *Oslobodjenje* had removed the dedication.

"Congratulations and I hope that this is a sign of a real move towards democracy," the man said.

"Thank you for your support," I answered. After all the angry diatribes from readers that he had had to field, Branko could not get over the fact that the first phone call I received was one of praise! However, I must admit that I also got my share of enraged calls, including an angry threat from a reader in Vogošća: "It looks as though we'll have to get our guns out to defend ourselves against you."

On that day I left by car to go to Belgrade, to the traditional New Year reception for the editors-in-chief of the Yugoslav media given by Prime Minister Ante Marković. Along the way, listening to Sarajevo Radio, I heard the youth call-in program on the subject: "What do the listeners think about the decision of *Oslobodjenje* to remove the dedication to Tito from the front page of the paper?" As I listened to the comments, I was heartened. "Well, it's all right. I think the result we have between those who are angry and those who approve of what we're doing is pretty much a draw," I said to the driver, Zoran Ivanović. "I guess I'll dare to go back to Sarajevo!"

At the reception, the major topic of discussion among Yugoslav and foreign journalists was the change in *Oslobodjenje*. Manjo Vukotić, the editor-in-chief of *Borba*, walked over. "Good for you!" he said congratulating me. "I know, perhaps better than anyone, how difficult that was. For months I have not been able to figure out a way of getting rid of that 'Proletariat of all countries, unite!'—and with Tito, the matter is even more sensitive. Tell me, who was it who really decided to do it?"

"I was."

"And what about your board? What did they have to say about it?"

"I didn't ask them. If I had asked, it would have been difficult for many of them. Some would have been opposed; others, while agreeing with me, would have found it difficult to say so at an official meeting. This was the most painless way."

All the papers in the country reprinted my "In Focus" comment, either in full or in excerpts. The removal of the oath from the header of *Oslobodjenje* was treated as an act of great significance. My colleague, Slavko Šantić, defended the move in a radio debate, saying, "It was very easy, and perhaps even politically useful, at the time that it was done, to place that slogan in *Oslobodjenje*. It was much more difficult, and delicate, to remove it. I am personally proud to belong to the editorial board of a paper where such a thing could happen." The only attack on *Oslobodjenje* in the press came in the pages of the Belgrade weekly NIN. Its commentator, Petar Ignja, in a comment entitled "Gorenje Instead of Tito" criticized us for, among other things, placing an advertisement for the products of a Slovenian company Gorenje, a large appliance manufacturer well-known for its refrigerators, televisions, and other similar products, in the spot previously occupied by the oath of allegiance.

The decision to place an advertisement in that space was, in fact, a product of yet another important change in the life of the paper at that time. When I was a candidate for the post of the editor-in-chief, I wanted the new manager to be chosen for his managerial experience and training. The policy then was to select people from various committees, none of whom had any business experience. The position of the manager of *Oslobodjenje* was just one more slot available for Party functionaries to fill. The newspaper did not work to get readers or advertising; instead, every effort led towards satisfying the wishes of the Socialist Alliance. This resulted in constant tension and competition between the editor-in-chief and the manager, since the latter would become involved in editorial policy instead of taking care of matters relating to business, finance, and development. This past experience pushed me to demand that we turn things around: we changed the statute and included the requirement that the director should no longer be a Party functionary but rather should serve as the manager of the firm, and should be chosen from among those who apply for the job on the basis of managerial skills and proven abilities. The job was thus given to Salko Hasanefendić, a business-school graduate who over the previous fifteen years had worked in various positions in *Oslobodjenje*—as the director of advertising, in the sales department, and as deputy manager of marketing. He knew all the major areas of activity within the company and had achieved a considerable level of respect even among the journalists.

One of the first things we did, as a team, was to create a combined editorial and business project to develop the paper and all of its vital functions. This entailed fundamental changes and modernization of the editorial concept, a modern marketing approach, a more productive employment of reporters and writers such that, with the same manpower, we would produce, in addition to the daily newspaper, two weeklies, *Nedjelja* (The Week) and *Svijet* (The World). In addition we would develop the correspondents' network both within the country and abroad, and significantly increase the number of pages of advertising. These changes produced very encouraging results: within the first year of this joint effort on the project (and a series of creative or "brainstorming" sessions with all the newsmen and correspondents of *Oslobodjenje*) we managed to maintain the circulation of the paper, which had fallen off by 5,000 annually over the previous four years, at the previous year's average and in the following year saw our circulation increase. At the same time, we had significantly higher earnings and made substantial progress towards solving the housing problem for our employees. And instead of being the state's or the Party's voice, *Oslobodjenje* became a truly independent voice of the public, developing its autonomy, and holding its own in the marketplace.

A DECLARATION OF INDEPENDENCE

THE FIRST YEAR had been a time of incremental, measured change—a step-by-step stretching of the boundaries of what was permitted. It was necessary to get the still powerful one-party state accustomed to criticism, uncomfortable questions and uncensored writing on what, up until now, had been forbidden topics and personages. For instance, in February 1989 we received an article in which filmmaker Emir Kusturica explained his critical approach towards Tito: "It is impossible to avoid (but we have been avoiding persistently for at least the last eight years) the fact that Josip Broz (Tito), in fact, is an integral part of the Yugoslav crisis, and that he is an inseparable part of that crisis, one of the generators of that crisis." Slavko Šantić, then the editor of the cultural section, came to me with this text: "I think that, as the editor-in-chief, in view of the sensitive nature of the topic, you ought to see this and decide whether or not we will publish it." Šantić knew that in Bosnia-Hercegovina no one had ever before publicly expressed such criticism of Tito, and that by running Kusturica's article we were likely to find ourselves in seriously hot water. I read it and said, "We will publish it, of course—we have no right to censor what people are thinking and saying." The very next day we were criticized at Party and veterans' meetings in the Sarajevo districts and received a number of angry letters with the basic message: "Hands off Tito!" Beyond this, however, there were no repercussions, and we had been able to extend a little further the territory of free speech and free exchange of ideas.

Similarly, in March 1989, on the "Tribunal" page we printed an entire series of critical letters concerning the "anti-Serbian positions" adopted by Fuad Muhić and Muhamed Abadžić at a meeting of the Central Committee of the League of Communists of Bosnia-Hercegovina. Both members had spoken critically of the increase of Serbian nationalism and especially of the politics and policies of Slobodan Milošević. Following the publication of the letters, the president of the Presidency of the Committee, Abdulah Mutapčić, called a meeting with the directors and editors of the Republic's media and upbraided *Oslobodjenje*:

"I think that the publishing of these letters was an editorial mistake. The letters have nothing but Serbs attacking and Muslims defending Muhić and Abadžić!"

"That is not an editorial mistake but quite possibly a realistic picture of the situation, and you ought to be grateful for the fact that, by publishing those letters, we are showing how seriously nationalism has taken hold," I answered, defending our position.

Oslobodjenje had been attempting to meet the challenge of the changing political climate in the country by playing a careful game of chess: making the first moves and not waiting for the changes to take us by surprise. Finally, in the spring of 1990, we decided we were ready to make the ultimate move and unilaterally renounce our connection with the Socialist Alliance: to forge a truly independent position in a future multiparty system a paper could not remain or be seen as, an appendage of any political party. Therefore, at a general editorial staff meeting on June 4, 1990, we adopted a document under the title "*Oslobodjenje* in the Multiparty System: Standards and Principles of

Editorial Policy" and published it in the paper five months before the first free elections were held in the country. The document defined *Oslobodjenje* as the independent, non-partisan newspaper of the citizens of Bosnia-Hercegovina. It took a clear position in defense of equal individual, national, religious, and all other rights and freedoms of the citizens living together in the Republic, and stated its support for the territorial integrity and sovereignty of Bosnia-Hercegovina and its equality with all other republics in the Yugoslav federation.

Underlining the "Yugoslav orientation" of the paper, the document committed *Oslobodjenje* to professional, objective reporting of all developments, and all opposing opinions, facts, and arguments pertaining to significant events in the country, and thus to an accurate reflection of public life. "As it has been critical towards the current party in power, similarly ... *Oslobodjenje* has both the right and the obligation to critically evaluate the activities of the new parties and their leaders and new organs of the government. In this regard, the daily editorial policy must be carried out with the most consistent and exacting separation of reporting and commentary." In the upcoming election the paper would allow equal space to all political parties and all political views and offer a platform to the public for dialogue on significant social and political questions. To maintain *Oslobodjenje*'s editorial and financial independence in its time of transition to complete economic autonomy, the document expected the Assembly of Bosnia-Hercegovina to serve as a guarantor that the paper would not become the object of takeover, monopolization, manipulation, or dictation of any party.

At the editorial staff meeting, we knew that our future position was not simply a matter of a document we adopted; rather, it would depend to a great extent upon the developments on the political scene. It was impossible to predict what the first free elections would bring: a truly democratic dispensation, another version of totalitarianism, or the return of the Communist government, albeit in some reformed, moderate incarnation. But we also knew that we would never again consent to being just "a means of information," a conduit for the political agendas of those in power. Our direct experience with Party control, together with the alarming spectacle—under the banner of "new democracy"—of the rush to take over the press in the neighboring republics (such as we saw in Croatia) was more than sufficient to make us understand that, in order to meet the challenges of an uncertain future, we would have to define in clear conceptual terms—as much for ourselves as for others—what we stood for.

In the editorial discussion on the document, it was clear that we had no illusions that the objectives we were setting ourselves would be easily achieved. Branka Milićević Mašić pointed out, for instance, that the position of being "above partisan politics" sounded too pretentious. "Our future status," she said, "will depend most heavily upon our ability, while separating ourselves from our past, to maintain the dignity of the paper which liberated itself and did not wait to be liberated by others." Mehmed Halilović wondered out loud whether overemphasis of our independence was perhaps "too large a turban" to carry: independence was established by professionalism and competence, and for *Oslobodjenje* the most important thing was that it remain a newspaper which could be trusted and believed. Ljiljana Smajlović suggested that, in our attempt to maintain objectivity and lack of bias, we would have to insist on standards of professionalism rigorous enough to insulate our work from our possible secret loves and loyalties to parties and influential personalities. Zlatko Dizdarević pointed out that our future independence would depend primarily upon how much our readers would believe us and not upon whether we put the term "independent" into our header. Ljubiša Jakšić, who was attending the editorial staff meeting as the president of the managing board, offered the sobering thought—one that we needed to take as a warning—that we had achieved our sense of independence in the conditions of a weakened and tired government, but that it was unknown how long this state of affairs would last. It was, nonetheless, extremely important that we had stipulated our position towards the multiparty system in Bosnia-Hercegovina well before the newly developing parties were able to stipulate it to us.

We had a glimmering of what we might expect in the future when, in the Spring of 1990, I received a call from Muhamed Čengić, the closest associate of Alija Izetbegović from earlier days. The founding convention of the Party of Democratic Action [SDA] was to be held and Čengić had phoned to let us know that he and Izetbegović would like to visit us at *Oslobodjenje*. "We would like to talk to you, to see what sort of treatment our party can expect from the paper," Čengić said to me.

This was going to be the first occasion for a meeting in our editorial offices with representatives of any of the ethnic parties being formed in Bosnia-Hercegovina. The emergence of ethnicity as the prime determinant of party affiliation was viewed with considerable dismay, not only by the Communist government, but also by a large cross section of the public and the media. In a commentary in *Nedjelja* I had expressed my own fears for the future, hoping that we would pause and think about the consequences before seeking refuge in nationalism as our first and last resort. Even if the idea of "brotherhood and unity" had been largely and clearly damaged by the rise of Serbian nationalism, which had done its share by scattering everyone in all directions with its all-or-nothing threats ("you will either go along with us or you will be destroyed"), was there not the risk, I had argued in my piece, that the appearance of parties based exclusively upon ethnic loyalties would only hasten the rending of everything that still constituted our common heritage? Some blame Izetbegović for being the first to organize an ethnic, all-Muslim, political party which, they argue, opened the way for others. The fact is that we already had a brutal drive for Serbian domination within the League of Communists and within all federal institutions which was clearly manifest in the "Serbization" of the military. The Slovenian, Croat, Muslim, or Macedonian drive for political representation and independence was essentially a response to a resurgent Serb nationalism. Nevertheless, it became clear in Bosnia-Hercegovina—at least to some of us—that organizing ethnically exclusive political parties, all-Muslim, all-Croat, all-Serb, was the step towards the disintegration of the Republic.

The catastrophe that awaited us, however, was still some distance away when I received our visitors, Alija Izetbegović and Muhamed Čengić. In that first encounter both sides approached each other with a degree of wariness but also with a measure of respect. For Izetbegović and Čengić, this was a meeting with the editor-in-chief of a newspaper which, in the not-so-distant past, had treated them rather badly. In the early eighties, *Oslobodjenje* was part of the officially orchestrated media campaign against Izetbegović and others who had been brought to trial on charges of "Islamic fundamentalism." Izetbegović paid a heavy price, spending eight years in prison for his writings.

"We are following your work with great interest. We know that the *Oslobodjenje* of today is not the *Oslobodjenje* of the past, and that last year it was voted the best newspaper in Yugoslavia. But can we expect fair treatment from it if the majority of the editors and newsmen there are Communists or up until recently were Communists, and if you are under the influence of the Party, which is spreading fear of 'nationalists' in order to maintain its monopoly on power?" they asked me, in a style of finishing each other's sentences.

"I can guarantee you fair treatment," I answered. "That does not mean that we will treat you 'more equally' than the other parties, that we will take sides and support you, but we have publicly made a commitment to provide the political parties with equal representation in our pages. We will treat all ideas, platforms, and individuals on an equal basis, presenting them and criticizing them, and leave it to the citizens to decide whom they will vote for and why."

"And about the Communist domination among the journalists?"

"We have already, as an institution, declined all sponsorship of any political party. Within the paper, for a few years now, there is no longer any party activity—nor will there be in the future. The political party that the journalists choose to belong to is a personal matter; they can vote for whomever they wish, but they may not support in their writing any of the parties, nor can they be a part of the leadership or a candidate for election. If they wish to be involved in party politics, during that time they will not be involved in the paper's political coverage, as reporters, commentators, or editors. I have personally and publicly defined our policy in specific detail. In elections, as in soccer, the reporter's place is in the press box. It is his responsibility to present, without bias or favoritism, information on how the game is played, who scores a goal, and what the score is, and that's all."

When I first met Izetbegović, his major opposition and the future president of the Serbian party, Radovan Karadžić, was still uninvolved in politics. In the spring of 1990, I had met him for the first time quite by chance. I was a member of the Presidency of the Soccer Club of Sarajevo—twice champions of Yugoslavia—and, although I usually refused the role of the trip leader for the team, preferring to spend what little leisure time I had with my family (usually in the country-side around what later became Serbian-occupied Pale where we were building a summer house), I had been talked into leading the team to the championship match at Rijeka. There was a part-time bench psychologist traveling with the team, who was introduced to me as Dr. Karadžić. He was excessively withdrawn for a man who was supposed to be able to motivate the team; for the entire length of the flight, he did not talk to anyone, but sat wrapped up in his raincoat, with an umbrella and the Belgrade paper *Politika* in his hands. The folks from Rijeka invited me and some others on the trip to a pleasant luncheon at a seafood restaurant, and I asked Karadžić to join us. He declined, saying, "I prefer to stay with the team in the hotel until the time of the game." We lost, one to nothing. I could not have imagined that this reclusive, seemingly innocuous person would soon mobilize a different kind of "team" and provoke some of the most horrible atrocities of this century.

In its political coverage, *Oslobodjenje* certainly attempted, as far as possible, to maintain its neutrality. In retrospect, though, I think we covered Izetbegović's SDA as the first ethnic party in Bosnia more cautiously than the other parties that subsequently appeared on the scene. And as events swiftly unfolded—and Radovan Karadžić's Serb Democratic Party (SDS) began to set its desperate terms for Bosnia—it became harder to be neutral. If *Oslobodjenje* had any political leanings, however, these tended towards the Alliance of Reformist Forces. It was not so much a matter of supporting the party in Bosnia-Hercegovina, but more a sympathy for the platform of economic and political reform of the founder of the party, Federal Prime Minister Ante Marković. Among their supporters, the Reformists had a number of prominent intellectuals and other public figures who were seeking an alternative to both the League of Communists and to the newly emerging nationalist parties.

Markovic's party, however, did not stand a chance in Bosnia-Hercegovina. He had little understanding or knowledge of the political conditions and personalities in the Republic and turned his highly reputable project over to the wrong hands. The president of the party was the same Nenad Kecmanović whose withdrawal from the election to the Yugoslav Presidency had been the subject of great controversy. In the political milieu of Sarajevo he had come to be known as a man who would give everything for his career. One of the party's leaders, Dragan Kalinić, had also tried out all the different political outfits and further confirmed his careerism by switching from the reformist party to become one of the ministers of Karadžić's self-proclaimed "Republika

Srpska." In addition to all of this, Markovic's party was further compromised by the selection of the undisguised nationalist, Todor Dutina, as spokesman for the reformists.

Before the election it looked as if the reform communists—Nijaz Duraković's Party of Democratic Change, which later became the Social Democratic Party—had excellent chances. We incurred the displeasure of all the ethnic parties when, in the last days of the campaign, we published the results of a scientifically conducted public opinion poll which showed a convincing victory for Duraković's party. "Once again the media is courting the communists!" they charged in attacking us. It seems to me that the problem was not in the poll but rather in those being polled: unaccustomed to free democratic expression, people had, "just in case," said what they thought would be most pleasing for the ear of the ruling party, although they knew perfectly well how they were going to vote.

In the closing days of the campaign, in addition to publishing extensive excerpts from the political platforms of all the parties in the race and introducing their candidates for the highest offices, we invited Aleksandar Tijanić, a journalist well known in Yugoslavia for his in-depth newspaper interviews, to talk with the leaders of all the leading Bosnian-Hercegovinian parties. These conversations were published as full-page interviews in *Oslobodjenje* covering a wide spectrum of issues. Judging from our readers' response, the interviews were received as a valuable contribution to the political debate and to our coverage of the elections.

After six years—and after 250,000 Bosnians have been killed and two million displaced—it is interesting to read some of the statements made in those interviews by the leaders of the three ethnic parties in the fall of 1990. Alija Izetbegović of the Party of Democratic Action (SDA) had said that he could not see any prospects for Bosnia ever becoming a Muslim state: "Nothing can bind us together better than a civic republic because we can't make Bosnia a nation-state. Let Serbia and Croatia move towards the creation of such states; we don't have the conditions for it in Bosnia. The only option we have is to create a civic republic or have a civil war." The leader of the Serbian Democratic Party (SDS), Radovan Karadžić, stated that "for a civil war there has to be a decision, a will, some goals. To me that is a mad and impossible idea . . . We can live here together; living together has created

some eternal values and the possibilities of continuing to live together."
The leader of the Croatian Democratic Union (HDZ), Stjepan Kljuić
was equally committed to coexistence: "Our position is that Bosnia-
Hercegovina is indivisible and that the Croats want equal rights, not
more and not less, as granted to other people . . . As far as I know, Mr.
Karadžić, Mr. Izetbegović, and I in the name of my party can assure
you that we are well aware that we have to live together."

With their leaders promising a model of coexistence akin to
Switzerland in Bosnia-Hercegovina, the nationalist forces scored an
easy victory in the elections in November 1990. The results were very
much like an ethnic census of the population: the SDA won 33.8 percent, the SDS took 29.6 percent, and the HDZ took 18.3 percent of the
vote. The non-nationalist parties—the reformed communists' Party of
Democratic Change, the Alliance of Reformist Forces, the Democratic
Socialist League, and the Democratic Leagues, as well as the Liberal
Party and the Muslim Bosniak Organization—managed a mere 18 percent of the vote with no real power to oppose the disintegration of the
country. The nationalist victory was one that the three parties, in the
final days of the campaign, had joined hands to achieve. The pitiful
irony, which often goes unnoticed, is that it was the Muslim leader,
Alija Izetbegović, who virtually backed the legitimacy of the party
which—a year and a half later—was to unleash its genocidal terror
against Bosnia. Speaking at the founding convention of Karadžić's
party in the summer of 1990 in Sarajevo, Izetbegović had said: "We
were waiting for you; Bosnia-Hercegovina needs you!" The day before
the election, the three leaders—SDA's Izetbegović and SDS's Karadžić
and HDZ's Kljuić—appeared together at a news conference and on
television and invited their followers to vote for the three ethnic
parties. This collaboration was not only a decisive strategic move
against the multiethnic reformist parties on the Left, but also a fatal
blow to the tradition of tolerance and multicultural living in Bosnia-
Hercegovina. With their coming to power, there began a dramatic new
chapter in the life of *Oslobodjenje*, and in the history of Bosnia.

CHAPTER TWO

Nationalists
at the
Gate

I N A MULTITUDE OF WAYS the
"first democratically elected governments" of the Yugoslav republics
reminded us of the earlier, much vilified leadership. The resemblance
was most obvious in their single-minded determination to consolidate
power by taking control of the media. In Serbia and Montenegro, a faction of the League of Communists, renaming itself the Socialist Party,
had held on and moved towards a politics of virulent nationalism.
Retaining its grip on all the instruments of power, it had made sure that
the media in its territory would continue to serve its purposes. On
March 9, 1991, a protest march organized by the opposition parties on
the Party controlled RTV Belgrade and the newspaper *Politika* had been
brutally crushed. In Sarajevo, on the other hand, there was no basis for
such a confrontation because the media had successfully fought their
own political battle, opening their pages and their airwaves to all well
before the elections, and before the new parties appeared on the scene.
Nonetheless, the victorious parties taking over from the Communists in
Bosnia-Hercegovina fired their first volley at the "information houses"
even before they had completely settled into their newly acquired offices.

THE SPOILS OF WAR

ONLY A FEW DAYS AFTER THE ELECTION, a program entitled "Media and the New Government" was broadcast on Television Sarajevo. Participating were Velibor Ostojić of the SDS, Muhamed Čengić of the SDA, and Ilija Žuljević of the HDZ. On the program these representatives of the multiparty coalition served notice that one of the first tasks of the government would be "the liberation of the Bosnian and Hercegovinian media" in order to ensure "independent news coverage." Towards this end, the government would assume the responsibility of appointing "competent and not accommodating" individuals to the principal editorial positions while the three parties would come to an agreement among themselves on the share to be allocated to each in the media. Clearly oblivious to their Orwellian descriptions of the new political order, Ostojić took the view that "a civil society with all the elements of democracy" could only be constructed if, like the railroads, the post office, and the telecommunications system, the media received "the patronage of the state" and were afforded "necessary conditions [for] completely independent, nonpartisan" journalism.

The program also included a brief conversation with me, which had been recorded earlier and therefore I had no way of responding to whatever would be said on the program. But in answering the question as to what the new government could expect from the media, I had said that they could expect the same dosage of criticism that we had been delivering to the previous government. Given that all three parties had elected to insert the word "democratic" in their names, we expected the new government to fulfill the promise of "democracy" and, therefore, to expand the area for freedom of speech and freedom of the press, and in no way to restrict it. Having achieved a considerable degree of freedom in the one-party system to write critically about the times in which we lived, there was no reason for us to abandon that freedom in a multiparty system. As a nonpartisan paper, *Oslobodjenje* would continue to respect the diversity of opinion and, of course, it was not to be expected that all the different voices we represented would appeal to every party, inside or outside the government. It needed to be emphasized, however, that the media in Bosnia-Hercegovina were on the side of democratic public opinion, had actively initiated and participated in the democratic process, and had every reason to expect that their full participation would continue. In brief, I said, "I think that it is the job of the government to act, to do its job, and to be responsive to the democratic expression of public opinion. I do not see any organic connection between the government and the media. Each must separately do their own work in a professional manner. I think that both are separately accountable to the critical judgment of the same public."

In the television broadcast, my recorded statement elicited an immediate angry response from Ostojić, the prospective minister of information in the new government:

> Listening to Kurspahić I noticed three things: First, he said that the means of information (media) have already achieved free expression. This is not true. He knows very well that he is at the top position in the institution where editorial policies are strictly controlled. Second, I noticed his tendency to want to put himself above the government and above the society—to be a power above society. Third, I noticed one inexactitude: namely, that the means of information—and there he particularly pointed to *Oslobodjenje*—were exceptionally objective in their pre-election coverage. So let me respond . . . We will specifically reach some agreement with regard to the so-called joint media that are supported by the budget because we have not been satisfied for four months with the writing in *Oslobodjenje*, and I was amazed to hear what Mr. Editor-in-Chief had to say. We have publicly declared that *Oslobodjenje* is an anti-Serbian newspaper, and I still stand behind that statement.

That evening, while the program was being broadcast, I was at a meeting with our correspondents from Hercegovina in Mostar. When I got home early the next morning, my wife Vesna was agitated: "Did you hear what the government officials had to say?" she asked. "It's incredible! They want to edit the newspapers, the radio, and the television. I taped the program, you can see for yourself." I was more tired than curious; I preferred to get some sleep. When I got into the office later that morning, I encountered the same atmosphere of dismay. Some of my colleagues were already considering me as good as "out." I said, "Don't worry, as long as we don't give up without a fight, they can't do anything to us." I finally did listen to the tape of the broadcast and, for the next day's edition of *Oslobodjenje*, Sunday, November 25, 1990, wrote a piece entitled, "The First Goal Scored Against Themselves by the New Government":

> The program "Newsmen and the New Government" broadcast Thursday evening . . . indicates that the Channel 3 news team has once again seized upon a hot topic, although there were two things about their approach that I would object to: first, that they approached their work in a manner of professional capitulation, as if it were natural that the new government should "organize things" in the press, and, second, that they merely recorded the statements of the media representatives and then left it to the guests in the studio, the representatives of the victorious parties, to interpret and chop to pieces those words, without the possibility of their interpretations being answered on the spot. For that reason, we printed a large part of what was said in that broadcast, so that the reader could know what was being discussed and so that we could show, point by point, how this is a replay of what we have already seen in our northwestern regions [in Croatia], where democracy has already been established. It is an attempt on the part of the new government to take over the media. Riding the wave of euphoria over its victory, it is seeking to replace the old one-party monopoly of the media, which has been out of commission for some time now, with a new multiparty monopoly.
>
> Especially offensive, first in claiming that something was said which in fact was never said, and then in disputing his own fabrications . . . was the representative of the Serbian Democratic Party in this program, Velibor Ostojić. He claimed to find "three inexactitudes" in the statement of the undersigned editor-in-chief of *Oslobodjenje* (printed in full in yesterday's issue of the paper). First, as regards "the freedom which we have already achieved in the one-party system" . . . Ostojić responds that this is not true. "He (that is, I) should certainly know that he is at the top of the institution where editorial policies are strictly controlled." Let's verify how true that is!
>
> Since I began my work in this position, the editorial policy of *Oslobodjenje* has been set entirely and exclusively by the editorial board of the paper, without any orders from any institution. As for

"Muslim domination," which is a lie repeated so often by Ostojić in this program that it might be assumed that there must be some truth to it, let it be a matter of record that the daily editorial team consists of one Muslim and five Serbs (to each of whom I sincerely apologize for this obscene categorization by numbers which I am forced to use against my will). The "freedom" which we are now offered by the representatives of the victorious parties, in fact, has already been won and accorded widespread recognition through-out Yugoslavia. There is absolutely no reason, nor any intention on our part, to relinquish what we have achieved—certainly not under pressure from people who belong to three different parties, each one of which describes itself as "democratic."

Furthermore, Ostojić saw a tendency on the part of this author to "wish to put himself above the government and above the soci-ety, to be a force above society." He probably puts that interpreta-tion on my statement that "I do not see any organic connection between the government and the media. Each must separately do its own work in a professional manner. I think that both of us are separately accountable to the critical judgment of the same pub-lic." This view had been accepted by the preceding government: *Oslobodjenje* was thus legally organized as an independent non-partisan institution long before this gentleman came along to "for-malize" the independence of the media. What I had to say is nothing more than common sense: in every democratic system one of the fundamental functions of the media is to gain access to the work of the government—a kind of public control—so that the government will not become enmeshed in intrigues behind the back and against the interests of the public …

From the statements made in the television broadcast, and from the statements of other representatives of the nationalist par-ties, it is clear that they think it to be completely natural that they can draw up some agreement between themselves on the division of their power over the media in the Republic. In other words, by some percentage formulation, they will be able to determine which editor of which branch of the media will belong to which national group. You will no doubt recall how many headaches and heartaches were caused by these percentage formulations in the not-so-distant past. I do not know what this would mean for the already acknowledged right of the journalists in the Bosnia-Herce-govina media to choose their own editor-in-chief and manager. The journalists of *Oslobodjenje* have already had this right put into law, and at any time, for whatever reason, they can have a vote of confidence (or of no confidence) for (or against) their editor-in-chief and replace him with a new one. But no one else can do so in their place, for whenever the government is able, as it once was, to decide on the fate of people in the press, it does damage to the practice of journalism … and it is harmful to the government. Very simply, we are no longer "the means of information" but rather, an independent part of the democratic process and no one can arbi-trarily deliver us from the hands of one government into the hands of another.

As for employing the budget as an instrument of blackmail, all one can say is that this ploy will not work. Not only because the participation of the Republic in the financing of the paper is only symbolic relative to the income from the market, but also because the money which we receive from the budget does not belong to the parties or their leaders, nor to the people in the government offices, but rather it comes from the pockets of the citizens of Bosnia-Hercegovina who have an inalienable right to a free, inde-pendent, and critical press. An attempt to monopolize this voice would be, therefore, the first goal scored against itself by the new government. We place our trust in the reasonable and democratic forces within that government.

The reasonable and democratic forces, however, were not heard from. Minister of Information Velibor Ostojić (formerly a proofreader and Party secretary at Radio Sarajevo where he gained notoriety for informing female job applicants that they would first have to pass the test with him) embarked on his "holy war" against the "anti-Serbian media." One of his principle targets, not surprisingly, was Yutel (Yugoslav Television) a news program edited by Goran Milić, who had found refuge in the city of Sarajevo at the time of the crackdown against the media in Belgrade. "Yutel is a foreign body in the Bosnian and Hercegovinian information system," the minister said, and he threatened that this "foreign body" would be removed. But the public in Bosnia-Hercegovina regarded the existence and survival of Yutel at

Radio and Television Sarajevo as an affirmation of the freedom and independence which the Bosnian media had achieved at a time when journalists in Serbia were physically threatened and transmitters were seized by force of arms. The media in Bosnia-Hercegovina no longer needed to get the approval of the minister for the things they wanted to do. Thus, in a "For or Against Yutel" survey, done by *Oslobodjenje* after Ostojić's statement, well-known Sarajevan personalities reacted with sharp criticism to the threat issued by the minister of information. But, clearly, this was only the beginning.

With the wholehearted support of the other two parties in the government, Ostojić doggedly pursued his aim of carving up *Oslobodjenje* and Radio and Television Sarajevo according to national percentages. The game, in accordance with the interparty agreement on the subject, was to divide up all positions—"from doorman to director" as Muhamed Čengić was reported to have said—among the three nationalist parties. Without wasting any time, during the preparations for the first session of the newly elected Assembly, Ostojić had been proudly leaking to the press, as "first-hand information," lists of the directors and chief editors who were to be removed and the names of the new appointees who were to take their place.

In the listing of the editorial positions, the position of manager of *Oslobodjenje*, which according to the interparty agreement was to go to the Serb party, was offered to Ilija Guzina, a newsman at Television Sarajevo (who, during the war, was to become a manager at the television station of the Serb extremists in Pale). "But why the manager? I have never been involved with management of a publishing house," he said to the party leaders who invited him to discuss the matter. "That's exactly the reason," was the reply. "You destroy them [*Oslobodjenje*] and then we will develop *Javnost* [the newspaper of SDS]. That's exactly what we want."

At that time *Oslobodjenje* was visited by various pretenders to the jobs of manager and editor-in-chief. They looked around and measured up our offices. Our onetime colleague, Mustafa Mujagić, who was then the deputy minister under Ostojić, came to advise us that it was all over and it would be best for us to reach the most favorable settlement that we could with the parties in power. "They won't quit until they have put all their own people in all the positions," he told us.

During those weeks, in a conversation with Muhamed Čengić, who was a candidate for the office of vice-president of the government, I had the opportunity to see what the practical shape of this three-sided division of key functions in *Oslobodjenje* would look like. Čengić showed me the document typed on a Cyrillic typewriter—in other words, in the office of the SDS—according to which the manager would be appointed by the SDS, the editor-in-chief by the SDA and the editor of the Cultural Section and the newsroom by the HDZ, and on and on, through the Political Section (SDS) down to the editor of the photo service (SDA).

"That place was originally to go to the SDS, but I remembered that this job was already being done by the excellent photographer, Salko Hondo, so I told them (SDS) to take the next position and we (SDA) would keep Hondo where he is," Čengić told me, explaining how this three-sided agreement was to function in practice.

"Such an artificial arrangement of the editorial staff would not last two days. They would be arguing over what commentary would appear on the front page; the Muslims would be working according to your instructions, the Serbs according to Karadžić's, and the Croats according to Kljuic's orders. We won't let you do it!" I told him.

"I don't see why you are complaining. Who else would we appoint as editor-in-chief?" he continued.

"We're not reaching any sort of understanding here," I replied. "When I said that we will not allow you to do it, I wasn't simply stating that you won't be able to replace us, but rather that you won't be able to appoint us. That is, quite simply, a professional and not a party matter." And we left it, literally, at that.

Officially, the manager, Salko Hasanefendić, and I had discussed the upcoming dispute between the new government and *Oslobodjenje* with the president of the Assembly, Momčilo Krajišnik, and the president of the Presidency, Alija Izetbegović. We told Krajišnik that a bill containing a statute for *Oslobodjenje* had been introduced some time ago and, since the Assembly was in charge of approving all statutes of publicly owned firms, we asked that this should be put on the agenda as quickly as possible.

"As far as I'm concerned, I have nothing against it. But, it will depend upon the agreement of the Clubs of Deputies of the three ruling parties," Krajišnik answered.

We also warned Alija Izetbegović that the carrying out of the interparty agreement on division of positions in the media would leave a very bad impression in the international media, where freedom of the press in Bosnia-Hercegovina had already been noted. Furthermore, it would put the government in permanent conflict with most of those working in the Republic's media who had chosen their own managers and editors. Such a conflict would have far-reaching and unforeseeable consequences; it would certainly lead, to the destruction of the media since editors run by remote control by the different parties would not be able to bring any coherence to the job.

"And in addition, Mr. President, I don't believe that you can legally win this dispute," I said, requesting him to organize a visit to *Oslobodjenje* by the representatives of the government, including the member of the Presidency for matters concerning the media, Stjepan Kljuić, the president of the Assembly, Momčilo Krajišnik, Prime Minister Jure Pelivan, and, of course, Minister of Information Velibor Ostojić. They would have direct face-to-face discussions with *Oslobodjenje*'s editorial board to clear up any possible misunderstandings. Izetbegović promised that such a visit would first occur "the week after next," after the first of a series of Yugoslav summit meetings in Belgrade of the presidents of all the republics, and then "in the last week of February [1991]," but those conversations never took place. Izetbegović was too busy from that time onward with matters of state in the crumbling federation, and the work was carried on in all three parties by hawks who considered it imperative to demonstrate their power by breaking the resistance of the independent media.

During this period the tension in the relations between the government and the press had grown to an explosive level. Especially harsh in his criticism of the media, and particularly *Oslobodjenje*, was the newly elected member of the Presidency of Bosnia-Hercegovina, Stjepan Kljuić. He did not miss any opportunity at the press conferences of his party, the HDZ, and even in casual encounters with his former colleagues from the paper where he himself had once worked as a journalist, to demonstrate his newly acquired power and to announce the government's intent to eventually and "finally introduce order there." I tried to comprehend the reasons for his animus towards us and wondered whether possibly long ago, before any of the current editors were even employed at *Oslobodjenje*, he had indeed been unfairly treated and driven from his job at the paper because he was a Croat, as he certainly seemed to be suggesting. Nonetheless, I was unable to mollify the obvious impatience which he demonstrated towards all of us generally, and towards me particularly. This much was clear: he had taken strong exception to the piece I had written as a rejoinder to the allegations made on television by Velibor Ostojić against *Oslobodjenje*.

His anger was triggered not by any particular regard for Ostojić but by my statement of the ethnic breakdown of the editorial board's membership—a statement made, it needs to be recalled, to give the lie to Ostojić's claim that the paper was dominated by Muslims. "Kurspahić should be ashamed to say that there are five Serbs and one Muslim who are determining the global policy of *Oslobodjenje*. And after such an admission I am expected to back him up?'" said Kljuić in *Večernje Novine* (The Evening News). It was becoming increasingly obvious that we could not please anybody—even if we tried. We could only keep on trying to set the record straight.

Therefore, once again, in *Oslobodjenje*, January 4, 1991, in the full swing of the confrontation with the new government, I wrote an open letter to Stjepan Kljuić, Presidency of Bosnia-Hercegovina, which, in part, made the following points:

> Even a superficial analysis of my impugned piece will show that Stjepan Kljuić managed to achieve three inaccuracies in just one statement. First: "Kurspahić should be ashamed . . ." The reader can easily see that I was, in fact, so ashamed at being pulled, very much against my own will, into ethnic categorization by numbers in this manner that I made an immediate and most humble apology for it—I have never judged the worth of anyone on the basis of his ethnicity, whether Croat, Serb, or Muslim. (As an aside, let me mention, since certain people cannot get along without such head counts: in the two years that I have served as editor-in-chief of this paper, in the total number of employees and in the number of editors, and in the number of regular and part-time contributors and columnists, there are more Croats today than there used to be in the past.)
>
> Second: "there are five Serbs and one Muslim who are determining the global policy of *Oslobodjenje*." Clearly this was not what I said, nor even what I might have said, because that would not be

true. I was referring to the daily routine of the paper, i.e. the daily operational matters, whereas the global editorial policy in this paper is determined by the whole editorial board and all the employees. . . .

Third, and most importantly: "And after such an admission I am expected to back him up?" No, I would not expect anyone from the government—past, present or future—to back me up in any shape or form. First, because I would not be comfortable with having them behind my back, a feeling left over from the police beatings in my student days in 1968. Second, because I think that every honest person, public servants and journalists especially, should have only one thing backing them up—their accomplishments. My work is out front every day for scrutiny by the judge—the public. It is represented by *Oslobodjenje*, which I immodestly remind you was voted "Newspaper of the Year in Yugoslavia in 1989," and by my regular columns in *Nedjelja*, which have been published under my full name for the last two-and-a-half years. Furthermore, if the government were making the decisions on the basis of ethnicity and the propensity for obedience about who could or could not work here . . . I would not want to do the job I do, so I don't want anyone at the top to "back" me up.

And last, but by no means least, I do not believe that the citizens of Bosnia-Hercegovina voted for Kljuić so that he could issue threats to members of the profession of which he was once himself a part, but rather so that he would, together with the other people and institutions in whom they placed their trust, focus on solving their more immediate problems—ensuring the regular monthly payment of their pensions and their salaries and improving their standard of living in general.

Press conferences by the nationalist parties had become, at the time, press conferences against the press. *Oslobodjenje* found itself accused within the same week by Radovan Karadžić of being under the control of the Muslim-Croat coalition and by Stjepan Kljuić of being under the influence of the Serbs. In responding at public venues to such mutually contradictory accusations, I would borrow the advertising slogan of the New York radio station which offended everyone but which everyone listened to: "If we weren't so bad, we wouldn't be so good."

The litany of complaints against us from all sides grew daily. The general secretary of the HDZ complained that *Oslobodjenje* did not represent the language and culture of the Croat people. I answered that in *Oslobodjenje* the authors wrote freely in the language and style of their choosing, and—as a clear example of the representation of Croats on the paper—I reminded him that the recently inaugurated Croatian biweekly, *Obzor* (Horizon), had a board of seven editors of which six were regular or frequent contributors to *Oslobodjenje*.

At a session of the City Assembly in Sarajevo, certain elected officials from the Muslim SDA, joining the party onslaught against the media, declared, "Kurspahić cannot represent the Muslim people." My response was that I had never been a candidate for the job, I did not participate in any election to represent anyone. My fear was, I said, that the people who had been elected for the job and were now sitting in the City Assembly were not going to live up to their own claims of representation.

At an Easter reception held by the Bosnian archbishop, now cardinal, Vinko Puljić, when I brought up the matter of the dispute between the government and the press with Prime Minister Jure Pelivan, he chided me in a friendly sort of way: "I don't understand why you are so hard-nosed in these talks. Couldn't we have agreed, for example, that the Assembly—as the founder—should appoint the manager, and you journalists choose the editor-in-chief?" No, it was not possible, I told him. "We have had a great deal of experience with the managers that were named by the so-called "Founder." Not one of them was the kind of manager that we needed—a businessman. Our manager today is a man with the requisite expertise and within two years we have succeeded in turning the company around. And that's the way we want to keep it. Besides, both you and I know that any manager whose appointment results from a party percentage agreement will arrive with party instructions. He will have the authority to give jobs and determine wages and payments and he will be thus in a position to make life miserable for the most democratically chosen editor-in-chief. For that reason, the deal is out of the question."

Chance had it that I should even have the occasion to discuss the matter with Radovan Karadžić. There was a popular series of open conversations with notable personalities, entitled "The Art of Living," conducted before a live audience in Sarajevo and broadcast on television. After one of these programs, its producers and my friends from Belgrade, Aleksandar Tijanić, Dragan Babić, and Mirjana Bobić-Mojsilović, invited me to dinner at the elegant Magnum restaurant in Sarajevo. Joining us were their guests on that evening's program: Stipe Šuvar, Stjepan Mesić, and Radovan Karadžić. I had a long and pleasant conversation with the two guests from Zagreb. Mesić had replaced Šuvar in the Presidency of the Yugoslav federal government and they were both talking openly about behind-the-scene Serbian maneuvering to impose martial law in the country for which Serbia always lacked the decisive fifth vote. After they left for their late evening flight to Zagreb we were left with Karadžić and his wife.

Mirjana Bobić-Mojsilović was the one who turned the topic to the relationship of the government and the press. "It would be a pity if the democratically elected government were to undemocratically take control of the media which is among the most open in all of Yugoslavia. For example, our conversations, in which people of very opposing viewpoints participate, would be possible only in Sarajevo," she said.*

"But we have nothing against journalists," Karadžić protested. "From the beginning we've said that we would push for their freedom. We are simply opposed to the editorial policies of the media from this area." The response was exactly in line with his party's approach which was to win over journalists with blandishments and affirmations of support and isolate their editors. "It is those policies that we have a problem with. People telephone me at home and ask, 'So, did you take over the government or didn't you, if *Oslobodjenje* can get away with constantly attacking you? What are you going to do about it?' Let Mr. Kurspahić tell you why his newspaper always publishes every letter which is written against me but never publishes one which supports me."

"Maybe because we don't get any letters supporting you," I said to Karadžić. "Our 'Tribunal' page is open to all readers. I could easily prove that the largest number of letters we publish criticizing various

---

* It would later turn out that not quite every viewpoint was welcome even in Sarajevo. When the program announced the guest appearance of the chetnik leader, Vojislav Šešelj, protest demonstrations were held, and the authors of the program were physically threatened, after which they did not return to Sarajevo.

people are written against me—often making the most serious accusations. Similarly we publish letters concerning you. And as for the supposedly unpublished letters which are written in support of you, let's immediately, on this restaurant's napkin, write up an invitation to the readers to send to you at SDS headquarters and to us at the editorial offices, a copy of every properly signed letter that we refused to publish, and I will either publish it or eat it."

From the table next to ours, one of Karadžić's bodyguards had been following the conversation with great concentration. At this point, he jumped in unceremoniously, "We know how you operate. Not only do you not publish favorable letters about Mr. Karadžić, you even concoct the letters against him!"

"That's a lie!" I exploded.

"No, it's not!" the bodyguard continued. "We looked for a certain Jovo Garojević, supposedly from Velika Kladuša, who wrote a letter against the doctor, and we established that such a person does not exist."

"Such a person does exist. We carefully verify the authenticity of all such letters."

Although I knew that the editor of the "Tribunal," Midhat Plivčić, always checked out the obligatory address to verify the authenticity of each author of the most sensitive letters, I wanted to be sure. The next morning I asked about the man who—fortunately for him—had not been hunted down by Karadžić's men. "Don't worry, he exists. I talked with him myself on the phone," Plivčić answered, confirming what I already knew without asking.

Meanwhile, Ostojić was continuing his crusade against the media. Rather than proposing to the Assembly, in his capacity as minister of information, that it examine the statute for *Oslobodjenje*, which was entirely compatible with the existing laws on information and public companies and which had been introduced in the previous Assembly a few months before the new government came to power, he prepared a proposal asking that the law be changed as an emergency measure, and only in the one particular article—the selection of the manager and the editor-in-chief. He proposed that the Assembly, and not the working journalists themselves, should decide the appointments. At the first meeting at which the government was asked to consider the proposal, the ministers—acting, perhaps, as independent public figures—with a majority vote rejected the initiative of the Ministry for Information. They said that such a change could not be undertaken without consulting democratic public opinion; that the election of the editor-in-chief could not be decided without the consent of the editorial staff which he would head; and that it would be advisable to organize a round-table discussion and have an exchange of opinion in order to arrive at the most democratic solution.

This admirable display of independent thinking and regard for democracy, however, was short-lived. Soon thereafter, it seems, the leaders of the parties whipped their men into line and the takeover efforts against the media were renewed. Instead of the promised democratic dialogue, a group of the top people in *Oslobodjenje* were invited to a conversation with Prime Minister, Jure Pelivan, his deputy, Rusmir Mahmutcehajic, and Minister of Information, Velibor Ostojić. It was then that they announced the plan to change the law by an emergency measure. We warned the representatives of the government that their decisions were running counter to what was happening elsewhere: it was the beginning of March 1991 and there had been massive and bloody demonstrations against government control over the media in Belgrade.

"For such appointments you will have to find the Bosnian equivalents of Mitević (then the director of Belgrade Television whose resignation was sought by the demonstrators), and you will not find them among any reputable journalists," I said.

"If I believed that there were anything undemocratic about this, I would be opposed. I value *Oslobodjenje* too highly to wish to bring it down; but this is a matter of the democratic control of parliament over the media," Mahmutcehajic argued.

"You cannot have your cake and eat it, too. You can't get the state subsidy (for the newsprint) as well as your independence," Ostojić chimed in with his "argument" on the budgetary assistance to *Oslobodjenje*—assistance which was given to all major dailies in all Yugoslav republics in order to keep prices of the papers low and thus affordable to the public.

"Then we'll do without the subsidy," was our answer.

We had, of course, come prepared. On February 14, 1991, anticipating a showdown with the government, the editorial staff had met to determine our course of action. A document, "*Oslobodjenje* in the Time of Change," had been distributed earlier for discussion, amendment, and approval, which included the proposal that we renounce any kind of state support, including the subsidy on the cost of newsprint, if it was to be used as a means of curtailing our professional independence. At the meeting, the document was adopted unanimously.

The strength of the journalists' opposition to anything that smacked of state or party control could be gauged from the decision by many to put their views in writing and on the record. At the editorial staff meeting, the editor of regional pages, Gordan Matrak, reported that the document had been reviewed and approved by all the correspondents' bureaus of *Oslobodjenje*. He also passed along numerous statements he had received from our correspondents across Yugoslavia and abroad. These statements essentially conveyed an unequivocal message: the journalists of *Oslobodjenje* had had a surfeit of state control and censorship; the last few years in which the paper had fought for its liberation had been exhilarating ones; they wanted to continue to work for a paper which had the potential, and was already becoming a truly independent, respectable, high-quality journal; they would therefore not allow the process to be obstructed and set back several decades. "Substantially and surely, the constraints on our freedom have fallen away. At this juncture, we are being asked to put our keys to the editorial office into the empty strongbox of the new government. In making such a move, the new government assumes the garb of its defeated competition, the old government. It is a pitiful spectacle," wrote Gordana Knežević from Cairo, her comments summing up the clarity of resolve at *Oslobodjenje* to defend the paper's independence.

The editorial staff meeting was a heated affair. Mirko Šagolj, for instance, found offensive the threats issued by some party leaders to have their followers boycott the paper: "Who has such power that they can dictate to the people what to buy and what not to buy, what to read and what not to read?" Zlatko Dizdarević wanted it to be understood that to divide up *Oslobodjenje* among the parties in power was to destroy it, "which would mean," he continued somewhat presciently, "a significant victory in the battle to destroy Bosnia-Hercegovina." Branko Tomić announced that "there [was] no good Serb, Croat, or Muslim who would be better than a good journalist in our trade." Hasan Fazlić was determined that he "would not back off by a single inch from what we have achieved in the last few years." Nagorka Idrizović agreed: "We are not fighting for any new or greater rights, but simply to preserve the freedom which we have already fought for and won."

At the end, Hrvoje Malić, our graphics designer, spoke with deep emotion of the time he had spent at *Oslobodjenje*. "I am probably the oldest person here," he said. "Watching all of this unfold and listening to you when I am approaching the end of my professional career, I can tell you simply that I am extremely proud and grateful. Thank you for the privilege of being here together with you and for the privilege of having worked with you in this publishing house." Hrvoje would spend more than two years of the siege of Sarajevo in the Serbian-occupied Grbavica neighborhood. He called me a few times from there while the phone lines still worked, for the last time to commend my open letter to the Croatian president Tudjman accusing him of joining Milošević in the common design to divide Bosnia. After that we lost all contact. I could not even ask our foreign colleagues, who were able to cross the dividing lines, to look for Hrvoje at Grbavica: if he was in hiding, to look for him would be to endanger his life. Even though we lived just few hundred meters away, it would take us several months to learn that he had died there. Not one of us was able to pay a decent last tribute to that great designer whose creativity had contributed so greatly to our efforts to remake the image of *Oslobodjenje*.

In retrospect, it would not be out of place to say that in resisting the partitioning of *Oslobodjenje*, as of the other media, we were defending the indivisibility of the institutions of Bosnia-Hercegovina into separate Muslim, Serb, and Croat entities while the divisive, nationalist impulses of the parties in power were paving the road to Bosnia's devastating partition (and their own path to perdition). The government, however, seemed blind to it all. Primitive triumphalism was everywhere as the new leaders pursued their separate but mutually reinforcing agendas, and claimed the exclusive right to speak for their "own" nation.

The ordinary folks who constituted these "nations," nevertheless, found their own ways to speak for themselves—through graffiti on the walls of Sarajevo.

"Tito, come back!" someone appealed on a wall in the center of the city.

"No, thank you. I'd rather not," was the response, signed: "Tito."

A DEFEAT FOR THE NATIONALISTS

ON MARCH 19, 1991, the government decided to move ahead with its decision to present its proposal concerning *Oslobodjenje* and Radio and Television Sarajevo to the Assembly. It asked that the proposed changes be enacted into law as "an emergency measure." The Citizens Council of the Assembly of Bosnia-Hercegovina convened on March 26, 1991. On that day, *Oslobodjenje* published an open letter to the delegates on its front page: "Vote No." It read, in part, as follows:

> Honorable Members of the Assembly: Today you are faced with your own personal test of democracy: with the choice to vote for or against a free, independent press—and, thus, to vote for or against the people who, in electing you, entrusted you with the honor and the responsibility of democratic government.
>
> The government of Bosnia-Hercegovina proposes that in an emergency bill, you should change the law concerning the public companies of *Oslobodjenje* and Radio and Television Sarajevo, specifically the article relating to the selection of the managers and chief editors of the Republic's media. This emergency proposal would give you, rather than the journalists and other members of *Oslobodjenje* and Radio and Television Sarajevo, the authority to decide who will be in charge of the media they work for. In this manner, the government shall draw you into sanctioning an antidemocratic measure which will place the media under the control of the government. [This proposal is being placed before you] at this precise moment when in Belgrade and in other regions of the country journalists and the public are fighting for their democratic right to free speech and a free press.
>
> We appeal to you, in the name of our profession and the people of this Republic, do not let a democratically elected multiparty parliament take away the freedom which the press has won under the one-party system. Vote no! . . .
>
> The proposal which the government is trying to foist on you today reveals its extremely arrogant and ignorant attitude not only towards those of us who work in the Republic's media, but towards the vast majority of the people of Bosnia-Hercegovina

who have unambiguously supported the position we adopted long before the election: that in a multiparty democracy, the media can only survive if it is truly independent and nonpartisan, open to all parties and platforms, ideas and individuals, and responsible only to the public—to its readers and its audience—and not to any government, past, present, or future. It needs to be remembered that it was the independence of the media which contributed in great measure to the full participation of the public in all phases of the first free election in Bosnia-Hercegovina. . . .

Those who are seeking to stifle the voice of independent journalism attempt to silence us with the argument that we cannot have our independence and a subsidy from the state at the same time. It is a bogus and insulting argument on two counts. First, if the Republic of Bosnia-Hercegovina supports and contributes to maintain the institutions of the media, it does so in the name of, and with the use of funds of, all of its citizens, and not with the money of the present or the future occupiers of government office. So it is both sensible and moral to support only a free, independent, nonpartisan press which does not function according to the dictates of the parties in power. Second, with regard to the facts, we have already publicly and unanimously declared that we will refuse support in the form of a newsprint subsidy (which amounts to ten percent of our income) if it is to be used by the government as an instrument of blackmail and a means of our subjugation. The reimposition of government control over editorial appointments at *Oslobodjenje*, even if it issues from this democratically elected Assembly dominated as it is by the often conflicting agendas of the parties in power, will be a dangerous step towards the destruction of this paper, which belongs to all the citizens of Bosnia-Hercegovina.

Those who ignore its voice will be answerable to a people who had voted for democratic change.

Respectfully, the Editorial Staff of *Oslobodjenje*.

Anticipating the worst, the journalists and workers of *Oslobodjenje* and Radio and Television Sarajevo prepared at the same time to hold a peaceful demonstration outside the Assembly the next day should the government's proposal be adopted and enacted into law. Accordingly, the public was informed and asked to join the protest. The Association of Journalists, the Union of Print Workers, various student organizations, and numerous other groups announced their support and, on behalf of press freedom and in a show of solidarity with the journalists, called for popular participation in the demonstration.

The representatives of the three ruling parties in the Citizens Council dismissed the gathering support for a free press as nothing but "the resistance of small unofficial groups within the media" and "an effort by those appointed in the past to hold on to their positions." The three parties had practically adopted the proposal at an earlier "test vote" in the representatives' clubs, so that the heated offensive mounted by the opposition parties in parliament to the Assembly's control of the media could only drag out the debate but ultimately not stop the passage of the government's "emergency measure."

Furthermore, in a move calculated to still all doubts—made probably at the insistence of Velibor Ostojić—the president of the Citizens Council, Professor Abdulah Konjicija, invited Radoslav Nešković from the Center for Development of Radio and Television Sarajevo to address the Assembly. Neskovic was not a member of the Assembly but was active in the leadership of the SDS. His role was to testify that he had in his possession "data and confessions" which indicated that the opposition to the measure was actually motivated by fear that the financial dealings and investments of the Radio and Television Sarajevo would be brought out into the open. "These drawers need to be opened as soon as possible," said Neskovic to the representatives in the Assembly. When Sejfudin Tokić of the Alliance of Reformist Forces asked why and in what capacity Neskovic was addressing the Assembly, Konjicija said that he had been invited to attend "as a knowledgeable person on the situation at Radio-Television." Tokić's sarcastic response—"then I must applaud you on the editing job you're doing on this session"—did not, of course, deter Konjicija, who had then proceeded to mislead the Assembly by stating that the representatives of *Oslobodjenje* and Radio and Television Sarajevo had also been invited to participate in this discussion but they had refused to attend. The truth was altogether different.

Several days before the meeting, on Thursday, March 21, Konjicija had called the editorial offices and spoken with me. He wished to express his dissatisfaction with some item that had appeared that day in *Oslo-bodjenje*, and in the subsequent conversation had gone on to express his support for the efforts of the paper to remain what it was. He suggested that I might participate in the upcoming session of the Council of which he was president. He mentioned even the possible length of my presentation and, if it were necessary, that of the manager of the paper, Salko Hasanefendić, "Be ready to talk for ten to fifteen minutes."

As agreed, I called him the next day in order to confirm our participation at the meeting. The offer, it turned out, was no longer open. "Unfortunately, we will not be able to go ahead with it," Konjicija informed me. "The Presidency of the Assembly has rejected the participation of the representatives of *Oslobodjenje* and Radio and Television Sarajevo. They said that the journalists would, in any event, be attending the session as reporters, but your participation in the discussion would set a precedent and break with customary practice. You can, if you wish, write a letter in the name of *Oslobodjenje*, and I will read it." The same message was conveyed to the manager of *Oslobodjenje*, Hasanefendić, and to the president of Radio and Television Sarajevo, Nedjo Miljanović, by Konjicija and the president of the Assembly, Momčilo Krajišnik, on the day before the session at a meeting held in Krajišnik's office.

A "letter" did not constitute participation in the debate: our open letter in *Oslobodjenje* was there for all to see. Having refused to allow us the opportunity to present and argue our case, the president of the Citizens' Council had proceeded to furnish his honest credentials with a lie: namely, that we were offered the opportunity to participate in the discussion and that we had declined the invitation! And then, as the crowning bit of evidence against "those top dogs in the media," there was introduced testimony of a member of the Executive Board of the Serbian Democratic party who in no way represented the institution where he was employed. Such were the conditions under which the first democratically chosen Assembly of Bosnia-Hercegovina—or rather its Citizens Council—with the 84 votes of the ruling three-party coalition in favor, adopted the government's "emergency measure." It should be said that the delegates of all the non-nationalist, opposition parties—the Alliance of Reformist Forces, the Social Democratic Party, the Liberal Party, and the Muslim Bosniak Organization—signaled their dissent by refusing to participate in the voting.

Needless to say, the Assembly's performance was not a surprise. Battered daily by the party hawks and their unrelenting nationalist arithmetic, constantly denounced as anti-Serb, anti-Croat, or anti-Muslim by those who had assumed the right to determine for everyone the measure and quality of their ethnic affiliation, we at *Oslobodjenje* did not expect this unholy brotherhood to relinquish control over the "means of information." If knowledge is power, our current rulers, like those who went before them, wanted to make sure that it did not become freely available to the people they severally and exclusively claimed to represent. But the battle was not lost. We could not conceive of surrender, for to do so was to accept the destruction of a paper which we had fought so hard to liberate from the control of the previous regime, where we had spent so many of our working years and felt the first breath of freedom.

The day after the farce at the Assembly, March 27, 1991, exactly at noon, on the open ground in front of the Assembly building, a huge protest rally was held. In attendance were journalists and technical workers of *Oslobodjenje* and Radio and Television Sarajevo; university students and faculty; members of the intelligentsia; and industrial workers. Over 5,000 people, representing the entire spectrum of Bosnia's multiethnic society had gathered to stand up and be counted. The speeches made at the rally are memorable not merely for the support offered to the cause of press freedom—which was there and desperately needed—but also for the passionate, angry defiance hurled at the parties in power who wanted to impose their own totalitarian "realities" on a people who had for too long been denied the right to think for themselves.

The first speaker was Gordan Matrak of *Oslobodjenje*. "This Republic has seen truth threatened since the dark ages," said Matrak. "Today, without the help of the gentlemen who are currently seated in the Assembly, when an unrelenting war is being waged against the media in this country, Bosnia-Hercegovina has taken the lead in transforming itself into the place where the truth can always be spoken to anyone. The pages of *Oslobodjenje* and the programs of Radio and Television Sarajevo are open spaces for democratic dialogue. It is here, more than anywhere else, that one can expect to find a clear and objective presentation of information." In the name of the journalists of *Oslobodjenje*, and to the accompaniment of thunderous applause, Matrak called for the resignation of the Minister of Information, Velibor Ostojić, and his deputy, Mustafa Mujagić, from the positions they were using to hound the press.

Željko Vuković, the president of the Association of Journalists of Bosnia-Hercegovina, said that the Assembly's action of the previous day had broken two of the principles without which democracy cannot exist: independent news reporting and an independent judiciary. "The journalists will not agree to be the spoils of war for the ruling parties. Our voices are an instrument of the people, not of the government. We will not agree to use our writing to deceive the people and to lie about reality according to the wishes of the government."

Zoran Popovski of Television Sarajevo, seconding the call for resignations, declared: "Either the minister of information does not recognize the seriousness of this profession and of the situation which he himself is responsible for creating or else he wishes to elevate his own undemocratic logic to the height of the highest democratic principle."

Zekerijah Smajić, an editor at *Yutel*, had come to the rally from the hospital where he was recovering from the injuries he suffered after being hit by one of Milošević's bodyguards while he was covering one of the federal summits. He was given a thunderous ovation when he said: "I am not the only reporter who has been hospitalized. Increasingly more of us are landing up there, and more will follow if we allow them to do whatever they want with us. We cannot allow them to soften up our heads. The time is past when they could get away with trampling over us, and every one of them who wants to do so must be removed from this beautiful Assembly building."

The president of the Union of Students of Sarajevo University, Dejan Mastilović, spoke of the students' unrelenting struggle against autocracy: "We fought earlier against an undemocratic government, and today we fight against the undemocratic undertakings of this democratically elected government." His professor, Božidar Gajo Sekulić, recalled a similar rally at the time of the student uprisings in 1968: "At this same place in Marindvor there was a word which was used as an appropriate label for the bureaucratic government. That word was "papani" (popular derogatory term which translated loosely means, "simple-minded peasants"). Today both the citizens of Bosnia-Hercegovina and the new government are at a higher level, but the impression remains that the years of regarding citizens as subjects has left a lasting legacy which dominates the mentality and disposition of the new government. We have had enough of being subjects; we want to be independent free citizens. And this we cannot achieve without a free and democratic press."

"Papani, papani," the crowd yelled at the functionaries whenever they made furtive appearances at the windows of the parliament to monitor the proceedings outside.

Zoran Milanović, the editor-in-chief of *Naši dani,* and his colleagues, Senad Pećanin and Pedja Kojović had brought a funeral wreath to the square in front of the Assembly, with the words on the ribbon: "In Remembrance of the Freedom of the Press." To loud applause, he raised the wreath above his head, and said: "When we brought this wreath, we did not know whose grave we would place it on. Now we know that it should go on the grave of ignorance and intolerance. If Messrs. Konjicija, Ostojić, and Čengić think that we are afraid of them, they are wrong. We have already been arrested and beaten, and, as [the writer] Abdulah Sidran has said, we have had a bellyful of fear and now there is no further space for it."

Other speakers came up to denounce the ruling parties' attempts to divide Bosnians into their ethnic parts. Professor Emil Vlajki stated, "We have not gathered here today as Muslims, Serbs, or Croats, nor does our ethnic composition interest us, but rather we want to finally receive what the bourgeois revolution managed to achieve more than two centuries ago: freedom of the press and freedom of speech." The filmmaker Ademir Kenović said: "When we see what darkness reigns over the press in Belgrade and Zagreb because of the blanking out of all that the censors there do not like, it is not difficult to imagine that the darkness to fall upon Bosnia-Hercegovina—with three 'ethnic truths' vying for space—would be three times greater!"

The editor of the *Yutel* program, Dževad Sabljaković, was equally contemptuous of the purveyors of ethnic truths. "On this day, those who are dedicated to the journalist's profession have decided," he declared, "that they will not be divided on the basis of anything—not on the basis of nationality, nor on the basis of party affiliation. We know that there is no such thing as a Muslim, Serbian, or Croatian truth, nor truth according to the SDS, SDA, or HDZ, nor is there such a thing as absolute truth and absolute objectivity, but there is such a thing as heading in the right direction. And this is the path that we choose to take, along which we will eat some very bitter, but occasionally also some very sweet, bread."

The next speaker was Professor Zdravko Grebo. "I do not know if this is the moment of truth, but it certainly is the moment of courage," he said. "The moment of courage in which I believe the men and women of the press in Bosnia-Hercegovina at last have a chance, after long years of fear in which this nation has lived, to show that they have understood that there comes a time in which the truth simply must be spoken. And without that speaking of the truth, any other social, political, and ideological achievement is utterly meaningless." He went on to add: "Someone yesterday asked a member of the opposition parties what it was in these adopted measures that constituted totalitarianism and repression. The answer very simply is that we have a government which believes that winning an election automatically confers on it absolute rights over society and our lives. This view [that political power equals absolute power] is totalitarianism. This is exactly what we had hoped that we had left behind us." Grebo then went on to propose that, in addition to other demands, we challenge the constitutionality of the new proposal to change the law before the Constitutional Court.

The last one to address the rally, I had a brief message for the demonstrators and the Parliament: "Have you ever seen a larger 'small group of people concerned for their own positions'—as they refer to us inside that building? They tell you that we want to enjoy both financial support and professional independence. And I declare now publicly, in front of you and in front of the cameras: Take from us the last dinar that you would give us if that is the price of independence and freedom of the press in Bosnia-Hercegovina."

At the end of the rally, a delegation of journalists went in to present our demands and to talk with the president of the Assembly, Momčilo Krajišnik, Prime Minister Jure Pelivan, and the president of the Citizens' Council, Abdulah Konjicija.* From the outset, Abdulah Konjicija tried to reassure the journalists, "You should know that you

---

* The following five demands were presented to the Assembly:

    1. We demand that the press and media be free, and that *Oslobodjenje*, and Radio and Television Sarajevo be independent and nonpartisan.

    2. We demand that the Assembly of Bosnia-Hercegovina respect the will of the democratic public opinion and, with the same urgency of the emergency measure,

are speaking with the three biggest believers in democracy in this building." Everything else he said was an attempt to prove the democratic character of the emergency change in the law. However, in the course of the discussion, agreement was reached on two points: first, that the Constitutional Court should be requested, also as an emergency undertaking, to determine the constitutionality of this change, and second, that the government should meet to examine the demand for the resignations of Ostojić and Mujagić.

Krajišnik was concerned that the journalists' dissatisfaction should not be used against the government to show that they have no respect for freedom of the press: "That is why we want to find a joint solution to this problem."** The next day, of course, nothing happened except for a new demonstration of the arrogance of power. In the official announcement following a meeting of the government, it was stated that participation of the government in the organization of the media was part of the government's overall program. The question of the resignations of Ostojić and Mujagić was not mentioned.

While the discussion between the representatives of the journalists and those of the government was proceeding in the Assembly building, I had an unusual encounter in the square in front of the Assembly. Three people were taking pictures of the wreath which had been placed there by the journalists of *Naši dani*.

"Do you know what that is?" they asked me in English.

"It is a wreath placed there by the young journalists of Bosnia-Hercegovina as a symbol of mourning over the death of the freedom of the press," I answered.

---

withdraw the change to the law which was adopted yesterday which took away the rights of the journalists of *Oslobodjenje* and Radio Television Sarajevo to choose their own management.

3. We demand that the government of Bosnia-Hercegovina meet and that their Minister of Information Velibor Ostojić and Deputy Minister Mustafa Mujagić submit their irrevocable resignation, because they have failed the first test of democracy.

4. We demand that the Assembly of Bosnia-Hercegovina discuss and approve the statutes of Oslobodjenje and Radio Television Sarajevo, which were adopted by secret ballot of all employees. These statutes call out, as an inalienable right of the employees, to select their managers on the basis of the law concerning organization of corporations and their chief editors by secret ballot of all journalists.

5. The journalists of *Oslobodjenje* demand of the government and the Assembly

I learned that the tourists were members of a delegation of the American Congress and the Commission on Human Rights who were spending the day in Sarajevo. Their official hosts in the government took good care that their schedule in the capital of Bosnia-Hercegovina would keep them away from the parliament building. But the three of them, including a Republican congressman from Florida, Clay Shaw, had come up to the entrance of the Assembly building with a video camera to see what was going on.

"Our official hosts in Sarajevo told us that this was an attempt by the Communists to maintain their control of the media," the congressman said.

"But they didn't tell you that the majority of the people in the new government, including the president of the Assembly, and the president of the Government, and the minister of information, are all former Communists. The ministers in the new government have a combined total of more than two hundred years experience in the League of Communists. That's the way it was in this country. Until a few months ago we had only one party, and no one had any choice: the majority of public figures were members of that party," I told him.

"But is it true that you in the media support the opposition and hinder objective news coverage for the new government, that you are under the influence of the Communists?" the Congressman continued his line of inquiry.

"Not at all. Communists for the last year or two have been bitter in their complaints about us. If we hadn't opened our pages and our programs to the presentation of all the parties, their platforms and

that they free them of all financial support and the status of a "public company" if this status and financial support will be used as a means of blackmail.

**At this point, it might be of some interest to note that Momčilo Krajišnik was to become a central figure, together with Radovan Karadžić, in the SDS's campaign to establish a "Republika Srpska." Following the Dayton "peace", he played the principle role in organising the forced exodus of the Serb population in the Sarajevo districts held by the SDS forces which were to be returned to Bosnian control. In the election of 1996 held under the provisions of the Dayton Accord, he was the party's candidate for the Serb representative on the Bosnian Presidency. In clear violation of the parameters established at Dayton, he openly and repeatedly declared his intent to secure "Republika Srpska's" complete secession from Bosnia-Hercegovina.

personalities, who knows whether the public would have ever learned about many of those who are now in power and whether they would have elected them. In other words, we enabled them, while they were a part of the opposition, to freely express their views, just as we are now open to the views of the opposition."

It is not clear what impressions the visiting American lawmakers finally went away with, but it was abundantly clear that the government was playing on its visitors' anti-Communist reflex to burnish their own democratic credentials and demonize our part in this struggle. It was pathetic propaganda and it gained few converts where it mattered—at home. Our continued resistance to a government takeover of the media drew exceptional support throughout Bosnia-Hercegovina and across Yugoslavia. The editorial offices of *Oslobod-jenje* and of Radio and Television Sarajevo were swamped with letters and telegrams urging us to stay the course. The message came in from ordinary citizens, from labor unions, professional associations, and, of course, from journalists everywhere.*

Meanwhile, ignoring the two-point agreement reached by its representatives with the press on the day of the rally, the government moved swiftly ahead with its plans to dispose of the "undesirables" in the media. At the end of March, a buoyant Velibor Ostojić appeared on television and challenged the leaders of *Oslobodjenje* and Radio and Television Sarajevo to demonstrate the support they claimed for

---

* The letters and telegrams that *Oslobodjenje* received at this time were in themselves a reflection of the insurrectionist mood around the country. Here is a brief sampling:

Journalists of *Front Slobode,* Tuzla: "Comrades! Don't give up! *Oslobodjenje* must be independent or it cannot survive. And then there will be no Bosnia, since what they are attempting is only a prelude to the conversion of the Republic into another Lebanon."

Zdravko Grebo: "Everything you are doing is not only brave but also beautiful. These may be only the first shots fired in the antinationalist resistance movement. If we have to, let us die together. But we shouldn't have to!"

Editorial office of *Borba,* Belgrade: "Comrades! Count us in. You have our support in your struggle to defend a free and independent press."

Slobodan Štrbac, Drvar: "Do not allow those who have made *Politika* (Belgrade) into Politikin Zabavnik (*Politika*'s 'comic book') to convert your newspaper into *Male novine* (a newspaper for children)."

Journalists of *Ekonomska politika,* Belgrade: "Keep up the fight, and we will keep up the support."

themselves. If the journalists were to vote in a secret ballot for their current leaders and not for him, he said, he was prepared to leave his ministerial office! The journalists of *Oslobodjenje* immediately took him up on his offer and organized a referendum in strict conformity with the rules of a secret ballot. The results were humiliating for the Minister: 204 votes against and five votes for him. But, of course, Ostojić did not leave. He made use of the reconvening of the Serb organization Prosvjeta ("Education") at Trebinje to say: "As an obedient servant of my people, I will no longer be silent. I want to state publicly that the means of information in Bosnia-Hercegovina are in ideological opposition to the Serb people, and are, at the same time, an anti-Serbian voice. For that reason I will not be content in my work until the top positions in this media are filled with democratically chosen, honest, honorable, competent, expert, and literate people, who will represent all the nationalities of Bosnia-Hercegovina. I will not submit my resignation to the Sarajevo dandies, and I will not submit my resignation to the anti-Serbian coalition. I will submit my resignation to my own colleagues, to my own people, if I do not do my job the way I should."

On April 22, 1991, the Citizens' Council decided to establish a commission for selection of candidates for appointment to the positions of managers and chief editors of *Oslobodjenje* and Radio and Television Sarajevo. *Oslobodjenje* responded by running a blank space in lieu of its usual "In Focus" column on the front page with the

---

The National Council for Defense of Bosnia-Hercegovina, Gradačac: "We call upon all citizens of Bosnia-Hercegovina to join the battle which *Oslobodjenje* and Radio and Television Sarajevo are fighting to protect the interests of us all."

Petar Luković, Belgrade journalist: "You have all my moral, intellectual, and professional support to carry on, and to win, in the battle against these comic Nazi characters, who are sure that providence and elections gave them the right to determine the limits of freedom. Journalism is not Serbian, nor Muslim, nor Croatian. Least of all is it something which belongs to the types of Velibor Ostojić and Abdulah Konjicija. In the war against such monsters, use all means: legal, illegal, institutional, non-institutional, streets, off-the-street, parliament, strikes, rallies (see S. Milošević's example). Victory must be yours, because defeat would be defeat for us all. Do not give up!"

Journalists of the independent Zenica newspaper, *Naša riječ:* "We give you our complete support in your just struggle; editorial policies in publishing houses must be determined by those who are members of the profession. We are hungry, but free."

Executive Board of the Independent Syndicate of Radio and Television Belgrade: "We support fully your battle for free and independent news reporting."

message in small letters at the bottom: "By the Government's will." On
May 7, the following letter from the Assembly's Commission for Elections and Appointments arrived:

> You are hereby notified that in accordance with Paragraph 1 of the
> Decision on the Composition and Conduct of the Appointments
> Commission for the nomination of the Manager of the public cor-
> poration *Oslobodjenje*, and the Editors-in-chief of the daily paper
> *Oslobodjenje* and the publications for our citizens residing abroad
> and for our emigrants (Official Document of the Socialist Repub-
> lic of Bosnia-Hercegovina, number 14/91), it is established that, in
> addition to the 11 representatives of the Assembly of the Socialist
> Republic of Bosnia-Hercegovina, the public corporation of *Oslo-
> bodjenje* is to appoint two representatives. In accordance with this,
> we request that you notify us as soon as possible of the names of
> your representatives to this Appointments Commission.

Only two days later, following the decision of the editorial staff
that we not, in any way, recognize the legitimacy of the government's
action, the manager of the paper, Salko Hasanefendić sent a response:

> With reference to your communication . . . I am informing you that
> it is the decision of the employees of the newspaper *Oslobodjenje*
> that *Oslobodjenje* will not designate any representatives to your
> Appointments Commission nor will the current manager and edi-
> tor-in-chief submit their names as candidates for your considera-
> tion for those positions, inasmuch as the employees dispute the
> constitutionality and legality of the change of the law, in connection

---

Professors Dr. Hasan Sušić and Dr. Gordan Srkalović, of the medical faculty in
Tuzla: "We are fortunate to have you. Do not allow them to get in your way, because
what they are trying today to do to you, they have left until tomorrow to do to us,
and therefore we are with you both today and tomorrow."

President of the Society of Journalists of Slovenia Andrei Poznič: "We support
your demands because we ourselves are also contending with attempts to control the
media. It is our firm belief that the objective measure of democracy under any
regime is not simply a free multiparty election and parliamentary order, but rather
autonomy and independence of the public voice of the media which can only be an
instrument of the public, and not of the legislative, executive or judicial powers."

with which a suit has been filed with the Constitutional Court of Yugoslavia and of Bosnia-Hercegovina, and likewise dispute the legality of the Commission formed on the basis of that change of the law.

The fact that out of a total of thirteen members on the Appointments Commission we would be able to name only two was corroborating evidence, if any was needed, that our participation in the Commission would have been entirely cosmetic. Not wishing to waste any further time sparring with the government, we got down to the business of preparing our case for the Constitutional court which we had filed immediately following the decision taken at the demonstration in front of the Parliament.

Our accounts on the property ownership of the newspaper and the corporation of *Oslobodjenje*, which we were obliged by law to present to the government, as a document of ownership of the company, indicated that in the preceding ten years since the construction of the new building of *Oslobodjenje*, from the earnings of the paper and of the corporation, we had paid off nearly all the debts which had fallen due and that the state's participation amounted to only 14 percent in the property ownership of the corporation (primarily in the printing press section) and 8 percent in the ownership of the newspaper. No interpretation of these accounts could possibly justify a monopoly of the state over *Oslobodjenje*.

As we braced ourselves for further moves on the part of the government—the parties in the coalition were already naming their representatives to the Appointments Commission—reprieve came with the news from Belgrade: the Constitutional Court of Yugoslavia, in a meeting on May 30, 1991, had reached a decision which would stop the implementation of all individual acts and work being undertaken on the basis of the order of Article 1 of the Law concerning the public corporation *Oslobodjenje*. In other words, until a final decision was reached, the disputed change in the law could not be implemented!

We now had a few months to rest, regroup, and repair some of the damage. The relentless onslaught of the government had had numerous repercussions for *Oslobodjenje* during that year. Business partners were reluctant to reach any long-term agreements with us because they were unsure about the strength of commitment they could expect from the new people who were expected to take over the paper. We ourselves avoided making major decisions because we worried that we might not be there to implement them. Everyone in the editorial staff had been drained by the battle. Exhaustion and a certain degree of demoralization had begun to affect the quality of the paper. Galvanized by the Constitutional Court's interim decision to stay the implementation of the disputed law, we quickly moved to liberate ourselves from the "founder's" embrace of the Assembly by taking a decision to transform *Oslobodjenje* into a shareholding company. According to the law, we could not go directly from the status of a public corporation to the status of a shareholding company, but we took the first step: the registration of such a decision. The final decision was pronounced by the Constitutional Court of Bosnia-Hercegovina after the hearing held on September 26, 1991.

At the hearing, drawing more upon professional principles than upon my own training in law, I represented *Oslobodjenje*. Speaking, first of all, on the reasons for our opposition to the change in the law, I said:

> Our dispute with the "founder" begins precisely on this point: who is the founder of *Oslobodjenje*? I submit that it was not the erstwhile Socialist Alliance, nor is it the current Assembly. *Oslobodjenje* was founded by the liberation and antifascist movement in the Second World War. In the light of this fact, we cannot, nor do we wish to be converted into a transferable commodity, passed from government to government as they see fit.
>
> What are our arguments in our claim that the change in the law is a violation of the Constitution of 1974.
>
> First, that the state monopoly over the media is inimical to the constitutional right to be informed—to the freedom of the press. The government, by assuming the prerogative to appoint the top positions in the media, establishes a control over the content of the media. Our decades-long experience shows that whosoever has the right to appoint and to replace the chief editors has the power to control editorial policy.
>
> Second, in our specific case this change in the law runs counter to certain other, fundamental, elements of that same law, according to which *Oslobodjenje* is established as an independent and nonpartisan daily paper. The amendments introduced to the law state in

black and white that the appointment of the manager and editor-in-chief would be based on the interparty agreement on appointment policy. How is it possible to maintain the independent and nonpartisan character of the paper if its top people are named according to an agreement among the victorious parties?

For us in *Oslobodjenje* the implementation of this change in the law will do serious and irreversible damage. It will paralyze and destroy the paper as one of the few remaining unified institutions of the citizens of Bosnia-Hercegovina. It is enough to look at how the executive branch of the government or the Assembly are functioning where this three-party coalition is dominant. Whenever there is any important subject on the agenda, the ministers and delegates of one of the three parties stage a walkout! How would we, as editors appointed by these three nationalist parties, be able to edit a newspaper and reach the necessary decisions as to what would go on the front page and what on the inside pages, what would go on the top and what at the bottom? How would we publish commentary critical of any of the three ruling parties or their members in government if the editor of the particular page or column where the commentary would normally be published were an appointee of the party in question? Similarly what kind of business and editorial policy would it be possible to conduct if the manager, appointed by one party or the other, were to have all the power to hire, fire, and pay the employees? And if the editor-in-chief technically had the power to appoint the editors of the various departments, how autonomous would these decisions be if the appointments had to conform to the inter-party agreement, with one editor designated by the SDS, the other by the SDA, and so on ...?

In short, our refusal to accept the dictation of the government in the selection of our top management is based both on professional concerns and on our commitment to the constitutional right of the citizens to freedom of information. It is our conviction that we in the media, as well as a democratically elected government, should be responsible not to each other but only to the public, which is to say, to the citizenry.

On the question of the property and ownership rights, the Assembly cannot have a monopoly on the management of the newspaper when its share of the ownership amounts to only 8 percent.

I believe that we do not fulfill the legal conditions to remain a "public company" because that is specified by law to be an organization established to serve a specific social interest, and in particular to secure "essential living conditions." We are, unfortunately, not part of the essential living conditions—if we were, we would have a circulation almost a hundred times larger than it is. We are willing to accept that the Assembly might participate in the appointments to the same degree that it participates in our financing and ownership, but that is by no means the proportion of 11 to 2 that the Appointments Commission is seeking! In fact, it is no more than 10 percent. . . .

I believe that this court will find itself confronted, in this situation, with numerous dilemmas: the will of the Assembly versus constitutionality; the government versus the public; a free press versus a controlled media; pluralism versus monopoly.

After I concluded this part of the presentation of arguments, the representatives of the government and the Assembly brought up the practice of the other republics where the Assemblies or even the Executive branch of the government appointed the editors and directors of the media. I responded by pointing out that surely we did not need examples from the other republics since we were all well acquainted with the extent of democracy that was available there: in Kosovo the Albanian language media in its entirety had been strangulated by policies issuing from Serbia; in Serbia itself, as in Montenegro, the press was being relentlessly targeted by the one-party dictatorship; and in Croatia, a democratically elected government was unashamedly seeking to subjugate the media. Why would we, as the most open and most liberal of the media in Yugoslavia, look for models in republics where press freedom is harshly circumscribed?

The government then changed tack and responded by arguing that the Constitution of 1974, in which freedom of information was defined, had been superseded and the provisions that it contained on the subject had no bearing on the case. I disagreed and countered with the observation that the progress of democracy in our country had not gone past or around but had, in fact, cut through the existing institutions of monopoly, transforming these or forcing these to yield to change. The Constitution of 1974 was at this stage the only constitution we had, and we must respect it and work from within it to secure enlarged democratic freedoms.

At the conclusion of the presentation of arguments, the observations and questions of the Justices of the Constitutional Court followed.

Justice Ćazim Sadiković spoke of the world's concept of the press as a "fourth estate" and pointed out that in the democratic world a clear distinction was made between the state and political parties. In other words, the state had separate and distinct claims that it made upon its citizens regardless of the political platforms of individual parties.

I agreed but pointed out that "here the state itself, represented by the Assembly, is not making that distinction. It is openly speaking about the interparty agreement on the control of the media. The Assembly itself is functioning on remote control, and it wants the media—newspapers, radio, and television—to function on the same basis."

"But then surely everything cannot remain the way that it was before?" the justice asked.

"Of course, it cannot. Up until last year we were the 'organ of the Socialist Alliance', and at our own initiative, long before the elections, we transformed ourselves into an independent nonpartisan daily. Furthermore, we had now taken a decision to convert *Oslobodjenje* into a shareholding company—you will notice that we are going from the state to the marketplace," I answered.

Justice Nedjo Milićević observed that the Assembly may not cite "social interest" as its justification for wanting to maintain control over *Oslobodjenje*, and at the same time relativize the Constitution of 1974, in which that "social interest is defined, when it suits its own convenience. Furthermore, why would the interest of the state be confined to *Oslobodjenje*, when, at the same time, the state declares no interest in, nor influence upon, the other newspapers which have a significantly larger circulation?"

Justice Ismet Dautbašić was interested in the percentage of ownership of *Oslobodjenje*. Salko Hasanefendić respectfully presented the breakdown of ownership in which the state's share amounted to approximately 8 percent.

"In what way does the appointing of the editor-in-chief and the manager on the part of the democratically elected Assembly threaten the freedom of the press which is guaranteed by the Constitution?" Justice Hasan Bakalović asked directly.

"This freedom would not merely be threatened, it would be destroyed," I answered. "By appointing editors of their choice, the parties in power will have a media responsible to those parties and not to the citizens of the Republic."

Justice Kasim Trnka asked, "How can the state protect the right of the citizens to freedom of information in conditions of the free market if one of the shareholders—on the basis of his ownership—achieves a monopoly over the paper?"

"It is possible, through a statute on ownership, to limit the percentage of ownership of individual shareholders: this is the case with the ownership statute of the *Borba* newspaper in Belgrade," I said.

Justice Alija Latić, at the end of the Constitutional Court's hearing, pointed out that the Constitution was older than the law on corporations which the Government was relying on, and he referred to Amendment 64 of the Constitution according to which "possession and work are bases for participation in the management."

The decision of the Constitutional Court arrived by fax on October 3, 1991, with the signature of the president of the court, Dr. Kasim Trnka. It read as follows:

It is confirmed that Article 1 of the Law on Amendment of the Law on Establishment of the Public Corporation *Oslobodjenje* ("Official publication of SRBiH," number 10/91), is not in accordance with the Constitution of the Socialist Republic of Bosnia-Hercegovina.

In accordance with Article 395 of the Constitution of the Republic of Bosnia-Hercegovina, this decision will be sent to the Assembly of the Socialist Republic of Bosnia-Hercegovina. This decision will be published in the Official Publications of SRBiH.

The battle was won. We had fought hard; the highest court in the Republic had upheld the justness of our cause. But this victory was not the end of the story.

TROUBLE AT *OSLOBODJENJE*

MY FIRST THREE YEARS AS EDITOR-IN-CHIEF had been years in which we had worked hard to establish new and higher professional standards at the paper. Professionalism was, for us, a refuge and a defense against all outside attempts to take control of *Oslobodjenje*. It was the journalists' answer to the political forces that laid claim to their loyalty on the basis of nationalism and it was the best way to achieve one's own liberation and maintain some semblance of sanity. The pressure of the three ruling parties upon *Oslobodjenje*, and then the mounting threat of war, in effect, concentrated our minds and our energy as never before.

Freed of the obligation to write according to the orders or expectations of any centers of power beyond the agreed-upon editorial policy of the paper, our journalists found themselves, many for the first time in their careers, confronting a challenge of an entirely different kind. They were now writing for a liberal, open newspaper, in the company of, and competing with, some of the best journalists in Yugoslavia, and were under pressure to produce well-written, well-researched articles and stories. The editorial demand for originality and excellence soon began to reveal the differences in the professional competence of different journalists, which previously had been submerged in the gray average. In the past, no distinctions were possible or apparent between the best and the mediocre; the talented and the ordinary; those who wanted to excel and those who were simply marking their time in a boring accumulation of days towards their retirement; those who proved their ability with every text they wrote and those who made up their lack of knowledge and talent with noisy demands for the correction of various "injustices." The development of higher and more rigorous standards of journalistic reporting and writing at *Oslobodjenje* was a cooperative effort by an editorial team which itself underwent a series of changes as the rising tide of nationalism and the war that it brought to Bosnia-Hercegovina began to take its terrible toll.

My first deputy editor, Drago Soldo—the paper's Moscow correspondent for eight years and an excellent authority on the trends and changes in Eastern Europe—knew how to read others' copy very critically, and had little patience with sloppy writing or inadequate research. Some of the younger colleagues did not always like his strict scrutiny and considered him "too demanding," even "boring" or "a nuisance." But his contribution was invaluable. Unfortunately, Soldo was only with me for a few months. He was retiring in September 1989 and we needed a new deputy editor. Upon his return from New York,

I offered Zoran Kurtović the job. I believed that his appointment to the position would strengthen the editorial team, since Kurtović, like myself, had been nominated as a candidate for editor-in-chief by the paper. For the two years that he worked as my deputy, he took charge of finalizing the paper in the newsroom. It was a very successful collaboration—we were in one mind about the conceptual framework of the paper—but, unfortunately, he could not stay. His wife had a job in Belgrade, his family lived there, and Yugoslavia was in the throes of war: in the fall of 1991, Zoran decided to leave for Belgrade to join his family but continued to work as a commentator for *Oslobodjenje*.

Following Zoran's departure, Miroslav Janković took over as deputy editor. Essentially an author, Janković had an original and fresh way of writing, full of common people's wisdom. Unlike Soldo or Kurtović, however, he was not an editor who would participate daily in the final setup of the first pages of the paper. But when he took over, the war in Croatia was already raging and tensions had mounted in Bosnia-Hercegovina as well; I therefore made a point of staying on after work every day myself until the first pages were completed.

In the summer of 1991, the very arduous and sensitive work of the editor of the newsroom, who worked with the editor-in-chief on editing the first six to seven pages of the paper, fell to Zlatko Dizdarević who until then had been the editor of the weekly *Nedjelja*. He had taken over from Fahro Memić, who had gone on a six-month leave of absence. Zlatko brought to the newsroom a much-needed element of sober professionalism at a time when the political crisis in Yugoslavia was pushing the country headlong into war.

The position of political editor at that juncture had been held by Ljiljana Smajlović. Young, intelligent, curious, and very literate, unwilling to settle for mediocrity, she had been doing an excellent job, insisting on tougher, higher standards in the political section of the paper. In the summer of 1991, however, she applied for the newly opened position as our correspondent in Brussels and was given the job. At that point, Gordana Knežević, who had just returned from her assignment as the paper's Cairo correspondent, took over. Gordana's arrival was to be a source of immeasurable strength to *Oslobodjenje*. A serious, dedicated journalist, she was a woman of many qualities. Her honesty, professional energy, and manner of relating and working with people contributed to the cohesion of the editorial staff during the exceedingly difficult times that came with the war. The same qualities won her the respect of, and helped her establish good working relations with, the government. And meeting and talking with the foreign correspondents who came through Sarajevo, she kept herself well informed and abreast of developments on all fronts, domestic and international.

Gordana was one of the real heroes of wartime *Oslobodjenje*: professionally indefatigable and always in action; privately in a desperate situation. In the first two years of the siege of Sarajevo, her family was torn apart, with her three children scattered across the world: her seven-year-old daughter, Olga, was sent to safety to live with family friends in Zagreb, Croatia, and, needless to say, missed her parents desperately; thirteen-year-old Boris stayed on with Gordana and her husband, Ivo, in Sarajevo but spent days alone at home even in the worst periods of shelling while his parents were at work; and fifteen-year-old Igor was living with a family and stranded, as it were, in Great Britain. But Gordana's enormous commitment to the multiethnic Bosnia we knew never wavered. She continued to work, assumed the responsibilities of deputy editor on Miroslav Janković's departure in 1992, headed the paper adeptly whenever I was away, and still found the time and the strength to come to the aid of countless people at *Oslobodjenje* and in Sarajevo. Finally, in October 1994, after two-and-a-half years of a very painful separation for both, she decided to leave so that she could be with her daughter in Zagreb. Her departure was a great loss to *Oslobodjenje*, but no one could have faulted her for her decision.

In sum, we were to find ourselves working, and struggling to maintain independence and excellence at the paper, in increasingly desperate times: first, besieged by nationalist hysteria and then, quite literally, under fire and in fear of our lives and the lives of our loved ones. While in the main our answer to the disorienting forces of nationalist warmongering was more professionalism, we could not run a hermetically sealed operation and there were bound to be areas of conflict which mirrored the fractured political landscape beyond the newsroom. The contagion of nationalism welling from the fissures in the federation would not spare us entirely. It would sap morale, subvert loyalties, cloud political judgment, and compel a few to leave. This sobering fact was first brought home to me by my deputy editor, Miroslav Janković, following the Constitutional Court's ruling in our favor.

Following the decision of the editorial board, I had written a commentary in *Oslobodjenje* stating that the paper would no longer feel obliged to publish every insult and accusation that was thrown at us at political party press conferences. Immediately afterwards, Stjepan Kljuić, the leader of the HDZ, explaining the failure of the crusade against the media initiated by his party, declared: "Our partners in the government from the SDA have their own people in *Oslobodjenje*, and they are no longer interested in going ahead with the changes." The next morning at the editorial board meeting, someone suggested that we ask Alija Izetbegovic at the SDA press conference whether this was true and request him to identify the "SDA people" at *Oslobodjenje*. "But didn't we publicly announce that we would not respond to these party allegations?" I reminded the editorial board, without giving any thought to the possibility that any of my colleagues—after our joint struggle for the independence of the paper—would have any reason to suspect my motives. At the meeting, all agreed that we would do best to ignore Kljuić's insinuations. However, disregarding the decision taken at our meeting, Janković called our reporter at the SDA press conference, Rajko Živković, and instructed him: "Go ahead, ask Alija!"

There was nothing that Izetbegović or anyone else could say that would have compromised me, but it was the suspicion, the mistrust demonstrated by Janković that delivered a hard blow to my illusions. Earlier on, in the summer of 1991 during my brief absence in Dubrovnik, he had run a two-part interview with the commander-in-chief of the Yugoslav National Army, General Blagoje Adžić, in *Oslobodjenje*. I was troubled by the interview, not because Janković had talked to the general and given him space in the paper, but because the queries he addressed to him were mild and generous, without any of the hard questions that would have challenged the JNA's ruthlessness in support of the Serb rebellion in Croatia.

When Janković took over as deputy editor from Zoran Kurtović, who was leaving for Belgrade, I was aware that he had close personal relations with people associated with the Serb nationalists in Bosnia but I did not consider that a disqualification for the job and I liked the way he wrote. Besides, I considered a diversity of opinion, democratically expressed, to be an advantage rather than a burden in a pluralistic newspaper, which is what I wanted *Oslobodjenje* to be. However, he was just one of several possible candidates I was considering (all Serbs and Croats, since I wanted an equal representation of all national groups on the editorial staff). I had had a private and exploratory discussion with Zoran, who was one of my closest associates and who occupied that position, but I had not yet made up my mind. I was surprised therefore when I returned from a short vacation and was told by Zoran, "I talked with Janković and he accepts the position." The decision had been taken and I accepted it. But the appointment became more of a problem in the months preceding the war. During my short absences to attend professional meetings abroad, he tried to impose his pro-Serbian slant on some of his other associates. In some of those editorial board discussions he began to use intolerant language and the particular target of his anger was political editor—and another Serb—Gordana Knežević. It therefore became increasingly difficult for me to separate the personal political affiliation of my deputy from his professional work as an editor. He often insisted on printing nationalistic pieces by obscure Serbian writers close to the SDS on the op-ed page of the paper. While I had no problem with printing their views, I felt that their proper place was the Letters page: the op-ed pieces had to meet higher standards of discourse and these included regular contributions from prominent Serb writers.

There were other instances which left some of us with an uneasy sense of the leanings of some of the reporters on our staff at a fateful time in 1991 when Parliament was having to take crucial decisions on the future of the Republic. For instance, during one of the sessions of the Assembly of Bosnia-Hercegovina that was debating the question of independence from or inclusion in a rump Yugoslavia, one of *Oslobodjenje*'s journalists had solicited the comments of Radovan Karadžić and, in a skewed piece of reporting, given the views of the SDS leader—who was not an elected member of the Assembly—the same weight as the considerations and decisions of the Parliament as a whole. Again, when the Presidency of the Republic made official announcements on matters of policy, the individual reactions of the representatives of the SDS in the Presidency, Nikola Koljević and Biljana Plavšić, were given prominent play in the paper as though their opinions merited consideration equal to the decisions taken by the Presidency itself. At this point in time, the two Serb representatives on the Republic's Presidency had declared that they would "freeze" their

status and not participate in the Presidency's work. They were protesting the Muslim and Croat members' majority decision to refuse to
recruit Bosnians into the JNA for the Yugoslav army's war against
Croatia.

My view was that the SDS representatives won the elections, as
did the others, to work within constitutional institutions to which they
were elected and not outside or against them; that they were elected by
Bosnia's citizens to represent them all and not to represent some separate "Serbian truth"; to improve and not to destroy constitutional
institutions. However, I also knew that the journalists of *Oslobodjenje*
did not respond to the invitations of the SDS to regular meetings of
Serb journalists. Only one member of our editorial staff, Ljubo
Grković, was actively engaged in the party—as chief of staff for
Radovan Karadžić himself—but he did no political reporting for the
paper. As for our relations with the government, we continued to
maintain our distance and our independence. It would have our critical support as long as its actions and decisions were in defense of
Bosnia-Hercegovina and the maintenance of its multiethnic, pluralist
political culture.

Some time later, in January 1992, as war raged across Croatia and
the government struggled to secure Bosnia's independence, Salko
Hasanefendić and I had a brief meeting with Alija Izetbegović. He had
agreed to give an interview to Miroslav Janković and Emil Habul for
Oslobodjenje and Salko and I had joined the two briefly to exchange
New Year's greetings with the president.

"I'm glad to see you again," Izetbegović had said, shaking hands.

"But, if things had gone according to your interparty agreement,
Mr. President, at least one of us would now be Karadžić's man, and, in
that case, we probably wouldn't be here," I had responded, not being
able to resist bringing up the memory of that dispute which had nearly
put an end to *Oslobodjenje*.

"I will be happy if you defend Bosnia-Hercegovina in the way
that you defended *Oslobodjenje!*" said the president.

This statement of recognition by the Bosnian president was welcome but in sharp contrast to the hysterical campaign waged against
Oslobodjenje, and against me, by some of Izetbegović's close associates
in his party and in the Muslim publications under his party's control.
The only "problem" was that we in *Oslobodjenje* were committed only

to our suffering country and its people and not to the individuals or parties in power—and especially not to their militant, fanatical ideologues. Most of us at the paper would face the trials ahead, grapple with our personal tribulations, and still stay the course. Sadly, Miroslav Janković and a handful of others could not.

While *Oslobodjenje* had survived, fought a hard battle for its independence, secured recognition, respect, and acclaim, and developed a professional team of journalists, all of this was going to be submitted to a fierce, harsh test in the horrible events soon to follow.

CHAPTER THREE

War and Resistance

T HE WAR DID NOT COME to Sarajevo completely without warning. But loving that marvelous city the way we did, serene in the belief that its diversity of cultures, traditions, and religions was a special blessing, a gift, and entirely secure in the respect that each one of us was raised to give to his neighbor, we refused to consider the possibility that something as devastating as a fratricidal war could ever happen to us. Our city and those who dwelt there, we thought, led a charmed life.

Having returned home in the late eighties after four years as correspondent in New York, I was reveling in the excitement of rediscovering Sarajevo. The days were long, filled with the challenging work of transforming *Oslobodjenje* from a dull and obscure Party organ into a liberal pluralistic daily with a growing and engaged readership. From the early morning planning sessions to the closing of the front pages in the evening, there were battles fought and battles won, and work had meaning. But life outside work was equally rich. Vesna and I had many friends in the vibrant cultural community of Sarajevo. We went to the theater and to art exhibitions, and spent long evenings with journalists, writers, and other friends at the Writers' Club. I liked to take Vesna for long walks through the heart of the Old Town district, down Vase Miskina Street, from the Eternal Flame to the bazaars of Baščaršija. Those unhurried evening strolls in Sarajevo were a social experience in themselves, for along the way we would encounter many people we knew, taking in the night air, pausing for an exchange of greetings or a bit of conversation. And then there was the city by night, its cafes and restaurants filled with Sarajevans enjoying good food and great music. Occasionally, we would join friends for dinner at a restaurant featuring popular Sarajevo musicians some of whom we also counted among our personal friends. On Saturday or Sunday mornings our favorite place was the Wiener Cafe in the Europa Hotel where dozens of well-known Sarajevans would gather for long discussions, convivial conversations, and a little gossip on everything under the sun—politics, soccer, the arts, people, and public life—over cups of perfect Turkish coffee or glasses of cognac.

Life was good and stretched out in a blue haze into the future. On Sunday afternoons my sons, Tarik and Mirza, would take me to one of the soccer stadiums, Koševo or Grbavica, to watch Sarajevo or Željezničar—both former Yugoslav champions—playing their First Division games. After years of strict parental supervision in Manhattan, the boys were enjoying a new sense of freedom to play all day long in their neighborhood and, more than anything else, to spend winter weekends on the Olympic ski slopes of the mountains surrounding Sarajevo: Jahorina, Bjelašnica, Igman. And we were building our weekend cabin in the hills above the village of Pale. Getting together over a barbecue with friends from *Oslobodjenje*, Branko Tomić and Dževad Tašić, who had also bought parcels of land next to ours for their homes, we would dream on—"one day, when we retire, this will be perfect place to relax, and to write"—never imagining that this idyllic spot would soon become the command post of those who would besiege Sarajevo and destroy Bosnia.

But then one day, brief years later, light-years ago—bang!—the world we knew was blown to smithereens and the unending nightmare began. Sarajevo, a place of light and grace and beauty, became one of the darkest, coldest places on earth. Its streets which had throbbed with life became sniper alleys, its parks and playgrounds became cemeteries, the darkened city an inferno of shattered glass and blasted lives as peo-

FRANK WARD

GLENN RUGA

THE NATIONAL LIBRARY WAS TARGETED BY SERBIAN ARTILLERY UNITS ON THE NIGHT OF AUGUST 25, 1992. AS THE STRUCTURE BURNED AND DISINTEGRATED, A NUMBER OF LIBRARIANS AND CITIZENS ATTEMPTED TO SAVE THE LIBRARY'S UNIQUE COLLECTION. WHILE THE FIRE RAGED OVER THE NEXT TWO DAYS, MANY WERE TARGETED BY SNIPERS AS THEY LOADED BOOKS INTO TRUCKS AND VANS. AIDA BUTUROVIC, A THIRTY-THREE-YEAR-OLD LIBRARIAN WAS SHOT AND KILLED. AN ESTIMATED 1.5 MILLION BOOKS BURNED. ACCORDING TO ANDRAS RIEDLMAYER OF HARVARD UNIVERSITY, THE DESTRUCTION OF THE NATIONAL LIBRARY REPRESENTS "THE LARGEST BOOK-BURNING IN HISTORY."

ple were murdered every day. Life was stilled: the music, conversation, laughter, argument strangled by the explosion of war.

It was not that we did not see and take note of the development of Serbian nationalism. For almost four years, week by week, writing my regular column "Calendar Pages," in *Nedjelja*, I had been recording its malevolent growth: Slobodan Milošević's ascent to power and the progress of his "antibureaucratic revolution" through highly orchestrated rallies and violent demonstrations; the consequent destruction of institutions of government in Vojvodina and Montenegro in pursuit of his project of "Greater Serbia"; his threats in the Belgrade media to export his "revolution" to Bosnia, Croatia, and even Slovenia; the gathering of hundreds of thousands of Serbs at Gazimestan at Kosovo Polje (Field of the Blackbirds) on June 28, 1989, to mark the anniversary of the battle lost by the Serb prince, Lazar, to the Turks six hundred years ago; and Milošević's address at the rally promising to carry out the Serb national program, if necessary through "armed struggle."

In retrospect, this could be interpreted as a veiled declaration of war against those who might stand in the way of Milošević's quest for power. On March 29, 1989, he had made unilateral and illegal changes in the constitution that took away the autonomy of Kosovo and these were followed by the imposition of docile leaderships in Serbia, Montenegro, Vojvodina, and Kosovo which "would either do what they're told or would no longer be," and the acquisition thus of four "automatic" votes in the eight-member presidential council of Yugoslavia. The unilateral decision, without asking or informing any of the other republics, to withdraw a huge sum of money from the federal coffers to pay pensions and agricultural bonuses in Serbia in order to avert social unrest was followed, in the summer of 1991, by the inauguration of a military campaign through the Yugoslav People's Army (JNA) to thwart the move towards independence by Slovenia and Croatia.

INTIMATIONS OF CATASTROPHE

THE DEVASTATION THAT WAS TO SWEEP across the lands of Yugoslavia had thus begun. In November 1991, after several months of incessant bombardment by the JNA and Serb militias, the Croatian city of Vukovar had been leveled to the ground. The "explanation" for its destruction and the mass killing of its inhabitants, provided by David Erne, the American lawyer and vice president of the Serbian Unity Congress in the United States, was available in the document distributed under the title "Historic Background of the Civil War in Yugoslavia." The Serbs did it, according to Erne, almost preemptively in order to prevent the reappearance of the Ustashe in Croatia.*

---

* Erne's document appeared under the cover of the UN's Commission on War Crimes.

In October 1991, the savage artillery attack on Dubrovnik, a jewel among the medieval cities of Europe, was already in progress.

We saw all of this, wrote about it, talked about it, worried about it, and were afraid. Only the willfully blind could choose to turn away from the storm that was rising in the country. In my column I wrote that Serbian nationalism—in the name of the defense of Yugoslavia—was actually destroying the federation and making life intolerable, and coexistence impossible, for everyone else. The growth of Serbia's nationalistic—and military—campaign was being reported and regularly criticized in the pages of *Oslobodjenje* and *Nedjelja,* in articles and columns by our own editors and commentators, and by guest columnists from all over Yugoslavia. Not surprisingly, *Oslobodjenje* became an early target for attack.

In the *Belgrade Express* an article entitled "For Serbs They Have Only Thorns" accused *Oslobodjenje* of "an anti-Serbian editorial policy." Milošević's major daily, the Belgrade *Politika,* began publishing real and imaginary letters from readers accusing me of instigating "anti-Serbian vengeance" through the pages of *Oslobodjenje.* We would respond by reprinting such letters without comment in *Oslobodjenje* which would often evoke replies from our own readers—many of them Serbs—pointing out that the criticism of the nationalist policy of the Belgrade regime was in no way aimed against the Serbian people but rather against their self-appointed leaders who had traded the name "communist" for the name "socialist" but continued to run a dictatorship.

It was around this time that I began to receive anonymous threatening letters: "If you go on writing against Serbia, the day will come when we will cut off your hands and your heads—you and your journalists!" Usually I threw such letters away without further thought. On one occasion my telephone at home rang and was answered by my younger son, Mirza. Frightened and in tears, he barely managed to give me the message: "Dad, a lady just rang and asked me to tell you that they are going to kill you!" The next day, in an attempt to protect my children from fielding threats over the phone, I applied for a new, unlisted phone number.

At a New Year's cocktail party, in the first days of 1992, the minister of police of Bosnia-Hercegovina, Alija Delimustafić, came up to me. "You really ought to arrange some security for yourself," he said.

"That's what we've got you for—to worry about things like that, so I don't have to," I responded jokingly.

"This is serious," he continued. "We have found a Serbian 'hit-list' and you are very high on it."

"Perhaps we at *Oslobodjenje* should request you to assign a bodyguard to him?" suggested the manager of *Oslobodjenje*, Salko Hasanefendić.

"Absolutely not!" I interrupted. "How would I manage to go around town, meet and talk to people if I had to take along an armed bodyguard? No, I don't want that."

"All right. Let's do it this way: I will lend you a revolver which you will always, just in case, keep somewhere handy," answered the police chief, and he persuaded me to accept his "Christmas present."

Until that day I had been implacably against keeping any weapons in the house. At the age of six, playing with my grandfather's hunting rifle, I had very nearly killed someone. It was the sort of childhood experience that puts real fear in your heart, and so, years later, I had not wanted any guns lest they attracted the curiosity of my own children. This time, however, I consented. The coming war was to change the way we lived and engaged with the world—this was merely the beginning. When Delimustafić gave me the "long nine" pistol—the sort carried by cops in American action movies—I decided to show it to my two sons, seventeen-year-old Tarik and ten-year-old Mirza. I wanted them to see what it looked like and where it was so that they would not try to go looking for it on their own. We agreed on a hiding place for it and also established that they were not ever to touch it or show it to their friends who came to visit. I hoped that I myself would never have to touch it again.

Not long after that another gun was to be added to the cache of weaponry in the house. Because of my job, I was one among a large group of editors and other workers of *Oslobodjenje* from all national groups who were issued 7.65 mm pistols under a decades-old law for emergencies enacted as part of Tito's "all people's self-defense." Accordingly, all the most crucial workers in all organizations, along with the organizations' territorial defense units, were supposed to get weapons for self-defense if there was an attack from outside. The law was designed to deal with the possible Soviet threat of invasion after

Tito broke with Moscow in 1948, and after the Soviet invasion of Hungary in 1956 and Czechoslovakia in 1968.

The pistols were issued to us after what came to be called the "dress rehearsal" for the Sarajevo siege soon after the referendum of March 1992. The referendum was held in fulfillment of the condition for the international recognition of Bosnia-Hercegovina's independence set by the European Union, after it had recognized the independent statehood of Croatia and Slovenia. The SDS had opposed the referendum. It announced a boycott and, in some of the regions where it was in power, had taken steps forcibly to prevent others from exercising their right to vote. Nonetheless, 64 percent of the citizens of Bosnia-Hercegovina voted for independence. The referendum had been held under the watchful eye of international observers who expressed their satisfaction with the procedure, and lauded the fairness with which it was conducted. One day after the results of the referendum were announced, Sarajevo woke up to find itself completely blockaded.

The pretext for the blockade was provided by a murder at Baščaršija, in the heart of the old quarter of Sarajevo. There had been a Serb wedding. The members of the wedding party, on their way to the small Serb-Orthodox church at Baščaršija, were singing nationalistic songs and waving the Serbian flag. "This is Serbia!," they shouted as they went along. A scuffle between the wedding party and a group of passersby ensued and someone (later identified as Ramiz Delalić-Ćelo) had, as the story went, pulled out a pistol and shot the fellow with the flag who happened to be the father of the groom. The same evening, ostensibly in protest against the killing, armed Serbian paramilitary forces had erected barricades at all the key points around the city and had halted all movement in and out of Sarajevo.

It was obvious that such a comprehensive blockade of a city of half a million people had not been conjured out of the thin night air without prior organization and planning—there was not a whiff of spontaneity about it. All of Sarajevo was to be held to ransom not to avenge the murder at Baščaršija, but to prevent Bosnia's separation from Serbia. With the full political and logistical support of Serbia, the SDS had been systematically arming its supporters, amassing automatic weapons and artillery, and organizing the paramilitary units which took part in the operation that laid siege to Sarajevo following the vote for Bosnia's independence.

The Bosnian government—which until the time of the referendum still included the SDS as a member of the ruling coalition—had been in a state of near paralysis. In great measure, this unhappy condition had been brought on by the fact that the SDS, in accordance with the three parties' power-sharing agreements, controlled one-third of every institution of the Republic and, in addition, exercised total power over districts that had Serb majorities. From this advantageous position, it had proceeded with some of its most blatant military preparations to bring war to Bosnia under the very noses of its partners-in-government who found themselves unable to do more than wring their hands in private and politely avert their eyes in public. It was surreal but it was really happening.

Thus when a truck loaded with weapons was stopped just outside Sarajevo with a civilian driver and a woman in the cab, without the documentation and markings required by law, the Sarajevo government accepted the explanation given to it by the JNA, the Yugoslav army, that the weapons were destined for the barracks in Visoko, 30 kilometers from Sarajevo. When a police patrol along the road near Bileća intercepted a truckload of weapons and ammunition, it found Dušan Kozić, an SDS member of the Bosnian parliament riding in the truck's cab. The shipment was not seized but, under pressure from the local Serb population, was allowed to be diverted to neighboring Montenegro. Near Bistrik, on the immediate outskirts of the old part of Sarajevo, when a convoy of trucks packed with weapons was stopped and found to have documentation for a large shipment of bananas, Muhamed Čengić, the deputy prime minister in the government in Sarajevo urged an enraged crowd of Sarajevans to disperse and permit the passage of the convoy in order "to avoid an incident with the Army." And as members of the JNA dug trenches for days and built artillery nests at Crepoljsko and on other hills around Sarajevo, the city's government politely, indeed helplessly, accepted the military commanders' explanations that this unusual activity was part of the "regular exercises and training of the JNA."

The absurdity of it all was compounded when the government instructed the Bosnian police to assist the Yugoslav army in disarming the Republic's Territorial Defense which, in Slovenia and Croatia, was a decisive force in the resistance to Serbian aggression. In the meantime, while the Republic's Presidency had issued a decree against the mobilization of Bosnian conscripts into the JNA for the war against neighboring Croatia, local Serb authorities in large parts of Bosnia continued to mobilize men of military age, mostly teenagers, under the threats of arrest or expulsion from schools or jobs. Meanwhile, the SDS had declared whole regions of Bosnia, even those with Muslim majorities, "Serbian Autonomous Provinces," setting up its own political and paramilitary structures.

In August 1991, quite by accident, I had learned that members of the Bosnian government were in possession of perhaps the most convincing piece of evidence of Serbian plans for the occupation of Bosnia-Hercegovina. Strolling through Dubrovnik, on a brief holiday with my family (barely two months before the bombardment of the city began), I had run into the vice president of the Bosnian government, Dr. Rusmir Mahmutćehajić, who was also there on a family vacation. Together we went to have a coffee at the Gradska Kavana Terrace.

"What would you do, Mr. Kurspahić, if you had a tape of a telephone conversation between Milošević and Karadžić in which Milošević instructs him to get weapons for the Serbian paramilitary forces from General Uzelac in Banja Luka?" Mahmutcehajic asked me.

"I would publish it, of course, and I think that *Oslobodjenje* would pay a good price to get such evidence," I said.

"Such a tape does exist," he told me.

When I returned to Sarajevo from Dubrovnik, I assigned a few reporters to work several angles to try to get our hands on this evidence. Wherever we inquired, we were told either that they did not know anything about it or that it was "still not the right time" for it. While our search for the elusive evidence were going nowhere, *Oslobodjenje*'s correspondent in Ljubljana, Zoran Odić, persuaded a Slovenian military expert, Teodor Geršak, to write a series of revealing articles about his knowledge of the army's plans for "Operation RAM." RAM (which means "frame") was a military code for the creation of new western borders for Serbia, inside Bosnia-Hercegovina and Croatia, which would enable all Serbs to live inside the extended boundaries of a single greater Serb state. A few months later, when there was an open attempt to overthrow the reformist Premier of Yugoslavia, Ante Marković, did the public finally learn about the details of that telephone conversation between Milošević and Karadžić that Dr. Mahmutcehajic had alluded to over coffee in Dubrovnik a summer before.

In the transcript of the conversation, which was partially published in the press, Karadžić complained that he did not have enough weapons...

> *Milošević:* Get in touch with [General]) Uzelac, he will tell you everything. Wherever you have any problems, let me know.
>
> *Karadžić:* I have a problem with Kupres. That's an area where a part of the Serbs are not very cooperative...
>
> *Milošević:* You will have everything, don't worry. We are the strongest.
>
> *Karadžić:* Yes, yes.
>
> *Milošević:* Don't worry. As long as the army is there, no one can touch us.
>
> *Karadžić:* The question of Hercegovina...
>
> *Milošević:* Don't worry about Hercegovina. Momir [Bulatović, the president of Montenegro] told his men: "He who is not prepared to die in Bosnia, step forward five steps." No one stepped forward!
>
> *Karadžić:* That's all fine, but what about the bombing!
>
> *Milošević:* This is not a good time for aviation; the meeting of the European Union...*

While the fate of Bosnia was thus being determined, the government watched—and listened—but was unable to summon up the will or find the means to take a single decisive step to counter it. And so the first blockade of Sarajevo came to pass. That night our trucks, for the first time, were prevented from delivering the paper across Bosnia. The paper had carried the news of the results of the referendum. The next day the city was hushed, in a state of shock. In the early evening, the stillness broke as the citizens of Sarajevo gathered; from all quarters of the city, from the Olympic villages of Dobrinja and Mojmilo, from Ali-pašino Polje, Breka, Vratnik, Bistrik, and Novo Sarajevo, columns of people moved out singing and shouting: "Let them hear in Serbia, and across Croatia, that our beloved Bosnia is a united nation!"; "We don't want division!"; "Down with the barricades!"; "This is Bosnia!"; "Bosna, Bosna, Bosna."

As tens of thousands streamed forth from the districts of Novi Grad and Novo Sarajevo and reached the barricades at the Marshal Tito

---

* Stipe Mesić, "Kako smo srusili jugoslaviju" (How We Destroyed Yugoslavia), *Globus*, Zagreb, 1992.

barracks, shots rang out. Someone was wounded. But the column of people, with greater rage in their hearts, kept moving forward and the Serbian terrorists withdrew. As this tidal wave of humanity swept over the city, other barricades also fell. All night long, the city celebrated the victory of an unarmed citizenry over those thugs who, with guns in their hands and stockings over their heads, had come to terrorize and bring Sarajevo to its knees. Serbs, together with Muslims, Croats and Jews, had stood up to Karadžić's armed militias with song. It was a moment of indescribable euphoria. Of course, we did not know then that this was only the beginning: longer, darker nights of terror lay ahead.

Only two weeks before the attack upon the city began, I had been at a seminar organized by the Aspen Institute in Berlin, where the crisis in the Balkans was the subject of discussion. There, I was telling the participants that the fundamental conditions necessary for a war to break out among us simply did not exist in Sarajevo, and if there were a war, it would certainly be the bloodiest conflict that the world had seen since the end of the Second World War. "Look at any of the Sarajevo residential areas, streets, apartment buildings," I said. "In every one of them there are Muslims, Serbs, Croats, and Jews living together. You cannot shoot at 'the others' there without shooting at your own people!" The fear of what the war could bring to a land of such interwoven people and fates such as Bosnia would be a sufficient deterrent.

Of course, I had failed to comprehend at the time the maniacal nature of the fascist "Greater Serbia" project, which was driven by the imperative "All Serbs in a Single State" and which was blind to the wishes, the happiness, the lives of the Serbs themselves—especially those who would not take up weapons to build a "Greater Serbia" by destroying Bosnia-Hercegovina. Nor had I been able to fathom the darkness of the hatred that gave meaning to the lives of men like Radovan Karadžić who, addressing the Republic's parliament, had threatened Bosnia with extinction were it to vote for independence. Such a vote, he had warned, might well "lead to the wiping out of an entire people—the Bosnian Muslims." Aleksa Buha, the self-appointed minister of foreign affairs of the self-proclaimed "Republika Srpska," had made the pronouncement that for Serbs "it [was] better to commit collective suicide than to live with others any longer." Stevo Medić, a member of the Bosnian parliament, had delivered a similar message to Sarajevo's "high-rise" Serbs: "Those high-rise [apartment] buildings are not your hearth and home, your fireplaces are not there, and you will not defend them." Death, genocide, suicide. For ordinary men and women, the pathology of such warped nationalism defied understanding.

So there I was, listening to the news one spring evening in May 1992 as mortar shells rained down on Sarajevo from the surrounding hills, and fires raged through the city. The voice of General Ratko Mladić came across the air waves. His commands to his artillery had been intercepted and taped and were being replayed over my radio: "Concentrate your fire on Pofaliće and Velušiće; there are not too many Serbs there!" In other words, kill everyone in sight—including Serbs—as long as there aren't "too many" of them. I understood then that Sarajevo and all that it symbolized was being attacked by barbarians, as it were, who had not been touched by the civilizing, life-affirming cosmopolitanism that had flourished in Bosnia's urban centers and shaped the social ethos of its people. Born and raised in isolated, godforsaken regions, crushed by the burden of a history in which the Serb was the eternal victim, they had never learned to coexist with "others." Some of these men had acquired academic degrees, professions or political careers—and a patina of urbane sophistication—but they despised the hybrid culture that defined Bosnia. They dwelt with myths and imaginary pasts, nursing the idea of revenge upon the Muslim "balija" (a derogatory term for Bosniaks) for the defeat at Kosovo more than 600 years ago or the Croatian Ustasha for the atrocities committed against the Serbs in the Second World War, even though their neighbors, their co-workers, their friends—like them—belonged to a different generation and time, and had no connection with or responsibility for either the Turkish conquests or the fascist war crimes.

As the Serb militias embarked on their mission to "cleanse" Bosnia, it became horribly clear how greatly we had underestimated the strength of the systematic campaign that had been conducted over several years in the Serbian media. Mixing history and myth, evoking fear, paranoia, bigotry, and all that huddles in the dank crevices of the mind, Milošević's propagandist mercenaries had duped far too many into accepting the lie that the Serbs were a "threatened people," targeted by a global "anti-Serb conspiracy." The imperative, blessed by the Orthodox church, that all Serbs unite in the holy "defense of the Serbian land" became a call to kill, harry, and destroy all that was deemed to stand in the way of "Greater Serbia." Vukovar was a testament to that fact. And now this madness, before our disbelieving eyes, had caught fire in Bosnia.

In the last week of March 1992, on my return to Sarajevo from Berlin, not suspecting the disaster that was about to befall us, I accepted an invitation from the peace movement in Sanski Most to appear, together with my friend from Sarajevo University Dr. Zdravko Grebo, at a public tribunal for a discussion on the fate of Bosnia. Sanski Most was the town where I had grown up. In the auditorium were assembled, together perhaps for the last time ever, both the Serbs and Muslims of Sanski Most, many of whom were my high school friends. As I addressed them that evening, a weight of tremendous sadness had settled in my heart: "Remembering as I do how together, in this town, we celebrated both Christmas and Bajram,* visited one another in our homes and shared holiday suppers, and how much richer we were because of that, I refuse to believe that you will allow all of that to come to an end."

On the way back to Sarajevo, outside Mrkonjić-Grad, the town where I was born, we were stopped at a checkpoint manned by soldiers in red berets. They were not wearing uniforms of the JNA but were special Serbian units from the Krajina in Croatia. As my driver from *Oslobodjenje*, Zoran Ivanović, was being questioned by the soldiers, I wondered whether "Operation RAM" had gone into motion. Headed for Sanski Most were a large number of military trucks, hauling big guns on trailers, and carrying everything including field kitchens to feed an army of occupation. The peaceful valley of the Sana River, as indeed all of Bosnia, was being overcome by the evil-smelling breath of a war in which entire cities, including Sanski Most, would come under attack, homes plundered and burned, mosques destroyed, and tens of thousands killed, tortured, sent to concentration camps, and driven into exile.

I would have regretted it terribly if I had not gone then to Sanski Most. It was my last chance to see the town I loved, the old house of my dear grandmother, Hasiba, where I spent three happy years of my boyhood. That night I slept in the house of my mother, Sena, in Prijedor, which she and my stepfather, Kemal Kolonić, were soon to be forced to leave, the town "cleansed" of all its Muslim inhabitants. I visited many

---

* Muslim festival marking the end of Ramadan, the month of fasting.

of the places of my youth which will never be there to visit again. It was a time to say farewell. Bosnia's season in hell was beginning.

REPORT AND DIE

THE FIRST NEWS OF SERBIAN AGGRESSION against Bosnia arrived at the editorial offices of *Oslobodjenje* on April 1, 1992, from Bijeljina. Our correspondent, Halid Rifatbegović, called me from his home:

"Horrible things are happening here. Arkan's men are on the rampage. They are killing and driving out everyone they come across. There has been a massacre in front of the mosque. They are shooting as they go down the streets—here, you can hear for yourself, they are shooting just outside my house! Look, I can't talk any further. I've got my phone down here in the basement, and I don't even dare to stick my head out. See if you can find a way, through the army or the police, to get me out of here." He spoke with the voice of a man who was staring into the face of death.

That day *Oslobodjenje* also had an experienced war reporter, Vlado Mrkić, on assignment in Bijeljina. The entire year he had reported from the front lines in Croatia and was witness to events which brought Serbia's war to Bosnia-Hercegovina. Together with our photographer, Danilo Krstanović, he was the first journalist to enter the village of Ravno in Hercegovina and to bring—in words and photographs—eyewitness reports of the total destruction of that tiny Croat hamlet in Trebinje district. He had gone to Bijeljina to report on the visit of the members of the Presidency of Bosnia-Hercegovina, Fikret Abdić and Biljana Plavšić, who were there ostensibly to attempt to "calm the situation." On that day in Bijeljina, when the cameras were recording the kiss Ms. Plavšić bestowed upon the notorious war criminal Željko Ražnatović-Arkan in the presence of high-ranking JNA officers, Vlado Mrkić was taken away for questioning by Arkan's men.*

---

* In 1996, Biljana Plavšić was picked by Radovan Karadžić to take over his position in the government of the "Republika Srpska" when Karadžić himself was compelled to adopt a lower profile by Slobodan Milošević who was seeking to placate the NATO powers who were resisting the demands of the International War Crimes Tribunal to arrest Karadžić (as well as General Ratko Mladić) to stand trial for war crimes.

He had been filing his report at the time, talking to *Oslobodjenje*'s stenographer, when he suddenly said: "I have to interrupt this. They've come to arrest me."

I put out the alarm—for both Vlado and for Halid—wherever I could. I called Minister of Police Alija Delimustafić, and asked him to see if the police connections were still working in Bijeljina and if he could get our people out. Likewise, through journalists who had their connections in the JNA, I tried to get help from the army. Both Vlado and Halid managed to leave Bijeljina alive. Vlado was probably the last civilian to safely transit the road from Bijeljina to Sarajevo before the siege cut the capital off from the rest of the country. Halid escaped to the neighboring town of his birth, Janja, and from there to a place of refuge abroad.

Warnings also came in from other parts. Karadžić's henchmen from his obscure party paper, *Javnost,* had broken into *Oslobodjenje*'s Belgrade offices, changed the name on the door, and occupied the apartment at 8 Hilendarska Street which, together with Radio Sarajevo, we had bought over twenty years earlier. At any given time, there were close to ten correspondents working at the Belgrade bureau. When our Belgrade editor-correspondent, Branislav Boškov, came to work that morning, he could not open the door. The locks had been changed. Although we requested protection from the police and the judicial system, and even won the lawsuit which we filed, *Javnost* continued its occupation of the offices "because the court judgment [did] not include an enforcement clause." Similarly, our bureau in Banja Luka "fell" to local Serb extremists.

With these ominous bits of news coming in from around Bosnia and beyond, the weekend of April 4, 1992, arrived. There had been a rumor spreading through the city—"Chetniks are preparing a bloody Bajram for Sarajevo." At *Oslobodjenje*, we might, perhaps, have confirmed the truth of that rumor had we asked our reporter, Snežana Rakočević Novaković, who had been reporting on the activities of the SDS, and on that fateful day had gone with her children to Romanija mountain near Sarajevo and never returned. We had not asked her, and she had not told anyone, not even her colleagues who had small children of their own, and we wondered afterwards whether she knew what a terrible scenario was prepared for Sarajevo. And thus it was that on the very day that Bosnia-Hercegovina was recognized as an independent state by the European Union, it was brutally attacked. Sarajevo, including *Oslobodjenje*, was completely surrounded and cut off.

"War in Bosnia," the headlines of the world media read. In fact, it was not really a war. For a war, you usually need two armies, fighting each other. But Bosnia-Hercegovina, on the day it was attacked, did not have an army. Instead, there was only the Yugoslav National Army (JNA) with about 100,000 troops and a huge stockpile of weapons and which had now become an army of occupation inside the newly independent country. Withdrawing from Slovenia and Croatia, which had earlier declared their independence, the JNA had entered Bosnia with all its destructive power which it now began to deploy against Bosnian towns along the river Drina: Bijeljina, Foča, Zvornik, Višegrad…

The pattern of terror was consistent. After the artillery finished its part, the towns under attack would be invaded by paramilitary units from Serbia—Arkan's Tigers, the White Eagles, and the storm troopers led by Vojislav Šešelj.* They were the ones to carry out the dirty work that came to be known by the antiseptic title of "ethnic cleansing": public executions, torture, rape, forced exile, plunder, the torching of houses, mosques, and churches, and deportations in cattle trucks to concentration camps. This was terror, arson, slaughter, genocide, but not war. The Bosnians could not defend themselves, protect their homes, their towns, their country because the world had crippled their capacity to fight back: by refusing them arms under an iniquitous arms embargo that made no distinction between the victims of aggression and the aggressor, it had become complicit in their destruction.

In the face of this renewed assault by Serbian fascists, once again, as before, Sarajevo rose to its feet. Once again columns of people from all quarters, joined by busloads of coal miners from Tuzla and Kakanj, steel workers from Zenica, as well as people from Mostar and other towns in Hercegovina, began to move through the city. Once again they raised their voices in protest and in rage, "No division," "This is Bosnia." Once again the song "Let them hear in Serbia, and across Croatia" filled the air. Arm in arm, despair in their hearts, the citizens of Sarajevo gathered on the large Marindvor plateau, in front of the

---

* Vojislav Šešelj was the president of the Serbian Radical Party in Milošević's Yugoslavia, an ultranationalist organization with a murderous political agenda.

modern building of the parliament and government of Bosnia-Herce-govina. In an extraordinary and unprecedented demonstration of unity, hundreds of thousands of people pleaded for peace.

Then shots rang out. Serb snipers from Karadžić's headquarters in the Sarajevo Holiday Inn were shooting at unarmed demonstrators. The crowd froze for a moment in disbelief, then a wave of fear and fury swept through it, and shouts of "murderers, murderers!" rent the sky. Tens of thousands, in pure panic, sought to find a hiding place; the bravest, the most reckless, headed towards the Holiday Inn to con-front, bare-handed, the criminals for whom "peace" was a dirty word, and who thought nothing of emptying their guns on civilians—men and women, young and old—who could not return their fire. They managed to capture some of the sharpshooters but, that same day, Karadžić escaped with his most loyal followers, withdrawing through underground tunnels and back streets from Sarajevo to Pale. From there they would begin their long and bloody siege of the city they could not appropriate, the city they hated so pathologically. From that day, they were described as the "Bosnian Serbs" by the world. The real Bosnian Serbs, however, included those 80,000 who remained in Sara-jevo and, together with all their fellow citizens—Muslims, Croats, Jews, and others—were subjected to the same terror which took the lives of 10,609 Bosnians in Sarajevo in three-and-a-half years of the siege. Karadžić's guns did not discriminate: they also killed Serbs who were Bosnian, both inside and outside Sarajevo.

I was in the editorial offices, preparing the next issue of *Oslobod-jenje*, when reports on the outbreak of terror started coming in. Sara-jevo was under fire. At the Vrbanja bridge, where the demonstrators were headed carrying messages of peace, Serbian gunners on the hill behind "Unioninvest" had shot and killed a young medical student from Dubrovnik. Suada Dilberović was the first victim of the war against Sarajevo—the bridge where she fell bears her name today.

News also came from my own neighborhood of Hrasno. The insurgent Serb forces of the Special Unit of the police had attacked the police school at Vraca, above the Željezničara Stadium, with machine guns and grenades. The explosions were shaking Hrasno, shattering windows in its apartment buildings. It was the first time, after which all of this and more became a recurrent nightmare for all of us who lived in that part of town.

On that day, my son Tarik had planned to celebrate his eigh-
teenth birthday with his friends—a typical motley crew of Sarajevan
youth—in their favorite neighborhood cafe and pastry shop, Palma.
None of them had any idea that within a few days their Palma would
be destroyed in an attack by Serbian forces on their neighborhood;
that the world they had known was coming to an abrupt end. The war
would prevent them from celebrating their high school graduation
and, indeed, from pursuing their dreams in their own country—university studies, music, sports, summer holidays, and the magical experience of first love. In fact, the war would rob them all of their youth.
Some would fight, and some would die, and some would watch others die. The youth of Bosnia would know terror, fear, pain, hunger,
exile. The loss of innocence would come too swiftly, too brutally, and
leave them forever scarred. "Watch out for the kids, tell them not to go
out, stay away from the windows," I called Vesna from *Oslobodjenje*.

I was finishing up work on a day that was going to be the beginning of an extraordinary two-year struggle to keep the paper alive in
the midst of the terror and mass destruction that was sweeping over
Bosnia-Hercegovina. In a certain sense, we had already begun to
prepare for what was coming to pass during the earlier blockade of

EVERY AVAILABLE OPEN SPACE BECAME A CEMETERY DURING THE SIEGE OF SARAJEVO.

Sarajevo which had served as a prelude to the siege that followed in April. Because many of the reporters were unable, in the blockaded city, to get through to the editorial offices, I had requested all the editors to draw up new address lists for all their staff with all the essential information: what part of town did they live in, did they have a fax machine at home or somewhere in the neighborhood, and was there some way that they could, in the event of another blockade of the city, transmit their stories and pictures—even through some "relay" system from one to another—to the editorial offices? On the basis of this information, I worked with Gordana Knežević to create a "map" of sorts, a "geography" of our reporters and our resources. Thus the reporters in Old Town knew that if they did not have a fax machine at home, they were to bring their copy either to Vedo Kantardžić at Mejtaš or to the cafe owned by Milan Borojević in Vase Miskina Street, where we had installed a fax for our staff's use; the reporters around Breka were to go to Dževad Tašić, those from Koševo and Koševo Hill to Gordana Knežević, in Marindvor area to Mehmed Halilović, and in Novo Sarajevo to my place. We also installed a fax machine at the home of our typist, Željka Ergelašev, so that reporters around the city and correspondents from other places in Bosnia-Hercegovina could, at any time, dictate the news directly to her, and she could then fax it over to us at the editorial offices.

In the days when the real siege of Sarajevo began, this "map" proved to be invaluable. *Oslobodjenje* continued to put out the news, even from those parts of the city which for days, weeks, and sometimes months, were completely cut off from the rest of Sarajevo, and, of course, the world. The reporters of *Oslobodjenje* who lived there, unable to move in and out of the "ghettos," still managed to stay in regular contact with the editorial office. Mehmed Husić was one such journalist. He was the editor of the weekly *Svijet* (the World) and lived in the new residential area of Dobrinja which had been built as the Olympic Village for the Winter Games of 1984. From the beginning of the siege in April of 1992, Dobrinja was completely surrounded by Serbian forces. Its apartment buildings were shelled day and night, no one could move around safely within the area, and it was hazardous in the extreme to attempt to leave or enter it. Deliveries of food or medicine were impossible. And there was Husić, reporting from his apartment on the life-and-death happenings in the encircled district under fire and in flames: the terror, the solidarity, the bravery of the defenders of Dobrinja, the wartime hospital founded by Dr. Joussef Hajir, the Dobrinja press center. Then one day Husić called me:

"It's all over. The Chetniks are entering my neighborhood!"

We agreed that we would call him every ten minutes. If he did not answer, it would mean that he had been captured or . . . Or what? We could not give utterance to it; the thought was like a muffled implosion inside our heads; we were both afraid, frightened by our utter helplessness. He was on the phone with me when the criminals, who had already carried out a massacre of the civilians at the airport settlement adjoining Dobrinja, broke into the settlement, and then entered Husić's building. Memica, as he was known by all his friends, was taken to the prison at Kula. He lived and was later freed in a prisoner exchange.

As for Dobrinja, it did not lose its tenuous link with the world. After Husić was taken, Muhamed Džemidžić, similarly trapped in that hellish place, stepped in and carried on. Where there was fear, there was also rage in the hearts of those whose lives and homes were going up in flames. From the neighboring district of Vojničko Polje or Soldiers Fields, we were receiving regular reports from Rajko Živković as the siege began. In addition to reporting for *Oslobodjenje*, he was also reporting for Radio Sarajevo. One afternoon, a JNA transporter—an armored personnel carrier—entered the settlement and began firing upon the surrounding buildings. From a shelter, which he shared with his frightened neighbors, Živković was reporting live to the radio and, at one point, without pausing for breath, shouted angrily: "And now I am talking to you, General Kukanjac (the commander of the JNA's Sarajevo corps)—get this "transporter" out of here or we will be compelled to destroy it with our bare hands!"

From the first days of the siege, *Oslobodjenje* itself had come under the unrelenting sniper and artillery fire of Serb forces who had taken up positions in neighboring Nedžarići. What separated us from them was a bare one hundred yards of empty space: vegetable gardens, a basketball court, a parking lot for our cars, and nothing else. I was sitting in my office, which faces Nedžarići, talking with some of the editors, when Gordana Knežević came running in with an Italian colleague who had been interviewing her.

124

"They are shooting at us!" she was screaming. "What are we going to do?"

"Don't worry!" I said lightly, trying to suppress my own sense of panic.

I picked up the phone and, imitating the accented English of the Indian commander of the UN forces in Bosnia-Hercegovina, General Satish Nambiar, began shouting into the receiver:

"Mister Ghali, Mister Ghali, help us, please! We came here to make peace, but they are making war. They are shooting at us. My men cannot get their exercise or play soccer outside the *Oslobodjenje* building! Please, get us out of here, Mister Ghali!"

We had a few moments of laughter, drank the last drops of whiskey left in the bottle I had brought from Berlin, and then I went to join the reporters and staff who had taken shelter in the corridor on the safe side of the building. The guard from *Oslobodjenje's* security was standing in the hallway outside my office with his binoculars trained on Nedžarići, and was talking to someone on a walkie-talkie:

"No, they're not coming towards the building. But we are ready."

I laughed silently, bitterly, knowing that with their pistols the four or five of them would not be able to do very much if the Chetniks opened an infantry attack on *Oslobodjenje*. In contrast to the neighboring building of Radio and Television Sarajevo, which was being guarded by an armored personnel carrier and a special unit of police—which subjected all visitors, including us, to careful searches with electronic detectors—*Oslobodjenje* had no such defense. We had hoped that the presence of the UNPROFOR troops, who had moved into the brand-new Dom Penzionera (retirement home) next door before the war broke out, would be enough to discourage a Serbian attack—and that was not saying much about our security situation.

With all this in mind, and knowing that anyone who came to work at *Oslobodjenje* from that day forward would be risking his or her life, I called an emergency editorial meeting to make a decision as to what we should do now. The Political Section had the largest editorial office and that is where almost the entire editorial staff assembled. I told them that it was the decision of the editorial and managing board that *Oslobodjenje* should continue to be published, regardless of the danger—we, in fact, had no other choice. These were times which demanded that we live up to the paper's long anti-fascist tradition and the confidence and respect we had struggled so hard to attain: if hundreds of journalists from around the world could risk their lives to write about the tragedy of Bosnia-Hercegovina, how could we possibly even consider withdrawing from the battlefield? But, I added, there were among us women who were mothers of small children—journalists and other staff members—and it was our responsibility to offer to arrange their evacuation from Sarajevo. We agreed to organize their transport to either Belgrade or Zagreb, according to their individual choices. There were not many who took us up on the offer; in the end, about a dozen who had very young children decided to leave; the rest remained to continue their work. But the war had other ways of taking away some of our best and brightest. As the towns along the Drina river fell into chetnik hands and were "ethnically cleansed," one by one we lost a number of our correspondents: first Halid Rifatbegović, then Kjašif Smajlović, then Šemso Tucaković.

Šemso escaped death itself: he had dropped out, forced to traverse the gauntlet of terror reserved for the citizens of Bosnia who were being uprooted from their homes. His was a singular example of "on the spot" reporting. Driven out of town with the people of Foča, he stayed with them in their forest hideaways, experienced all the horrors

OSLOBODJENJE'S WAR TIME EDITORIAL BOARD MEETS IN FEBRUARY 1994. CLOCKWISE FROM LEFT: GORDANA KNEŽEVIĆ, RASIM ĆERIMAGIĆ, MIRKO ŠAGOLJ, KEMAL KURSPAHIĆ, BRANKO TOMIĆ, FETO RAMOVIĆ, MIDHAT PLIVČIĆ, AND EMIR HRSTANOVIĆ.

of exile, and—through ham radio operators—carried on reporting to Radio and Television Sarajevo and *Oslobodjenje*. Even when his seventeen-year-old son, Haris, was killed on the streets of Sarajevo by a mortar shell, Semso continued to send his reports. It was his way of fighting the murderers, of truly bearing witness. In his commitment to his calling, first from the town of Foča itself and then from the escapees' desperate sanctuaries, Šemso Tucaković set a rare example of dedication to the profession of journalism even in the most difficult conditions.

Reading and listening to his reports, I was constantly reminded of the repeated demands of the Minister of Information (in the prewar coalition of nationalist parties), Velibor Ostojić, that I get rid of "that Tucaković, because he is stirring up things in Foča, always putting himself forward on the Muslim side, and so the Serbian readers are requesting that the Ministry should have him removed." My response was always the same: Ostojić had to point out the evidence of the charges he was making in the stories that Tucaković wrote—examples of his malice, prejudice, chauvinism, or whatever else he was being accused of by the Foča SDS. "He's not the only one who is controversial. You need to also get rid of that autonomy fanatic, Dušan Vijuk, in Novi Sad, and the anti-Serbian Slobodan Racković in Titograd, and your correspondent in Moscow, Vlastimir Mijović. They are ruining the relationship of Bosnia-Hercegovina with Serbia and Montenegro!" The minister would expand the list of undesirables in *Oslobodjenje* every time I saw him. And now, this former minister in the first democratically elected government of Bosnia-Hercegovina—the same man who had denounced *Oslobodjenje* as "an anti-Serbian newspaper," in that same town of Foča where he was demanding the head of our correspondent—had become one of the arch perpetrators of some of the most brutal acts of "ethnic cleansing." In a police report, Ostojić and his associate, Vojislav Maksimović, together with Petko Čančar, were accused of kicking a severed head around as a soccer ball and of being the masterminds behind the systematic rape of Muslim women in Foča. While Ostojić was thus "playfully" engaged, Šemso Tucaković was fighting alongside those who were hounded out of town, their world destroyed, fighting for their right to exist.

By the middle of April, the magnitude of the catastrophe that was sweeping across Bosnia-Hercegovina had become tragically, painfully evident to those of us working at *Oslobodjenje*. It was at that time, one afternoon while I was sitting at my desk, that I received a phone call from the son of Kjašif Smajlović, our correspondent in Zvornik.

"Uncle Kemal, my father has been killed!" he said in a stricken voice.

"Wait a minute, are you sure? Who told you so?" I asked, not really knowing what to say.

"We checked, and it was confirmed from two sources. There's a woman we know—she doesn't want her name mentioned. She saw him dead, being dragged out of his office by his feet, like an animal, she said. And then, the director of community services in Zvornik told my mother that my father was buried in a mass grave with other Muslims who were killed, and that he was marked with a number, so perhaps someday we can give him a proper burial."

The young man, a university student in Sarajevo, had been living in exile with his mother in Mali Zvornik in Serbia, on the other side of the Drina, after Kjašif had put them on a truck just before the arrival of Arkan's men in the city on April 8. The truck carried old men, women, and children out of Zvornik to get them out of harm's way before the coming slaughter. Kjašif had known of the impending storm but had stayed behind to report what was coming to pass and to die while doing so. The day before his death, he had sent three reports to *Oslobodjenje*. "Three Arkan men arrested in Zvornik," ran the headline to the most ominous of the three. "The men claim that they came to Zvornik because of their concern about Muslims being armed." A professional reporter to the end, he was being meticulous about presenting all the facts, including "the other side" of the story—which came from those who had arrived as the advance party for the units who would, just one day later, murder him. On the morning of April eighth, when the paramilitary forces from Serbia, already notorious for the crimes they had committed in Vukovar and other towns in Croatia, crossed the Drina and began their bloodletting in Zvornik, Kjašif was broadcasting live on Radio Sarajevo. In closing his report, in the voice of one who recognized the close breath of terror, he said: "What can I say? They are coming and—that is all."

He had called in that morning, as was the procedure, to notify *Oslobodjenje*'s regional office in Tuzla of his plans for the day. To the astonished secretary, Sevleta Mujkić, who was on the other end of the line, he announced: "If I manage, I will report on the attack on Zvornik, and then you won't hear from me again." He did not manage to file that last report. The murderers from Serbia broke into his office, on the ground floor of an apartment building along the major highway running from Belgrade through Zvornik to Sarajevo, killed him while he was sitting behind his typewriter, and then, as witnessed by the neighbor who did not want her name mentioned, dragged him out by his feet and buried him in a mass grave of those slaughtered in Zvornik. (There was also a report that he had been tortured, and died when they smashed his head in with the typewriter.) According to some who kept a count, there were 95 such murders on that day in the town of Zvornik.

With the news of Kjašif's death, I called together a commemorative meeting in the editorial offices which was joined by many of our colleagues from Radio and Television Sarajevo. As I spoke, I could not hold back the tears. I was weeping for a friend, a good man, a peace-loving man, who had had no malice in his heart. In my frequent traveling between Sarajevo and Belgrade, I had often stopped by his office in Zvornik. He knew his town, its people, kept his finger on the pulse of life there—and did his job well. Once, when I visited him early in the morning on my way to Belgrade, he had told me: "You know, life is becoming increasingly difficult. I had a friend who used to stop by in a cafe every morning and order a coffee and two cognacs. Now he has barely enough to get his two cognacs." I knew who that "friend" was. But that need for a glassful of conversation never affected Kjašif's work. I remember his excellent dispatches from the Bosnian-Serbian border along the Drina on the day Serbia began to enforce its economic embargo against Bosnia-Hercegovina, reducing to small change what little we still had in common in the still officially united Yugoslavia. He reported on the exact number of trucks, and what goods they were carrying, parked on each side of the Drina River, what the drivers and the owners of the cargoes had to say about it, and what the consequences were for the customers left cut off on both sides of the Drina. It was exemplary, not literary or elegant, but professionally accomplished and comprehensive reporting on what was, indeed, the most urgent topic of the day.

A STREET SIGN IN MOSTAR SAYS "DON'T FORGET." A JEWEL OF TRA-
DITIONAL BOSNIAN ARCHITECTURE, THE CITY WAS DESTROYED IN
1992–93 BY SERB AND CROAT EXTREMISTS, WITH OFFICIAL SUPPORT
FROM BELGRADE AND ZAGREB.

Kjašif Smajlović, murdered in the correspondents' office of *Oslo-bodjenje* in Zvornik on April 8, 1992, was the first of dozens of journalists killed in the aggression against Bosnia-Hercegovina. There were others who paid the price for their stubborn commitment.

Mugdim Karabeg, the editor of the regional correspondents' office for Hercegovina in Mostar, was passionately in love with his beautiful city. When the air force, called in by the half-insane Serbian General Momčilo Perišić, began its bombing runs over Mostar, Mugda was the first to report, on Bosnian radio and in *Oslobodjenje*, the magnitude of the destruction that was being wrought. Against the deafening noise of exploding bombs we heard him shouting, "the Mostar you used to know no longer exists." His younger colleagues, Alica Behram and Nenad Žujo, had been reporting on the events in Mostar for the regular column, the "Mostar War Journal," published in *Oslobodjenje*. When the telephone connections were no longer working, they made their way through the mountain passages to a small town in neighboring Croatia so that they could file their report. At that time, in the first year of the war, they did not know that the Serbian attack on Mostar was just a beginning: the destruction of the city would be completed by the HVO (Croatian Defense Council) and the Croatian army which opened its assault in the first days of May 1993.

Taking a leaf from the book of the Serbs, who had used force to create their illegal "Republika Srpska," the Croatian extremists, under the direct leadership of Mate Boban and the more distant control of Croatian President Franjo Tudjman in Zagreb, decided to create their own nationalist state within a state, the "Croatian Union of Herceg-Bosna." They attacked a large area in central Bosnia and in Hercegovina, reserving a special viciousness for the city of Mostar to destroy the cosmopolitan spirit which it had shared with Sarajevo or Tuzla or Zenica. It was declared the capital of their "Croatian Republic" in Bosnia-Hercegovina and became the base of the Croat militias own "ethnic cleansing" campaign. Entire families were liquidated (among them, my cousins, Mustafa and Maida Sefo). People were driven out of their homes and villages. Thousands ended up in the prison camps at the Heliodrom (a field for army helicopters) and at Dretelj, where they were tortured in the same ways that the detainees of the Serbian camps in Omarska and Manjača had been. ("They kept people in an overcrowded, underground former military storage area, left them without water until they started to drink one another's urine, then the drunken HVO soldiers began shooting through those closed doors, killing and wounding large numbers of them at random," I was told by a British colleague who was among the few journalists who managed to get to see Dretelj.)

Mugdim Karabeg ended up in the Croatian concentration camps. His fate, as well as the fate of all Mostar and many other cities under Croat attack, was in the hands of a man who had once been his student: Jadranko Prlić. As a young man in the early seventies, at a time when Karabeg was the editor of our regional pages in Hercegovina, he had been a freelance correspondent for *Oslobodjenje* in Mostar. And he had been friends with Nenad Žujo. Twenty years later, when Karabeg was imprisoned in a concentration camp and Žujo and his wife and children were driven out of Mostar, Jadranko Prlić was the president of HVO forces responsible for the terror and a "prime minister" of the "Herceg-Bosna" government.* Karabeg survived and he called me after he was released from the camp, from some small island in Croatia and, as if his suffering was of no importance, asked me: "How are my colleagues at *Oslobodjenje* doing, are they alive and well? Tell them that I am proud that you have kept the paper going."

He could equally be proud of his student, Alica Behram, and *Oslobodjenje*'s photographer in Mostar, Ifet Kapdžić. Alica had continued to report from besieged and devastated East Mostar, and whenever he could find a courier, Ifet continued to send us pictures cataloguing the destruction of the city—of the bridges blown up over the Neretva River, the destroyed Bristol and Neretva hotels, the ruins along Šantićeva street, and later the deep emptiness left by the destruction of the famous Stari most, the Old Bridge, a masterpiece of Ottoman architecture.

While our correspondents continued to take risks and tried to seize all possible means to send in their dispatches to *Oslobodjenje*'s editorial offices, the siege of Sarajevo had made it impossible to deliver the paper outside the city. Faruk Midžić, our correspondent in Zenica, came up with a plan to get the paper past the iron curtain surrounding Sarajevo and have it "published" in other Bosnian towns. "Send me the newspaper via fax, and I will post it in visible

---

* I could not believe my eyes when I saw him at the Holocaust Memorial Museum in Washington in September 1994! The Croatians had nominated him the Vice-Prime Minister of the Bosniak-Croat federation brokered by the United States in March, and he had accompanied the Bosnian prime minister Haris Silajdzic on an official visit to the United States in September. I was invited—together with Silajdzic—to speak at the opening of the exhibition, "The Faces of Sorrow," and was overwhelmed by the irony of finding the man who was in charge of concentration camps in Hercegovina visiting the museum built to commemorate the victims of the Nazi holocaust.

"He doesn't belong here!" I said to Silajdzic. "The presence here of someone who ran concentration camps is an offense to all the victims of fascism."

"But we have to live there and if his being part of our government might prevent new camps and sufferings, I'll have to tolerate him," the prime minister responded.

In his speech that evening Silajdzic compared Nazi camps in the Second World War to those ran by the Serbs in Bosnia like Omarska and Manjača. As the last speaker, facing Prlić who, as an honored guest, had been seated in the front row, the very least I could do to keep faith with memory was to add Dretelj to the list of camps being mentioned where people had been robbed of their humanity and their lives. Prlić was later named Bosnia-Hercegovina's foreign minister.

locations around Zenica, in store and shop windows, so that people can see that *Oslobodjenje* is still coming out, and they can read what it says," he suggested in the first days of the siege of Sarajevo. And we readily complied. Whoever was on duty in the Communications Center of *Oslobodjenje* would get the scissors out, cut the pages of the day's issue into quarters, and fax them over to Zenica, where Faruk, helped by his co-workers as well as numerous other friends of *Oslobodjenje* in Zenica, would copy the pages, paste them together, and get them displayed in windows around the town. A similar fax publication was occasionally distributed in the first months of the siege in other Bosnian towns as well: Jajce, Bihać, Tuzla. We were as proud as children are of their art work when we saw a televised news story showing dozens of Tuzla's citizens standing in a line in front of a barbershop in the old part of town in order to read *Oslobodjenje*.

Exhilarated by the success of his plan, Faruk came up with yet another idea. Together with friends in Zenica, he organized the publishing of a review of selected stories from the war issues of *Oslobodjenje* in Sarajevo and then distributed tens of thousands of copies throughout the free territory of Zenica, Mostar, Tuzla, Travnik, Bugojno, and other parts of Bosnia-Hercegovina. And when the Croatian occupation of parts of central Bosnia made the distribution of the "war review" impossible, he proceeded to print the paper, in a somewhat condensed version, in Zenica itself. The same thing was done by our correspondent in Tuzla, Mato Bikić, even though the *Oslobodjenje* he printed mostly carried local Tuzla stories. Their work was enormously valuable since it helped keep the name of *Oslobodjenje* alive, not only in Sarajevo, where we continued to publish each day, but also throughout the entire war-ravaged territory of Bosnia-Hercegovina. Emerging from the besieged, bombed-out building in Nedžarići, our voice could cut through the bunkers and barricades and reach our readers in other parts of the country.

A number of *Oslobodjenje*'s correspondents continued to maintain their links with the paper from outside Bosnia-Hercegovina. Branislav Boškov in Belgrade would send a dispatch whenever he could regarding important developments in Serbia. He also tried as best as he could to help his colleagues who had ended up as refugees in Serbia or their families—parents, wives, and children—delivering

WITH ITS EDITORIAL ROOM AND PRINTING PRESSES CRAMMED INTO AN UNDERGROUND BOMB SHELTER BENEATH THE RUBBLE OF WHAT HAD ONCE BEEN A TEN-STORY BUILDING, *OSLOBOD-JENJE* PUBLISHED EVERY DAY THROUGHOUT THE SIEGE.

messages, sending packages of medicines, and so on. In Zagreb, Darjan Zadravec found ways of getting through with the most important bits of news even when Sarajevo was under a complete communications blockade. It was our correspondents office in Zagreb which served as the "relay station" for other correspondents' around the world. They would send their daily reports by fax to Zagreb, and our secretaries, Gordana Vekić or Amra Hondo, who had taken their children to the safety of Zagreb, would read these reports to us through connections made by ham radio. This was how we got reports from Ivica Mišić in New York and Ljiljana Smajlović in Brussels (until that office had to be closed since *Oslobodjenje*'s lack of foreign currency did not allow it to guarantee a regular salary for the correspondent and Ljiljana moved to live with her mother in Belgrade, joining the independent weekly *Vreme*). Likewise, Vlastimir Mijović from Moscow kept in touch, and later kept himself by creating a Bosnian newsletter based upon the news from *Oslobodjenje*, and selling it to interested institutions and individuals in the Russian capital. From Podgorica in Montenegro, in spite of threats by local ultranationalists, Slobodan Racković consistently documented and reported the complicity of Montenegrin politicians in the aggression against Bosnia-Hercegovina. We also continued to receive reports from Zoran Odić from Ljubljana, Dušan Joksić from Skopje, and many others.

Oslobodjenje survived the war because there were enough people, both in Sarajevo and in small beleaguered towns across the country, some of whom I have mentioned here and some of whom I have not, who made enormous personal sacrifices to keep the paper in print. It was their way of offering resistance to the forces that were seeking to destroy Bosnia.

THE BATTLE FOR *OSLOBODJENJE*

FROM THE DAY *OSLOBODJENJE*'S offices came under fire, it became increasingly dangerous to come to work and to go home after work. All day long, from our windows we could see the snipers from Nedžarići shooting at everything that moved—cars, bicyclists, pedestrians—through the major intersection that led east into the center of town or west to Ilidža or south to the airport. Bullets hit the asphalt, the lampposts on the street, the gas station nearby, the carwash, the David restaurant. A woman shot and killed near *Oslobodjenje* lay where she had died for three days, and no one, not even the UN soldiers who ferried foreign dignitaries in and out of Sarajevo in their armored vehicles, dared to take her lifeless body away. A city which had throbbed with life late into the night was being turned into a graveyard. Moving through Sarajevo at night was to experience the threatening emptiness of deserted streets, with not a living soul anywhere in sight.

On one such evening in early April 1992, Salko Hasanefendić and I had gone to the Ministry of Internal Affairs to see the minister, Alija Delimustafić, about possible arrangements for increased protection around *Oslobodjenje*. We found him in an insoluble dilemma. A blackmailing ultimatum had arrived from the chetnik headquarters in Pale: the Bosnian government must release the snipers in its custody or it must prepare for the shelling of Sarajevo to commence at precisely 6:30 P.M.*

"What do you think we should do?" Delimustafić asked in haste as he prepared to go off to a meeting with the Presidency of Bosnia-Hercegovina.

"I don't know. Civilized states normally don't negotiate with terrorists or yield to their blackmail, but we've been a state for a just a few days. I don't know if you have the resources to resist this kind of force. Whatever you decide, you'll be making a mistake," I said, unhelpfully, adding that personally I would not give in to their demands for that would allow them to get away with anything.

We were offered a drink and we stayed, waiting with trepidation, our eyes on the clock. Exactly at 6:30 P.M. the first explosion went off—first in Baščaršija, in the heart of the old quarter, and then where we were, in the city center. Shells had hit the old city brewery, family dwellings, and small shops in Baščaršija, and were falling ever closer to the police headquarters at the Internal Affairs Ministry. When Salko and I headed for the exit, thinking that we would go home under the protection of nightfall, the police from the Special Units, wearing helmets and carrying automatic weapons (until then, still an unfamiliar sight) warned us: "Don't go anywhere, it's dangerous out there!" As if to punctuate the warning, one shell exploded a hundred yards from the door where we stood, on the stone steps going down the Pavla Goranina Street. The stones that were hit exploded, and a cloud of smoke and dust spread through the air. "The apartment building over there in Radićeva Street has been hit, too. Wherever you go, you're gambling with your life," the policeman continued.

We went back into the building, to the office of Zoran Milanović, formerly a journalist, who had been appointed Assistant Minister of Internal Affairs for Public Relations. The explosions were becoming a little less frequent, and we decided that after we had one more coffee and another half hour's conversation, we would head for home. At the exit we were again reminded that we were leaving at our own risk, but

---

* The snipers had been captured just days earlier firing from the windows of Karadžić's headquarters at the Holiday Inn on citizens demonstrating against the siege of Sarajevo. Among those arrested was one Rajko Kušić, who was the personal bodyguard of Karadžić's right-hand man, Nikola Koljević.

life—if possible—had to go on. From that day on, the citizens of Sarajevo would have to take their chances. As we stepped out I saw for the first time young men wielding automatic weapons on the streetcorners of Pavla Goranina, Boriše Kovačevića, Dalmatinska, and Titova, who had assumed the job of defending the city.

These defenders of the city were a story in themselves. Bosnia-Hercegovina did not, at the time, have its own army—not one single tank, one multibarrel rocket launcher, one mortar, one anti-aircraft gun or cannon, not to mention a plane. All the heavy weaponry belonged to the Yugoslav National Army, was operated by JNA officers and was used to its full capacity in the Serbian drive to "cleanse" and conquer Bosnian territory. With the excuse that the JNA was in Bosnia-Hercegovina to "prevent ethnic conflict" or—as later rephrased by Chief of General Staff General Blagoje Adžić—to "protect the Serb population," the army had become an army of occupation in the country from the day the Bosnia's independent statehood was recognized by the international community. The responsibility for the defense of Sarajevo in those early days of the war had thus fallen upon the Special Unit of the police under the command of Dragan Vikić. During the first months of the siege, "Vikić's Men," as the unit was known among Sarajevans, went out to all of the most seriously threatened lines of defense and countered the attacks of the Serbian armored vehicles and infantry. Soon the Sarajevans were singing a song about them: "Carry the flag, I will follow you; together we will celebrate victory, dear Dragan Vikić." Before the war Vikić was a famous martial arts champion, a man of impressive build and strength. When the war came, he became not only a legend in the story of the city's desperate resistance but also—because of his Croat background in predominantly Muslim Sarajevo—an embodiment of the defense of Sarajevo's multiethnic character.

Apart from "Vikić's Men," there were other regular and reserve units of the police force, but since these were stretched thin on the ground and were mostly assigned to the defense of the front lines around the city, other groups emerged to fight in the defense of Sarajevo. The earliest of these groups was the "Patriotic League," which was organized as an underground force by defecting JNA officers to prepare for war in Bosnia following the JNA's offensives in Slovenia and Croatia. Once Bosnia came under attack, in all the Sarajevo neighborhoods there was a spontaneous appearance of new units of young men ready to defend their homes and communities. These self-organized "irregular" units—which were subsequently integrated into the Territorial Defense and, later, into the new Bosnian Army—were often led by the boys who had been small street gang leaders, socially neglected youths who had lived on the edge of the law, selling contraband on the street, dabbling in the black market, and engaging in petty theft. When the war came their anonymous, dreary lives were transformed: some of them would fight and become local heroes and they would also profit enormously from the conditions of war. Thus in the first few weeks of the siege, with the police units dispatched to the front lines, all stores and warehouses in Sarajevo were looted, and the stolen goods surfaced in a black market for sale at skyrocketing prices.

Until the Bosnian army emerged to establish its hegemony, these units operated autonomously and played by their own rules. But the people of Sarajevo quickly came to regard them with trust and respect, even when they knew that some of them were involved in looting and war profiteering. The citizens were simply grateful that there was anyone at all willing to stand up to the heavily armed forces attacking Sarajevo. Those early defenders of the city paraded through the city wearing fancy sunglasses, driving the most expensive Mercedes and Audis they could find, commandeering them from companies and private owners "for the defense of the city." No one really knew whether some of them were more involved in fighting at the front lines in the hills around Sarajevo or strutting their stuff through the city streets, but there were many songs celebrating their heroism. Jusuf-Juka Prazina and Ismet Bajramović-Ćelo were among those first heroes of Sarajevo's defense in the spring and summer of 1992. And, like some other celebrated heroes, they departed—their meteoric rise to fame and fortune swiftly consumed by the war that spawned it. Juka was even accused of joining the Croat forces in terror against Mostar the following year and was later killed under mysterious circumstances, apparently by his own bodyguard, and found dead in his car on a highway in Belgium. Ćelo was shot near the heart, but nobody knew exactly whether the bullet came from Bosnian Army or Serb positions. He survived miraculously after being transported for a medical treatment abroad. Some like Mušan Topalović-Caco and Ramiz Delalić-Ćelo, became outcasts, terrorizing the city with their units. Caco was killed and Ćelo arrested in a Bosnian Army drive to restore the order on Sarajevo streets in the fall of 1993.

It needs to be said, however, that in those early days—when there was no army to fight in the defense of Bosnia—the defense of Sarajevo was nothing short of a military miracle. It took extraordinary courage, for instance, on the part of the boys in my neighborhood at the Square of the Heroes to stop Serbian tanks. Sometimes they had just one antitank grenade and they could not afford to miss the first of the advancing tanks. The bravest among them organized in commando units and better armed and trained than the rest of the Territorial Defense, would wait until the tank came so close that they could stop it with that single grenade, thus blocking the advance of the tanks at the rear. Once, in the summer of 1992, special units from Niš in Serbia joined the attack on Hrasno. They wore special armored uniforms and helmets and the defenders called them "turtles." "We couldn't stop them with bullets, so we used rocket-propelled grenades," the boys in the neighborhood told me, explaining how in a single day, defending Hrasno, they killed dozens of "turtles" from Niš. We could see the bodies still on the fence of Željezničara Stadium several days after the battle because the Serb units were afraid to come to collect them.

On that distant April evening of 1992, as Salko Hasanefendić and I drove away from the Ministry of the Interior, in the dark along the deserted streets of Sarajevo, it was these young men, and others like them, who seemed to be the city's only line of defense against the besieging forces on the surrounding hills. Going home, I felt a shiver of fear, the first sense of direct contact with immediate danger, the awareness that Sarajevo was so utterly vulnerable and might be utterly destroyed. There was little time for reflection, however. As long as the city existed and we were alive, we would find ways to carry on and the siege would teach us new lessons in survival.

In May, when he had just turned eighteen, my son Tarik decided to join the defenders of the city. He announced his decision to Vesna after a twelve-year-old girl, Snežana Radonja, the sister of one of his best friends, Srdjan, was killed by shrapnel while watching television in her apartment. Tarik went to express his sympathy to Srdjan. He felt the horrible nature of the terror which did not spare anyone and he said to his mother: "They are killing kids in their beds, helpless people in their houses, and I don't want to be just another target, I don't want to wait for them to come. I'm going to the nearest unit of our Army!"

Vesna tried, like any mother would, to tell him that she understood his feelings and motives, but that he was never trained to take a gun in his hands; he was just finishing high school and was too young for service in the Army. I was caught between a deep understanding of her feelings, which were mine too, and respect for the person he was: he would not forgive us if we stood in his way. So, he went to the neighboring unit under the command of Safet Tokača and, in the nights when all of Hrasno was shaking under artillery and infantry fire from Hrasno Hill, we would know that he was somewhere there among the young fighters defending the neighborhood.

On a late afternoon that May, after finishing our work on the front pages for the next day's paper, three of us set out in my car to head for home: two of my associate editors, Zlatko Dizdarević and Fuad Kovačević, and myself. I drove them as far as the bridge at Dolac Malta, where I turned to go to Hrasno, and they were planning to walk from there to the city center. As soon as I turned at the bridge, I saw that something was afoot on Ivana Krndelja Street. People were running in a panic, hiding behind the buildings and taking shelter under the eaves. While I was parking my car in front of the building, bullets started whistling by. My neighbors were waving at me from behind half-closed doors, urging me to hurry up. They were getting ready to barricade the doors. Among them were two women from the adjoining entrance. The shooting was so fierce that they were unable to run the fifteen yards or so to get to their own hallway. As soon as I got in, I turned around and saw Zlatko and Fuad. Bent down, as if they were swimming through the grass, they were running across the small island of foliage between my apartment building and Ivana Krndelja Street and, completely out of breath, made it to the door. There, in the space behind the elevator, on the stairs, all of my neighbors were gathered.

"We need to figure out how to protect and defend this entrance!" someone proposed. The building I live in is eight stories high with four apartments on each floor—in other words, 32 families for one entrance. It was decided that the residents themselves would organize a round-the-clock watch in shifts of two men every four hours. Those standing guard would be armed. For that purpose, everyone who had a gun in the building was to register it and make it available. Besides my two pistols there were another five or six volunteered.

Zlatko and Fuad stayed that night at my place. We established telephone contact with *Oslobodjenje*'s journalists in various parts of the city and turned my apartment into an editorial office: reporters called us with various reports, we talked with them and noted the most salient details, and then put it all together into a front-page editorial report on the night's attack on Sarajevo. It was at this time that we introduced the first security measures in the editorial offices. In the first few days, the journalists on duty, waiting for police protection, had tried to create some sense of security for themselves as they worked in the huge, empty building in Nedžarići by improvising an "advance warning" system: they placed empty beer bottles through all the long corridors so that if the Serbs came to occupy the building in the night, they would be alerted by the sound of falling bottles. During the day, the paper was being prepared by the regular team at the *Oslobodjenje* newsroom: Zlatko and I, together with the make-up editors, worked on the front pages, and we would be often joined by the editor of the political section, Gordana Knežević, and the editor of the "Sarajevo Chronicle," Josip Vričko, to finalize the pages. However, with news of developments arriving around the clock, we decided that we needed an editor to stay in the building all night. He would talk with the correspondents from all over Bosnia-Hercegovina as well as reporters in the city and incorporate their reports into the paper. A space of forty-five lines of text on the first page would be reserved for a late-night summary of the most important events of the previous day, and the entire back page for coverage of happenings during the night until the early morning hours. I would regularly write the day's summary, sometimes crouched in the tiny hallway of our apartment to which Vesna, Mirza, and I would routinely withdraw when the shelling and infantry fighting around Hrasno was at its heaviest. Until the telephone lines were cut off, the summary would be based upon whatever was included in that day's paper, as well as upon late evening conversations with journalists in Sarajevo and correspondents from other towns, as well as the news on foreign radio stations about diplomatic activities concerning Bosnia.

Our round-the-clock editorial watch, which was originally to be rotated among all of us so that every editor would serve, became the exclusive preserve of the oldest and most experienced *Oslobodjenje* editor, Adil Hajrić, who volunteered to do the job himself. He stayed alone in the editorial offices and occasionally—as happened when a gasoline truck exploded in front of the Yugoslav Army barracks in Mostar or when the oil refinery in Bosanski Brod burned throughout the night or when, at the end of May, all of Sarajevo was burning in the most vicious artillery attack upon the city—he managed to include in the next morning's issue the news of the night's developments while they were still unfolding. *Oslobodjenje* had never managed in its normal peacetime existence to be as current with the news as it did in these worst days of terror. Adil carried out this work for weeks at a time by himself, but it became more and more difficult for him to stay there alone. One night, the Serbian forces in Nedžarići, probably after having loaded their brains sufficiently with brandy and beer, decided to play a "game" with *Oslobodjenje*. They telephoned the newsroom.

"Did you order thirty-two mortar shells?"

"Hello, who is this?" Adil answered, not believing his ears.

"We will deliver them right away!" the chetnik said, laughing at the other end of the line.

And sure enough, within a short time, the building of *Oslobodjenje* was being shelled.

"I think that they did not 'deliver' as many as had been 'ordered': I counted and they were short by one," Adil told me, half-jokingly, when he recounted this experience.

It was important to minimize—and to distribute—the risk of death or injury. It was also important, as the attack on Sarajevo intensified, to ensure that we would be able to get the paper out in some shape or form even if we lost our communication lines or our correspondents could not make it to work. We therefore decided to improvise the seven-day shift program, which would keep a skeletal staff on the job at all times. A group of ten editors and reporters would take up residence at the offices in Nedžarići from Monday to Monday. The group would be organized in such a way as to include editors who were also good proofreaders, at least one reporter who could use radio and television news to "reconstruct" all the major events of the day, an experienced commentator who could write the front page commentary if the regular columnist were unable to get his copy to us, and a photographer who, if no pictures arrived that day, would be able to shoot pictures off the television screen to illustrate the day's stories. We formed three such teams so that after a seven-day stay at

TO MINIMIZE THE DANGER FROM SNIPER ATTACKS THE PAPER'S STAFF WORKED ON SEVEN DAY SHIFTS. DURING A PAUSE IN THE SHELLING, ONE OF THE SEVEN-DAY TEAMS GATHERED IN FRONT OF THE NEWSPAPER IN THE SUMMER OF 1992. BACK ROW: MUHAMED PAJEVIĆ, BRANKO TOMIĆ, BORO SIMIĆ, MIDHAT AJANOVIĆ, MILAN STOJAKOVIĆ, DRAGAN RADCVIĆ. FRONT ROW: AMIRA ŠCHIĆ, ZDENKA BRAJKOVIĆ, ŠLAVKO SANTIĆ, AND SLOBODAN STAJIĆ.

the "*Oslobodjenje* Inn Hotel," our basement newsroom-bedroom, each shift would have a two-week respite. After a day or two of rest, most of them would then join the reporters in town covering events of the day, and they would work out of the offices rented in the administration building of Bosnia-Hercegovina Railway, opposite the Presidency building in the center of Sarajevo.

All the time, however, in all the shifts, we had one person who had taken up residence at the building: Boro Simić, a prewar stringer in our "Sarajevo Chronicle" department whose family lived in a small town in Central Bosnia. He recorded and transcribed hundreds of radio and television news reports, and often received and typed up the reports from city reporters and correspondents. He also took on the responsibility of preparing the day's death notices which, unfortunately, were vastly more numerous than ever before. In the forty-two

143

months of Sarajevo's siege 10,609 people were killed—more than perished over the four-year period of fascist terror in the Second World
War. It was always painful to open those last pages which carried the
obituaries—very often I would find names and faces of people who
had died the day before, people I knew well. When telephones in the
city did not work, which was often, those death notices brought to
Oslobodjenje were the only way of letting friends or family know that a
loved one had been killed.

There were some changes, caused by the departure of several
journalists from Sarajevo, in the teams operating the shifts in the first
two years of the siege. The evacuation of a few was arranged by *Oslobodjenje* while others got out by risking the deadly run across the
sniper-covered and UNPROFOR-policed runway of Sarajevo airport. *
Most of those who remained in Sarajevo were angry with those who
left. I was more understanding about the difficult decisions most of us
had had to make. Although I came back after every trip abroad even
while my own family had been evacuated to Croatia, I knew that those
who left had to decide between their responsibility to their work at the
paper and responsibility to their spouses and children who were not
welcome anywhere as Bosnian refugees; between remaining with their
families or returning to the uncertainties of life in the besieged city;
between risks of trying to start a new life elsewhere or risking death in
Sarajevo. Some of them simply had to leave. Boro Radosavljević was
one—his wife Smiljana had died at the beginning of the war after

---

* The airport was under UN control, and it was the only piece of "no man's land" in the
area, separating Bosnian Army positions in the Dobrinja neighborhood from the village of Butmir across the runway, just under Mount Igman. For people trapped in
Sarajevo, there was no other way out except to use the cover of night to sprint across
that distance from the trenches of Dobrinja to the front lines of Butmir and then over
the mountainous Mount Igman road through Bosnian Army and HVO-held territories towards Croatia. Since UN soldiers patrolling the airport often showed excessive
"zeal" in preventing that "illegal" crossing, their reflectors sweeping across the runway
to spotlight the silhouettes of those making the desperate run—either to reunite with
their families or bring back food to stave off hunger—the Serb snipers surrounding
Dobrinja were afforded ideal conditions for target practice and many were wounded
or killed making the crossing. In desperation, Bosnian Army units from Dobrinja and
Butmir invested many months of hard labor in 1993 to dig a "Communication D-B"
tunnel less than two yards high and two yards wide under the runway connecting
Dobrinja and Butmir and thus providing a lifeline which Sarajevans could use to
bring in some food, arms, and ammunition or get across to the free territories.

a long illness, and his two small children, Nikola and Lana, were left with her parents on the Pelješac peninsula in Croatia; after a year of continuing to work at *Oslobodjenje* he had to go and look after them. We told him that there would always be a job waiting for him whenever he was willing to come back. Amira Šehić was hit by a sniper bullet from Nedžarići while in the company van on her way into town; her arm did not sufficiently recover its use, and we helped to send her to Paris for medical treatment. She was joined in her journey by Zdenka Brajković who was shot in the leg by a Serb sniper while she was inside our building and was going to get a cup of coffee. Some had gone away with the permission of the company and then decided for different, mostly family reasons, not to return. A few simply "disappeared"— went somewhere safe.

But there were always more people at *Oslobodjenje* who wanted to work than there were productive positions to assign to them since, owing to the shortage of newsprint, we had been compelled to reduce the number of pages of the paper. From a prewar staff, which numbered 180 in Sarajevo including administrative personnel, we were now working with a daily staff of about 70, in addition to a large number who were on the waiting list, ready to fill in if needed. After a year of working with the seven-day shifts, the need for augmenting the teams arose when the Agence France Presse (AFP) gave us their daily news service and, later, Reuters agreed to donate their services for both news and photos. I then assigned one English translator to every shift. They not only translated the foreign wire services' stories, but often, with the assistance of other colleagues who knew foreign languages, hosted the numerous journalists and diplomats who frequently visited *Oslobodjenje* during their stay in Sarajevo.

The seven-day shifts turned out to be the most reliable guarantee for the regular appearance of the paper. Even if the rest of us, in the worst days, were prevented from coming to work, we could be sure that the paper would get printed. At first the teams were still able to work in our editorial offices, although day by day the job became increasingly hazardous. The shells fired from Nedžarići had practically destroyed one side of the building. My office was the first to be hit, targeted by incendiary bullets which broke all the windows, riddling everything with holes—furniture, shelves, cupboards, paintings on the wall. On that day, a Television Sarajevo crew came to take pictures of the damage.

"We know who did this and where they are firing from. Those are the houses over there," I pointed out the location for the camera which panned across Nedžarići. "We will not tolerate such treatment from our neighbors and will be forced to respond in kind."

I knew, of course, that we did not have any means of retaliation. Just a few months before the outbreak of the war, *Oslobodjenje*, like all the other large firms in Sarajevo, had had its own territorial defense unit with weapons which could, indeed, return fire if fired upon. But then came our unilateral disarmament when the JNA—with the assistance of the Bosnian police under instructions to cooperate—had collected the weapons of all territorial defense in Bosnia, which therefore ended up in the hands of the Serbian terrorists instead of the military stockpiles of a Bosnian defense force. My "threat" on the television screen, however, did have an unexpected effect.

The very next day, three people came to *Oslobodjenje*. "Please don't destroy our houses in Nedžarići!" they pleaded, as if we really could have done so. They explained to the policeman at the door that they had been living in those houses and that Serb extremists had chased them out of their homes. They gave us the names of those who had moved into the houses and the names of the commanders of the Serb paramilitary unit in Nedžarići. Thus, although we had not known who were shooting at us when I claimed on television that we did, they had now been identified for us. But the knowledge, of course, was of no practical use to us. The firing only became more and more fierce, opening up gaping holes in the walls and clearing a path for the bullets which streaked through the building into the offices on the other side which, in the earlier phase of the attack, had been relatively insulated from the attack. It was then that we decided to move *Oslobodjenje* underground, into the large bomb shelter in the basement.

The entry to our new location was through a massive steel door in a dark underground corridor. The room was both long and wide, designed as a secure shelter from nuclear fallout, with showers and toilets to provide for a long stay. When the building was built in the late 1970s, we joked about the Communists' paranoia which forced us, by law, to build such a shelter. "That's really a waste of money; who would ever need such a large shelter?" we asked. Now, in the spring of 1992, under the onslaught of the Serbian artillery, this was the only place where we could safely work and ensure that *Oslobodjenje* would be printed every day.

THE INTERIOR OF *OSLOBODJENJE*'S OFFICES JUST BEFORE THE BUILDING WAS TARGETED BY INCENDIARY ATTACKS AND BURNED TO THE GROUND IN JUNE 1992.

In those days, I would come to work in the morning and, still preferring to stay upstairs, usually go to the manager's office in the "safer" part of the building, my own office already having been completely destroyed. One day while I was sitting there in the company of a small group of other editors, writing one of my "Letters from the War," an explosion went off which was bigger than anything I had experienced before. The entire building shook, rocked, and twisted; glass shattered, and the aluminum squealed. This was not just a powerful projectile hitting the building but a sound that went on for several long, terrifying seconds, like the howling of some tormented animal.

"It's a tank. That's a tank firing!" Branko Tomić, the on-duty editor, burst into the room shouting.

They had indeed brought a tank to the small hill next to the student dormitories, just a hundred meters or so from *Oslobodjenje*. They had trained their barrel on us and fired once, twice, three... seven times.

"You can't sit here, everyone go down below!" Branko shouted in a commanding tone.

"Branko is right. You should all go below and leave me to finish what I'm writing and this glass of what I'm drinking," I said, not because I was less frightened, but because, even at home in Hrasno, I did not like going down to the basement when the Serbian attacks were on. Usually I sat and wrote, or in the worst cases took refuge in our small windowless hallway inside the apartment, knowing that if I let the terror force me down into the basement I would become paralyzed by fear and would not be able to continue my work.

The attacks upon *Oslobodjenje* became so routine that the editors on duty stopped calling me at home. Artillery, automatic weapons, snipers' bullets had become commonplace stuff—a nasty nuisance, nothing more. Something much more serious and out of the ordinary would have to happen to make them call me, because they knew that at my place in Hrasno the same fireworks were on display. But on the evening of June 20, 1992, just as I got home, the on-duty editor, Feto Ramović, called me:

"The building is on fire! They have been shooting with incendiary bullets and now the building is aflame," he said.

The fire had engulfed the twin towers—ten stories high—which had housed our administrative offices in prewar Sarajevo. When the firemen arrived they were joined by the journalists and printing press workers on the weekly shift. They unrolled the fire hoses through the stairwells and along the hallways, helping the firefighters through smoke and flames, risking their lives while the murderers in Nedžarići continued shooting at the silhouettes of men battling with the fire they had started.

They were sopping wet, dirty from the smoke, and exhausted.

Feto called me that night every hour: the upper two…three… four floors were burning. One of the firefighters was killed; Fahro Memić, one of our editors, was wounded.

"Now," Feto said, "we are putting water on the floors which still haven't caught fire to prevent the fire from spreading."

"The fire has finally stopped. Four of the floors on the one side and six floors on the other side have burned," I was informed at exactly six o'clock that morning.

Only five minutes later, the phone rang.

"The presses are rolling. The paper will be on the streets again."

Sarajevans had watched the late evening news on television showing the *Oslobodjenje* building in flames, via an amateur video camera in the hands of our reporters, Vlado Mrkić and Rajko Živković, who had been filming from the nearby residential area of Vojničko Polje. No one believed that from those flames a newspaper would still emerge the next morning. But it did. It was June 21, 1992. In its tribute to those who had battled the fire, Television Sarajevo said: "Today, with the appearance of a new issue of *Oslobodjenje*, the aggressor has suffered his worst defeat since the beginning of the siege of Sarajevo!"

That morning we had a surprise visit from the poet, author, and screenwriter, Abdulah Sidran. Inspired by our achievement, he had braved the dangerous path between the television building and *Oslobodjenje*, hurrying past the sniper and machine-gun nests in Nedžarići, to come shake our hands. He was frightened only when he came to the point where there had once been an entrance to the building. Instead of a wide and well-lit entryway and reception area, there was only a dark sooty emptiness.

"Kemal, Kemal," he called out, "Avdo Sidran is here. Where are you?"

He wanted the guards to hear him so that they would not wonder who it was moving among the piles of rubble, and shoot him. When they heard him and escorted him to the room where we were going over all the horrors of the previous night, he handed a book to me. It was a copy of his *Sarajevska zbirka,* a volume of selected poems, with the dedication: "To Kemal, my brother, from Avdo—towards the end of the war, 21 June 92." We all hoped, of course, but the war raged on.

Everyone working on the seven-day shifts experienced many nights of terror. But the team led by Feto Ramović was always the one on duty when the worst events occurred. They experienced the three biggest fires and the collapse of first one, and then the other, of the twin towers. Fuad Kovačević, who was on the shift, remembers the day when the first tower collapsed as the most dramatic of all the days and nights he spent in the building. Since early morning a tank from Nedžarići was targeting the tower which had already been burnt to a shell. Hit a number of times, it finally fell in a thunderous mass of dust and smoke, crushing several of the cars parked in front of the building. Fortunately, not one of the journalists and printing workers on duty was injured. It was August 28, 1992, also the day when Sarajevo's historic hundred-year-old National Library, housing thousands of rare books and manuscripts, went up in flames, and the day when the London Conference—one of the many futile international conferences that were to follow—reaffirmed Bosnia-Hercegovina's "sovereignty and integrity." Three weeks later the other twin tower collapsed—what remained standing among the rubble was the metal elevator and staircase shaft, raising a defiant fist to the sky.

Everyone experienced his own personal drama. Adil Hajrić recounted to me the story of the fire he survived at *Oslobodjenje*. That night he was sleeping in the documentation room, and he did not awake even when the entire floor where the newsroom was located was enveloped in smoke and several rooms were in flames. All the other members of the team, who were sleeping in the newsroom, had been awakened and had taken refuge in safer areas. While everyone was running for cover, not even stopping to get dressed, the editor in charge of the next shift, Branko Tomić, remembered that Adil was sleeping in the other room. He came through the smoke to him and woke him up.

"Let's get out of here, Adjo, everything is on fire!" he said, as he shook him awake.

"That saved my life, because the smoke would have suffocated me while I slept. And it proved to me what I already knew: that I was working with people who would never abandon me," Adil went on to say.

Adil, Pliva, Branko, Feto, Mirko, Fahro, Slavko . . . each of them could write a book from their journal notes of wartime *Oslobodjenje*. But, in a way, that was also true of the other reporters who were on duty in the city. In the cramped quarters of the space we rented in the center of town, they worked under the supervision of the political editor, Gordana Knežević, and her first co-editor, Rasim Ćerimagić (the latter became political editor after Gordana assumed the position of deputy editor). Some thirty journalists worked with them, writing about the happenings of that day in the city: the shelling of Sarajevo, the killing of its citizens, human tragedies, and the heroism of Sarajevo's doctors, firemen, police units, and the operations of the Army of Bosnia-Hercegovina, the activities of the Presidency and the Government and its representatives, diplomatic initiatives and visits, activities of UNPROFOR and UNHCR, the state of the supply of water, electricity, food, and the impressive spiritual and cultural resistance of Sarajevo by actors, writers, musicians, artists, and others who gave life and hope to the badly wounded city.

It is a truism that adversity can bring out the best or the worst in human beings. The war and the siege put all of us to the test. As I write this, I cannot but be impressed by the number of journalists at *Oslobodjenje* who gave their best to their paper and their people. Vlado Mrkić was among them. He was tireless. When he was not writing some of the most powerful stories of loss and suffering (eventually compiled into a book), he was at the front-lines covering the battles fought or— sometimes alone, sometimes with an equally dedicated Rajko Živković—he could be found delivering the paper around town, bringing bread from the bakery for his colleagues, and even driving people wounded on the streets to the hospital. One day he found himself driving a badly injured girl from one of the city's working-class neighborhoods to the hospital with a desperate man in the car begging him to speed up—"Faster, faster, my child is dying!"—only to discover, once the girl was taken care of in the emergency room of Koševo hospital, that the man did not even know the name of the child. He was just a passer-by and, like the war reporter, had acted to save the life of an unknown child. ("I read that story last night in Mrkić's book and couldn't sleep at all: I was thinking of my granddaughter and of so many children killed and wounded in this war," Alija Izetbegović once told me.)

In the summer of 1992, the telephone lines went dead in Sarajevo. This meant that we could not send stories or photos, either by fax or telephoto. They had to be physically delivered to the editorial offices in a city blanketed with artillery shelling and sniper fire. Again, Vlado was most often the one who would wait for all the others to finish their stories and bring their pictures; he would gather all the material together and, in the late afternoon, bring it over to our bunker at Nedžarići. On several occasions, his car was hit as he made the crosstown run, a bullet once ripping through the shirt he was wearing, missing him by a hair's breadth. In the first two years of the siege, sometimes for weeks or even for months the city was without telephones or electricity, and it was through such countless courier runs that pictures and copy for the next day's paper were delivered to their destination.

Being without a phone, of course, made my job considerably more difficult: I could not call from my office (or from my home) to organize the day's columns or stories or even reach the on-call editor at the newsroom. It did, on the other hand, sharpen the professional sense and reflexes of the journalists. Every one learned to function as his or her own editor—they thought about what might be expected of them and often figured out exactly what was best to do. Gordana Knežević had an interesting story to tell. She and Rasim, neighbors at home on Koševo Hill, had been talking about who might write on what topic for the regular "In Focus" column on the front page that day. When they got to the *Oslobodjenje* offices, they found waiting for them the author they had wanted with the very piece they had been wishing for in hand.

There were others. Šefko Hodžić was on the 24-hour "line" with the units and headquarters of the Bosnian Army, witnessing and reporting all significant battles around Sarajevo. Ramo Kolar wrote numerous human interest stories about Bosnia's defenders and their lives. Later they were published as a book, *Sarajevo War Stories.* In the daily reporting—until November 1992, when we arranged for them to take their children to a safe refuge in the Czech Republic—much of the work was carried out by Arina Šarac and Branka Milićević-Mašić, and they continued to write for *Oslobodjenje* even as refugees. Elvedin Kantardžić was often at the right place at the right time for dramatic events in the first year of the war and was always available to the on-duty editor for "emergency coverage." Nada Salom wrote hundreds of stories on cultural events during the war: theater performances, exhibitions, concerts, literary events. She was chronicling the story of Sarajevo's will to transcend barbarism, its spiritual resistance to the war.

A special chapter should be devoted to the veteran photography editor, Salko Hondo. He was utterly devoted to the paper, very reliable in his work, a man who would not quit until he had accomplished his assignment. I had known him for over two decades. As a young reporter, I had traveled around Bosnia-Hercegovina with him, covering various political and Party events in Yugoslavia. On such occasions, Salko would entertain dozens of reporters in the evening with his imitations of Hollywood's western cowboy heroes. One day, sometime in the 1970s, his familiarity with Westerns reached the point of antagonizing the *Oslobodjenje* management. He had created an entire film script in which the major roles were played by members of the *Oslobodjenje* staff. His "film" was told and re-told and added to among the journalistic circles. There were stories on the love and political affairs of *Oslobodjenje*'s editors and journalists which circulated widely and drew a devoted following. Everyone working at the paper would discuss the evolving screenplay and would ask Hondo for as best a role as possible for themselves, adding ever new episodes to the movie in endless sessions at Lutvo's Club in *Oslobodjenje*'s old building. Finally, half-jokingly and half in earnest, the editor-in-chief at that time, Aziz Hadžihasanović, called him and in a dead-serious tone told him: "Hondo, tear up that screenplay of yours, dismiss the cast, and stop the filming!" "Yes, Sir!" Salko answered, with a military salute in his voice. And from that point onward, no more "work" was done on the film—it was, to continue the metaphor, canned.

Before the war, he had been seriously ill and had undergone surgery to remove the cancer in his colon. So, when the blockade of Sarajevo began and we were putting together teams of on-duty journalists, I suggested to him that he stay at home on half salary and with full benefits. "No, please, if necessary, I'll make the coffee for all of you," he said, "but I can't stay at home. I want to be here with the rest of you." He was one of the most conscientious of our workers. One day, in the middle of July 1992, he went on an assignment to the residential area known as "Ciglane" (where the old brickworks had been) on Djure Djakovića Street, near the center of town, to photograph the line of people there waiting for water. He never returned. A mortar shell once again sought out a group of civilians gathered in one spot, and this time it took Salko Hondo's life as well. Gordana, who had sent him on that fatal assignment, was so desperate and distraught that for days she could not bring herself to ask anyone to go out on any assignment again. I tried to console her by reminding her that Sarajevans were being killed all the time—in their apartments, in bread and water lines, or walking down the streets. "If Salko wasn't there taking pictures, he could easily have been there, standing in that line, queuing up for water," I told her.

On the anniversary of his death, I visited his wife, Nura, and took a few small gifts with me. At the time of the Muslim holiday of Bajram in 1993, she brought an entire feast for the whole staff of the newspaper: several different kinds of homemade specialties, including some meatballs, pies, baklava, and a liter of the popular Bosnian liqueur, the home-produced plum brandy called "Šljivovica." "This is a bottle

SALKO HONDO, *OSLOBODJENJE*'S PHOTOGRAPHER AND BELOVED FILM "DIRECTOR," WAS KILLED IN JULY 1992 BY A MORTAR SHELL WHILE ON ASSIGNMENT IN THE CENTER OF SARAJEVO.

which Salko kept for special occasions. I know he would have liked to have shared it with you, so I brought it here," she said.

I was especially impressed by the commitment of a number of the youngest members of our staff who had been hired just prior to the beginning of the war or in some cases, after the war began. Marija Fekete was a reporter and Senad Gubelić a photographer who would go every day to the UNPROFOR headquarters or to the peacekeepers' units and report on their activities. I watched them every day with my heart in my mouth as they would return to Nedžarići, trying to find hiding places along the way to escape sniper fire, running through the destroyed gasoline station, then racing across the open space, often accompanied by the staccato beat of a machine gun or the dust raised from bullets hitting the ground around them, and finally ducking into the ditch which would shield them from the gunfire. Marija later married a wounded foreign correspondent whom she met in wartime Sarajevo. She left the city with him but remained in touch.

Later the reporting on UNPROFOR and general diplomatic activities concerning Bosnia-Hercegovina was carried on successfully by Vlado Štaka and Džeilana Pećanin. Although they were the youngest of our staff in seniority, the two of them became the most reliable reporters on daily events for *Oslobodjenje*. First Džeilana, and then Vlado, left the city after three years of hard work. Senka Kurtović, like Vlado and Džeilana, also became one of our best reporters, writing some of the most moving stories about the human tragedies that made up the daily life of Sarajevo. Among those stories was the one about the deaths of six children, killed by a Serbian mortar shell while sledding in the snow among the high-rise buildings in the working-class neighborhood of Alipašino Polje. Then there was Juso Prelo who, until he left Sarajevo, wrote a regular satirical column, entitled "From the Dead Corner," and Memnun Idžaković, who wrote in a personal, bitter-humorous way, about people in the war. Especially notable was the open letter that he, as a former Yugoslav handball star, wrote to his teammate from earlier days, Djordje Lavrnic, who reportedly had become the Chetniks' "vojvoda" (duke) in the Doboj area.

And we had our cartoonists who helped sustain our sense of humor and put the war in some sort of perspective. There was, for instance, the cartoon by *Oslobodjenje*'s Božo Stefanović, which encapsulated the entire tragedy and the spirit of irony of the capital of Bosnia-Hercegovina: a Sarajevan with a rope tied around his neck, looking for a tree from which to hang himself to end his misery, wandering through a park where all that remained were stumps of trees that had been cut down for fuel by his fellow citizens.

A very special mark was left by the work of *Oslobodjenje*'s leading columnist Gojko Berić. During the war, he wrote some of the most sharp-witted, incisive analyses of the causes and manifestation of Serbian fascism, which were later published as a book entitled *Sarajevo at the End of the World*. He did most of his writing at home, never leaving his apartment in Vase Miskina Street, except on rare occasions to go to the nearby rented office space of *Oslobodjenje*. But since he would not go out to "greet" the war, the war had come to him when a mortar shell exploded in his bedroom. In the summer of 1993, when the Union of Journalists of Bosnia-Hercegovina voted him "Journalist of the Year," I had to talk him into going to receive the award, and

I came by car to pick him up and take him there. At the awards ceremony, he paid a special tribute to the city of Sarajevo:

"The fact that I, a Serb, am being given an award as journalist of the year in the capital of Bosnia-Hercegovina, speaks most clearly as to the nature of this country and this city," he said. "Try to imagine, if you will, whether it could happen that in the town of Banja Luka, under the control of Karadžić's forces, a Muslim or a Croat might be declared journalist of the year or in the town of Grude, under the control of Mate Boban, a Serb or Muslim might ever receive such recognition."

Foreign journalists who came to Sarajevo often expressed the wish to meet Gojko. I was at his place once with Maggie O'Kane, the *Guardian*'s correspondent. "How is it possible for you to describe so precisely the developments of the war and never leave your home?" she asked him.

"I live under siege; I talk with many people who visit me just as you are doing now; I listen to the radio—Serbian, Croatian, and foreign broadcasts; and then I analyze the information I thus gather," said Gojko. "The fact that you are writing under the gun, in fear that any moment another mortar shell can hit your apartment, really sharpens your thoughts."

I added that some of the most respected columnists in the West did not have to journey to Sarajevo to understand the nature of Serbian terror, and Gojko—like all other Sarajevans—was experiencing it in the most direct way.

If the goal of the Serbian attacks upon *Oslobodjenje* was to silence us or to make it impossible to publish the newspaper which not only spoke on behalf of a multiethnic Bosnia-Hercegovina, but also represented such a Bosnia by the composition of its editorial staff, in this regard, it suffered a total defeat. *Oslobodjenje* continued to be published every day. It was not only the daily paper of Sarajevo, *Oslobodjenje* soon became, for hundreds of foreign journalists, a symbol of resistance in a city under siege. A number of *Oslobodjenje*'s journalists appeared in television programs in dozens of countries, had articles published around the world, and contributed in some measure to a clearer understanding of the nature of the war in Bosnia-Hercegovina. In February 1993, we began the publication of an international edition which was distributed across Western Europe and North America to reach the Bosnians who had been compelled to leave their homes and seek refuge abroad.

WHOSE WAR IS IT ANYWAY?

THERE WERE, HOWEVER, other journalists who stopped reporting for *Oslobodjenje* from the moment Bosnia-Hercegovina came under attack. A case in point was Zijad Žuna in Jajce: long after he ceased sending us reports, the young reporters for Television Sarajevo, Gordana Ristović and Amir Hadžiosmanović, continued to report from Jajce even until the very moment when chetnik forces started to enter the town itself. I will always remember their last report as an act of extraordinary professional bravery: "This is our last report. We will not be able to report from Jajce anymore," they said before escaping from the occupied town in the fall of 1992. Some did not send a single word on the horrors in their regions, even though they were themselves compelled to leave the towns which had fallen to Serbian forces— Prijedor, Bihać, Doboj, Brčko—and to seek refuge elsewhere. The position that Boro Grubić took in Prijedor was particularly disillusioning. Not only did he quietly observe the mass murders and displacement of people from their homes, the destruction of houses and mosques, the murder of all of Prijedor's intellectual elite, and the devastation of entire suburbs such as Kozarac and Puharska, but he also began to give routine reports for the propagandistic Serbian media, adopting the line that the war against the Muslims was nothing but "the defense of age-old Serbian settlements."

There were still others, such as Nikola Bojić from Goražde, who simply told us that they could not continue to work for *Oslobodjenje*. Nikola sent a letter explaining why. After referring to "communications" and "technical" reasons for his two-month-long silence, he wrote:

"Keeping . . . in mind the fatal and dirty media war which is also going on in B-H, and being allied to truth, justice, and democracy, regardless of the conditions in which I find myself (without the basic conditions for survival), I cannot and do not wish to write anything but the truth about any people or nationality, including my own (Montenegrin and Serbian)! If I did, I would be, it seems to me, adding to the agony of the peoples and nationalities of Bosnia-Hercegovina! As long as this madness of war does not end, so that people, including journalists, can be free to decide what they want to do, and *Oslobodjenje* finds itself able to carry the remarks of nonpartisan and democratic voices of citizens of all nationalities of Bosnia-Hercegovina, I can do little except continue to remain loyal to truth, justice, humanity, and democracy! At this time, unfortunately, there is almost none of that left! My ideals are collapsing!"

Here was angst, self-pity, a holier-than-thou moral judgment, a plea for understanding, absolution—anything but an admission of weakness, cowardice, fear. Nikola was dropping out. Did he expect us to understand, to commiserate, and to hang our heads in shame? My response to him—in an open letter, "The Truth Still Lives Here"—was a response to those fellow journalists who had abandoned the struggle for Bosnia:

Dear N, . . . I use only an initial for your name because the letter you sent me represents the misfortune of a number of (former) colleagues who have only now, in this war, come to realize that they have not matured sufficiently to fill the shoes of responsible professional journalists . . . After so many years, all of a sudden, when for the first time in their lives they are confronted with a real challenge, with the call to bear witness to horrible human suffering and tragedy, they have simply run away, seeking safety, hiding themselves in silence in a profession in which the only ones who survive are those who have the courage to speak out.

. . . I do truly sympathize with you in your misfortune as a person fated to be left in life without ideals, but their collapse is by no means the fault of the newspaper for which you have worked, and with which you have lived, for the last two or three pleasant decades.

For example, there is absolutely no one here who is asking you to write anything but the truth about any people or nationality. But it is true that we did expect you to write to us, as a man of established professional reputation and experience, to report the news from your region, to answer the questions: who, when, where, how and why—the five questions that are supposed to be answered in every news article, even written by a rookie reporter. Who attacked your city and the towns in your region, who undertook the devil's work of killing and driving out of people from their homes, so that regions inhabited primarily by a Muslim population would now be "freed," cleansed, burnt . . . to create a territory for some ethnically pure republic or republics? Nothing else, in other words, but to let us know what is happening there, and who is doing the killing of whom—only that terrible truth which you claim to be so dedicated to. And we do not ask you to write anything at all, and certainly not anything that is not the truth, against any people or nationality, not even about the two that you say you belong to at the same time. It would be the biggest insult for anyone, including ourselves and yourself, to blame all Serbs and Montenegrins for those monsters who, for the past two months, in your city and region and in mine, have been committing enough crimes to fill books, museums, and courtroom dockets, (let alone an ordinary, truth-telling, newspaper article such as we have been waiting to receive from you.) For a full two months we have been waiting for such news, from you and from others like you, whose ideals are probably also collapsing since they have nothing to report on the suffering of the people in the cities where they are living.

You have been able, however, like everyone else who works for this paper "to freely decide what you wish and want to work on," with the simplest conditions and requirements: that you follow the truth which you say you are committed to, and the rules of the profession that you are engaged in, and absolutely nothing else. The fact that you do not dare to write the truth is in no way the problem of *Oslobodjenje* or those of us who continue to publish it every day in spite of everything. You will have to discuss it instead with those self-appointed representatives of the "people and nationality" that you say you belong to, who only acknowledge the truth according to SRNA [the Serbian News Agency of Pale].

And finally, as to the question of whether *Oslobodjenje* can, as you say, "carry the remarks of nonpartisan and democratic voices of citizens of all nationalities of Bosnia-Hercegovina," if you had been in touch with us, if you had remained with us, you would know that for the entire two months *Oslobodjenje* has been undergoing the most terrible ordeal—machine-gun fire, shelling of its building, a total blockade of all routes into and out of the city, sniper fire at all the city's intersections—just because of the fact that its staff of all nationalities, Serbs, Muslims, Croats, and others, have been writing day and night, preparing the paper for the press, printing it, packing it, delivering it, selling it . . . this paper dedicated to all those noble principles that you claim to cling to, but deny that we are respecting. I am sorry, dear N, for you and all the rest who have, in such a cowardly fashion, run away from the truth at the time when the need was greatest for you and for all of us to stand up and bear witness. Unfortunately, I cannot help you.

While Nikola mourned the loss of his ideals, Ranko Preradović, our correspondent in Banja Luka, decided to appear on Television Banja Luka, controlled by the self-proclaimed Serb "government," to advertise the "Republika Srpska" as an "irreversible achievement and fact." Ranko was my old friend from the days of my youth. I had met him when I first began writing for *Oslobodjenje* as a sixteen-year-old high school student in Sanski Most. I had published some poetry in the *Banja Luka Glas* (The Voice), and he wrote me a friendly letter and suggested we should meet when I next came to Banja Luka. That was the beginning of a decades-long friendship. We would meet at the gatherings of young Bosnia-Hercegovinian writers at Mrakovica, Srbac, and Mrkonjić-Grad, we attended literary evenings together and worked for *Oslobodjenje*, I in Sarajevo and he in Banja Luka.

A year before the war broke out, in the summer of 1991, Ranko Preradović came to see me in my office in Sarajevo, together with a common friend from Prijedor, Idriz Jakupović. "We would like to request you, as a participant of the early literary meetings at Mrakovica, to speak at the opening ceremony of this year's meeting," they said to me. I accepted, feeling this to be an obligation to our shared youth. At Mrakovica, on that occasion, a large number of people had gathered, including a number of partisans who had fought and broken the fascist offensive at Kozara, in the Second World War. Among such an audience, gathered on the Kozara mountain, it was appropriate to remember Skender Kulenović's poem, "Stojanka the Mother." Kulenović was a famous Bosnian poet and his "Stojanka" was a Serb mother grieving for her lost children in the Second World War. As I spoke at the meeting, I had referred to the "tears of Skender's Stojanka" as "the tears of all our mothers who watch over their children with fear in their hearts while new terrors of war are rolling towards the Kozara valley." Ranko Preradović was still my friend then, but I lost him when the war came to Bosnia.

Bitter, disillusioned, I had written yet another of my "Letters from the War," this time to those friends who had gathered at the literary soirées at Mrkovica, saying that in my view they had wasted their time, eating, drinking and spending entire summers at Mrakovica praising "Mother Stojanka" if today they could not see the new crimes that were being committed in the Kozara region. Ranko was angry with me for having written the letter—or, perhaps, it merely came as a welcome excuse to ease his own conscience over his decision to appear on Television Banja Luka. For here he was, this friend from my youth, praising the "Republic" which was being built on mass murder and enormous human suffering—and which took the life of our friend, Idriz Jakupović, who had been with us at Mrakovica barely a year ago. Idriz disappeared after being tortured, his arms broken, in the Serb concentration camp at Omarska.

Thus was the network of *Oslobodjenje*'s correspondents stretched and torn.

My deputy editor at the time of the outbreak of the war, Miroslav Janković, left us in the first few weeks. He left without even saying good-bye. It had been by no means easy for him to come to work from his home in Osijek, a village near Ilidža, which was soon swarming with chetnik forces, and return through the many checkpoints on both sides. It would have soon become impossible. The only thing he could have done would have been to move from the area under Serbian control into the free territory of Sarajevo. Many others who were committed to Bosnia and to the paper had done so. But knowing him as well as I did, I think he decided that "this was not his war." And so, he left. To my knowledge, he had not spoken or written against *Oslobodjenje* in the first year and a half after his departure. I was, therefore, surprised when Tom Gjelten, the correspondent for the American National Public Radio, who was writing a book about *Oslobodjenje*, told me about his meeting with Janković in Belgrade.

"He told me that you are an Islamic fundamentalist; what do you say to that?" Gjelten asked me.

"I don't have to say anything. The best thing would be for you to see what Janković himself said on the subject just two years ago," I responded, and pulled out an article from the newspaper about a protest meeting of the journalists of *Oslobodjenje* in March 1991, when we were fighting against the decision of the newly elected government to establish control of the media in Bosnia-Hercegovina. Joining our resistance, Janković had stated at the time that in the last two years, since I had become the editor-in-chief and Salko Hasanefendić the manager, *Oslobodjenje* had based itself upon two strong foundations: first, its modern, European, pluralistic editorial policy which enabled various opinions to be heard, and second, its success in the market-place, because *Oslobodjenje* was one of the most successful companies in Bosnia-Hercegovina.

"I leave it up to you to determine whether I have changed, in the last two years, from a 'modern European editor' into an 'Islamic fundamentalist' or whether, for himself and for others, he had to find some justification for leaving *Oslobodjenje* when the paper was going through its most difficult times," I told Gjelten.

In the summer of 1994—on the occasion of the fifty-first anniversary of our paper—Janković, as the editor-in-chief, published the first issue of the Serbian "*Oslobodjenje*" from Karadžić's headquarters at Pale. It was perverse, to say the least, to name the paper of the occupied territories *Oslobodjenje* or "Liberation." The main difference, of course, was that *Oslobodjenje* in Sarajevo still advocated a multiethnic Bosnia and equal rights for all its citizens while the Serbian "*Oslobodjenje*" was in favor of an exclusively Serb statelet created on the ruins of other people's lives and property.*

---

* In September 1995, CNN's Moscow correspondent Eileen O'Connor introduced her viewers to the imposter "*Oslobodjenje*," without a mention of the fact that the name had been stolen from the original newspaper. A few days later she also introduced the "colleagues" from Television Pale who had been consistently propagating hatred and separation. Was it just bad taste or judgment on the part of the journalist who wanted to present the "other side of the story" by bestowing respectability on those who had been promoting the impossibility of coexistence between people of different ethnic or religious backgrounds or some editorial decision to support partition in Bosnia in order to ease the conscience of those in the Clinton administration who had decided to accept and legitimize Bosnia's "new realities"?

Together with Janković, and likewise without a word of farewell, *Oslobodjenje's* foreign policy editor, Mile Duvnjak, also left. He had experienced some very difficult times in the first weeks of the war. His wife and daughter were in Mostar. The reports on the destruction of the city, the bombing and killing of the civilian population, were coming in and he was unable to reach them, even by telephone. In Sarajevo, he had had some trouble with the Bosnian police. He had been visiting the owner of the apartment he lived in at the time the police came to look for weapons, and—since they found weapons and evidence that the landlord had participated in arming members of the SDS—both the landlord and Duvnjak had been brought in for questioning. He was freed only after our intervention and reassurances that it was the editorial office that had rented the apartment, and Duvnjak had been assigned the right to live there as a tenant but had not, himself, been involved in negotiating the lease. He lived through a number of days of difficult personal trauma, staying at home alone in his apartment, and then, together with Janković, simply "disappeared." They took along, in the same car, another colleague from *Oslobodjenje,* Momčilo Bekan, who was still reporting in the first few weeks of the war from Karadžić's temporary headquarters in the Ilidža Hotel Serbia.

And finally there was the case of the "defection" of Miroslav Kurtović, who worked in our political section and then found himself cut off in the occupied section of Sarajevo known as Grbavica. One day in May 1992, he called me with a broken voice:

"I have to tell you, Kemal, that I am being forced to go to work for SRNA (the Serbian News Agency). They have come by a number of times to recruit me into their army, and I refused, telling them that I was a newspaper man. And finally they said to me, 'If you can't handle a rifle, then you can handle a pen!' I don't know what to do!" he said, almost sobbing.

"Miro, you'll have to do the best you can, but keep your head on your shoulders and keep your soul intact," I answered, not being able to do much to help him in a very difficult situation.

Ironically, his work—he was a speleologist by training—had contributed to the ideological framework of Serbian nationalism and the aggression it spawned. In the year before the war, Kurtović had participated in the SDS's project of opening up the mass graves of the victims of Ustasha atrocities in the Second World War. The Serb nationalists would open those graves, excavate the bones of the dead, and then carry those bones in processions through Serb villages in Bosnia organizing mass rallies at which the priests and politicians of the SDS, as well as leaders from Serbia and Montenegro, would offer the remains of those who were killed half a century ago as evidence of a new conspiracy to exterminate the Serbs. The excavations were thus part of the campaign to prepare the Serbs for the war that was to follow; to make them believe that the killing, humiliation and expulsion of their neighbors, Muslims and Croats, even those born long after the Second World War, was essential to the just and legitimate "defense of threatened Serbhood." Miroslav Kurtović was honored for his role in excavating the bones with the high "Serbian Order of Saint Sava" and, for some reason, he was proud of it. But working for the Serbian media at that time was indeed a very humiliating experience. He had to decide which would be worse: to have them lock him up, and keep him in prison as a traitor if he refused to be recruited into SRNA and thus the SDS's propaganda machine or to join them and betray his conscience and his profession.

For those of us on the receiving end, SDS's war journalism was an assault on the senses. I remember well the reporting, for instance, of Dragan Božanić from the Prijedor region on Television Pale. While the camera showed the smoldering ruins of entire villages, and the burnt remains of once beautiful homes in the small town of Kozarac, this former foreign-policy journalist and anchor of the major news program of Television Sarajevo was interviewing the representatives of the "Serbian government" as saviors and liberators—in a region where they had tortured and killed thousands, among them all the most highly respected Muslim intellectuals. The elected Mayor of Prijedor, Muhamed Ćehajić, had disappeared in a Serbian camp, as had hundreds of other Prijedor residents, and there were countless others who had been deported to the concentration camps of Keraterm, Omarska and Manjača.

Božanić had not been forced to go to work in Pale. He had lived in the elite residential area of Ciglane in Sarajevo, near the center of town; his wife was a teacher of English in the city, and he was one of the most influential editors of Television Sarajevo. But he chose to leave for Pale. We watched him on television later, in the summer of 1993, as he stood with a microphone in hand on Mount Igman and interviewed

General Ratko Mladić, asking him about his "heroic" soldiers who, in withdrawing from the mountains, had burnt down the Olympic hotels and sports facilities built there ten years earlier. Mladić cautioned him in passing that his enthusiastic interviewer might be dispatched to the front lines if he did not report "properly" on his Army's successes.

SDS's broadcasts were offensive not only because they presented barbarity as defense of civilization, but because its journalists participated in pure fabrication and lies. In May 1992, for instance, Television Pale had stated that "in last night's fighting in Sarajevo, the city's maternity ward was hit." There had been no fighting in Sarajevo that night, but instead, as was the usual case, Serb artillery had been relentlessly shelling civilian targets in the city. The maternity ward was not simply damaged by some wayward misfired shells, but rather was systematically targeted, two stories of the building were utterly destroyed, and six babies were killed because the incubators that they were dependent upon had been burned. Even that monstrous act was in a way part of the "Greater Serbia" project: Karadžić had declared that the Serbs in Bosnia were being threatened by the higher birth rates of others.*

This primitive propaganda on Serbian television was carried on with special enthusiasm by the one-time newsman and editor of Radio Sarajevo—Risto Djogo. His broadcasts included such imaginary happenings as the "vicious murder in Sarajevo" of the former soccer star and very respected citizen, Svetozar Vujović—who reported for work on the following day as director of the Sarajevo Soccer Club. When a few months later Vujović died of a terminal disease, a commemorative meeting was held in Sarajevo Holiday Inn. It was attended by hundreds of Sarajevans of all ethnic backgrounds who braved the hell on the streets of Sarajevo to pay their respects to their favorite soccer player. That moving ceremony was itself symbolic of the multiethnic Bosnia that men like Djogo were recruited to "deconstruct" with their lies. After the marketplace massacre in Sarajevo in early February 1994, which killed 68 and wounded and maimed many more, the news from Pale was that it did not happen—the mayhem on the street was faked; the dead and wounded were not really dead or wounded. And so Djogo,

---

* SRNA, meanwhile, inventing one morbid story after another in order to sow greater hatred, had reported that "in the Sarajevo Zoo Serb children are being fed to the lions."

on his evening news program, had proceeded to enact a grotesque
"comedy": he lay down on the floor of his studio, imitating the supposedly fake victims at the marketplace, and then raised three fingers
to the camera, a sign of Serbian victory.

Sarajevans had a joke in the worst days of terror reflecting their
feelings about Djogo's crass "journalism" in the service of his over-
lords: "It would be so nice if our Army arrests Karadžić. Then we
would exchange him for Djogo!" But Djogo was killed, most probably
by the same criminals he was regularly portraying as heroes. It was in
September 1994. There was a "cultural event" in the occupied town of
Zvornik, a concert of the Serbian folk music star, Svetlana Ceca
Veličković, and Djogo was introducing her to the public. That evening
he went to his motel overlooking the river Drina, and disappeared. A
few days later his body was found at the Drina dam a few miles down
the river. The security for the concert was provided by the units of
Željko Ražnatović Arkan—the same units which in April 1992 had
"cleansed" Zvornik and other towns along the Drina and had been
hailed as "liberators" on Television Pale. According to the testimonies
of his friends, Djogo was executed either because of the criticism on
his television programs of Serbian President Milošević for his sanctions against Karadžić's "Serb Republic" after the SDS rejected yet
another peace plan for Bosnia or—the more likely story—because he
tried that night to get too close to the singer, "Ceca the Beautiful," who
later became Arkan's wife in a wedding which was a primitive spectacle, flaunting the newly acquired wealth of Serbia's war profiteers.

In sum, while Sarajevans endured the rigors of the siege, were
cold and hungry and cut off from the world, they could "feast"—if
they desired—on the surreal fare of Serbian television on which
broadcasts on the world and the war according to the SDS were livened
by advertisements such as the one in which beautiful women who
looked like they had walked off the sets of *Dynasty* sat at tables stacked
with delicacies, crab, shrimp, oysters, and freely flowing champagne.
"Let us separate and live in luxury again," intoned the voice-over from
Pale. The population in the areas occupied by the Serbs was subjected
to such fare even before the full-scale war on Bosnia began. With the
assistance of the JNA, the SDS had taken over and turned towards Belgrade all the receivers and transmitters for radio and television in the
Bosnian Republic. (In their assault on the Vlašić transmitter a Radio

and Television Sarajevo technician, Bajram Zenuni, was killed at his work.) And once the attack on Sarajevo commenced, the director of SRNA, Todor Dutina, once a poet and the spokesman for the Reformist Party in Bosnia, called the director of Radio and Television Sarajevo and threatened him: "Free up the frequencies for the Serbian radio programs or the Radio and Television Sarajevo building will be shelled!" Sarajevo did not yield, and the artillery on the hills opened up.

Sarajevans therefore watched Television Pale and listened to their radio more for the sake of seeing which ones of the Sarajevo newsmen had sold their souls to the devil, rather than for the sake of finding out what went on in the world. In the summer of 1993, the SDS opened a witch-hunt against the Serb journalists working in *Oslobodjenje*. In a television commentary by former Sarajevo tabloid journalist Dragiša Ćosović, an entire list of "traitors" working in the "Muslim media" was broadcast. The names of a number of my close associates were on the list, and those who had families in Serbia or Serb-occupied territories were reminded of the fact—"Branko Tomić and Vlado Mrkić are working in the Muslim paper while Serbia feeds their families"—in a not-so-veiled threat to their continued well-being. Branko later decided to take his wife and two sons as refugees to Sweden, and Vlado for a long time could not write his reports on the war.

The three and a half years of the siege had put loyalties, convictions, principles to a severe test. While dozens of people left and many new ones were hired—and most of those who endured the entire siege in the city, from the bread-line massacre in May 1992 to the second Market Place massacre in August 1995, drew sharp and unforgiving distinctions between those Sarajevans who were "in" and those who were "out"—each individual story about those who left and those who stayed was a painful one.

Some, like Miroslav Janković or Gordan Matrak, left because—for all their advocacy on the Editorial Board of *Oslobodjenje* of economic reforms in Janković's or professional discipline among regional correspondents in Matrak's case—they had accepted Milošević's drive for "Greater Serbia" and ended up editing Serb-only newspapers at Pale and Banja Luka. Some others, like Preradović in Banja Luka, Grubić in Prijedor, or Puhalo in Doboj, were compelled by fear. Deeming, perhaps, that discretion in this instance was decidedly the better part of valor, they decided to join up as media advocates of the new authorities, for they had seen the local ultranationalist Serbs' determination and brutality in implementing the "Greater Serbia" project and had seen also that torture, imprisonment, and murder was the fate of anyone who stood in the way. Some, like Milan Borojević or Radmilo Milanović, decided to take less public assignments at *Oslobodjenje*, the former distributing the paper in the first two months of the siege and the latter opting for anonymous copyediting over more visible reporting, until they got the opportunity to leave Sarajevo to join their families. Most of the others stayed for a year or two, even three, torn between their professional obligations in Sarajevo and their personal commitment to the loved ones whom they had managed to send out of the city at the beginning of the siege.

Life in Sarajevo was unbearable by all human standards: no food, no electricity, no heating, no running water, and no place to escape the shelling and sniping which could either kill you or drive you to the edge of madness. And for those whose families left it was even worse. Sarajevo was cut off from the rest of the world, with no telephone lines and no mail so that you could not even send or receive a letter. Once you managed to leave Sarajevo to see your spouse and children some place abroad—where most often you had to contend with the fact that you had no means of income and therefore no means of supporting your family—you were faced with the agonizing choice: your paper or your family? There were many of us at *Oslobodjenje* who nevertheless continued to return to Sarajevo but there were also those who asked for an extension of their leave for a month or two or three, before deciding that they had to stay and take care of their families.

And, finally, I also know that for some of my colleagues—especially the Serbs on our staff—it was more and more difficult to continue to live and to work in an increasingly unsafe city. We all shared the terror of Serbian artillery but my friends Branko Tomić and Rajko Živković—whose apartments were repeatedly hit and then destroyed by fire—had additional problems. In the summer of 1992, Branko was twice harassed by the Bosnian police. Once a self-styled "Special Police" unit led by Jusuf Juka Prazina, searching the papers left by one of the SDS activists who fled to Pale, had found a list with dozens of Serb names and decided to pick up and interrogate those who were on it. Branko was one of them and he was taken for questioning at Juka's

PHOTO SERVICE/*OSLOBODJENJE*

WORKING TOGETHER AS BOSNIANS ON WARTIME ASSIGNMENTS ARE DANILO KRSTANOVIĆ, SENAD GUBELIĆ, AND DARKO BABIĆ—A SERB, A BOSNIAC, AND A CROAT. THE NEWSPAPER'S CONSISTENT REFUSAL TO PERMIT ITS STAFF TO BE DIVIDED ON THE BASIS OF ETHNIC NAT-IONALISM REMAINS THE PROFESSIONAL AND POLITICAL ETHIC OF *OSLOBODJENJE*. A PHOTO-GRAPH OF SALKO HONDO, *OSLOBODJENJE*'S SENIOR PHOTOGRAPHER, CAN BE SEEN IN THE LOWER RIGHT-HAND CORNER. HE WAS KILLED DURING AN ARTILLERY ATTACK ON THE CENTER OF SARAJEVO IN JULY 1992.

headquarters. The list proved to be nothing more than a collection of addresses of all Sarajevans from Drvar, a town where 98 percent of the population was Serb, so that all those listed were Serbs. Juka's people recognized Branko as a prominent sports journalist and escorted him home apologizing for the inconvenience. Soon after that, however, another police unit stormed his neighborhood arresting dozens of Serbs whom the commander of that unit—also a Serb—wanted to exchange for his family captured by the nationalist Serbs elsewhere in Bosnia. Alarmed by the raid, I immediately went to find Branko. He was safe but very perturbed. Together with *Oslobodjenje*'s manager Salko Hasanefendić, I visited the chief of Sarajevo police, Bakir Alispahić, and protested against the harassment of my close friend and associate. In our presence, Alispahić telephoned Branko apolo-gizing for "unauthorized actions for which there will be disciplinary measures against those responsible. I promise that something like that won't happen again," he told Branko. As if that was not enough,

Every day at the Nedžarići offices, I would work with the on-duty team, planning the contents and major themes of the paper; meet with numerous foreign correspondents and visitors; and visit the nearby units of the Army and the police who were responsible for sending reinforcements in the event of a Serb attempt to take the *Oslobodjenje* building. Sometimes, if I could not return home before the curfew at 10 P.M., I would end up staying with those units for the night. And I was writing more than I ever had before. In the first two months of the war, I wrote a series of articles for *Oslobodjenje*, my "Letters from the War," which were addressed to those who could have and should have taken a stand against the war that was destroying Bosnia. Some of those letters were published in part or in whole in foreign newspapers, and in this manner I hoped that their message reached at least some of those for whom it was intended.

Those were the days and months of living dangerously. Preoccupied with work I rarely stopped to think of the death or injury that lurked at every corner. To dwell on one's condition was to invite paralysis, and so doggedly one carried on with the next task on the list. My family and I lived in a neighborhood that was constantly the target of Serbian attacks. When their forces occupied the neighboring residential area of Grbavica, the only Sarajevo neighborhood which fell to Serbian control, Television Pale showed a Serbian officer outside the Grbavica Shopping Center, just a few blocks from our home, announcing the intended takeover of our district as well: "With God's help, soon we will be speaking to you from the Serbian territory of Hrasno," he said to the reporter, pointing in our direction.

And, indeed, they attacked nearly every day and every night. Snipers practically had all of Hrasno in their sights and the number of dead and wounded rose daily. From positions in the high-rises of the shopping center and the hill of Hrasno, their gunfire raked the entire area in front of our apartment complex and bullets streaked across the broad Ivana Krndelja Avenue up to the bridge at the Dolac Malta intersection. Going out of the building, crossing the street, the bridge or the intersection was usually a hazardous operation. One day in June 1992, I was at some business meeting at a nearby restaurant when Vesna called to tell me that our son Tarik had come home to see us after spending two weeks at the defense lines at Hrasno Hill. "He has to go back this afternoon," she told me. I wanted desperately to see him and decided to walk home since the car that was to fetch me was not expected for another hour. I was crossing the bridge and had almost reached our bank of the Miljacka river, when I heard the familiar sound of sniper fire and then felt the bullets whistling past my head. Looking for shelter, I lunged behind a huge yellow road sign. It was not much of a shield, however, since the sniper was now shooting directly at the road sign, puncturing it with holes where I stood. I moved then, as fast as I could, scrambling to the left through the yard of the nearby mosque and the police station and behind the Nolit bookstore, and finally made it to my apartment, shaking from the encounter. I lived, but there were far too many among my neighbors whose luck ran out.

When John Burns, the *New York Times* correspondent, came to visit in the summer of 1992, I led him to our battle-scarred balcony and, taking care not to expose ourselves to the snipers, showed him the entire "geography" of murder in the area. In the tall building across the way, with the Nolit bookstore on the ground floor, twelve-year-old Snežana, the sister of Tarik's friend, Srdjan, had been killed in her apartment. Srdjan had given his parting salute to his sister at her funeral, saying: "Farewell, my little Walter." Walter was the nom de guerre of a Partisan resistance hero and defender of Sarajevo who died fighting the Nazis in the Second World War. Together with his father, Dragan, Srdjan joined the defenders of the city. The father, a Serb, died while fighting in the Bosnian Army. In the building adjacent to ours, three people had been killed: Sadžida Toholj and her friend, Muhamed Pašić, who had gone with their neighbor, Dragica Pilipović, to the neighborhood post office, at Dolac Malta, to exchange their Yugo-dinars (former Yugoslavia's currency) for the new Bosnian certificates. As they were on their way home, in front of the cafe at Dolac Malta, a mortar shell struck and killed all three of them on the spot. I never saw my younger son, Mirza, cry so much. "Dad, you can't imagine what a good person that lady, Sadžida, was; she always wanted to help every-one," he explained through his tears. Her son, Senad, who was at the time serving in the Bosnian Army, later told me: "My mother died because of a few German marks!" The salaries that we were earning in wartime Sarajevo were so insignificant that we were really only pre-tending that we were working, earning, and spending money, but no one except the war profiteers, who were skinning everyone of their life-time savings, ended up having anything.

Our own apartment building had its own victims. The 33-year-old Javor Butina was a friend of ours, whose wife, Smiljka, used to go with my wife, Vesna, on a daily "run-for-your-life" across the street to try to get bread. She finally left to join their three-year-old daughter Barbara, who was staying with her mother in Kraljevo, in Serbia. Javor worked in the humanitarian organization, Caritas, at Stup, and one day, he called me from work: "I'd like to come home, but I'd like to know if it is safe. Is there any shooting going on?" he asked. "Right now there isn't," I told him. "I'll come tomorrow, *ako-Bog-da* (If God allows)," he said and hung up. I remember that I noticed his use of the phrase because it was not his usual way of speaking and mentioned it to Vesna. The next day, his brother, Dubravko, called me and said, through tears, "Javor was killed right there, near your house, while he was running across the bridge; a sniper shot him in the head, right above the temple."

In the grassy area beneath my balcony, children had been playing soccer in April. A mortar shell landed among them, killing one of the boys and taking off both legs of another. Around the corner, a shell had struck a group of people waiting in line for the distribution of humanitarian aid. Six of them were killed, two Muslims, two Serbs, and two Croats, including one twenty-one-year-old student, Oleg Majušević, a Serb, who was a friend of my son, Tarik. Mirza had witnessed his dead body being carried into a vehicle that had been brought to pick up the dead and wounded. And some distance from us, in the Pere Kosorić Square, now called the "Heroes Square," dozens of people were killed or wounded. Two of the five 21-story apartment blocks on the square had been completely gutted in the fire started by artillery attacks. In one of those apartments, five members of one Muslim family had perished: grandfather, grandmother, and three grandchildren, as well as their neighbor, a Serb woman who had stopped by for a coffee. Eight hundred people were made homeless and lost all their possessions. While the buildings burned through the night, we could see silhouettes of people in a desperate struggle to stop the fire, and then watched a huge fireball rolling down from the upper to the lower floors, spreading the fire, until the entire building was a terrifying mass of red flames—the intensity of the light and heat from the fire was so great that it even filled our apartment. All night I watched people leaving that place in tears, with not a shred remaining of what constituted their lives to carry away with them. And there, standing guard at the Square, one twenty-one-year-old student from Bihać was massacred by a missile fired from a tank. His name was Adnan Midžić. He had come to Sarajevo as a university student, and was renting a room in Hrasno. When he came to volunteer for the unit defending the area, they told him, "You don't need to—you just came here recently." But he wanted to join the defense and was on guard together with my neighbor, Muhamed Bikić, in the line closest to Grbavica. "Suddenly there was a huge flash of light around us, I couldn't see anything for several seconds, and then there was nothing but dust everywhere. I called out to him: 'Ado, Ado,' and then, in the pile of cement, plaster, and dust I saw his leg, which had been severed from his body," he told me.

"Everything around here," I told Burns who had turned fifty that day and was sharing a glass of cognac with me, "was just one horror story after another." After hours of peppering the neighborhood with sniper fire and heavy artillery, the Serbian forces would undertake an infantry attack upon Hrasno in the evening, believing that they had softened up the defense forces. Then the bullets would fly like flocks of birds, whistling all around the buildings, bouncing off the walls, often streaking through shattered windows, destroying the lives of those who had lived there. In our own apartment we had moved wooden doors, a king-size mattress, and bookcases in front of the windows to shield us from the bullets. I derived grim satisfaction from the thought that the eleven leather-bound volumes of the military encyclopedia, an award from the JNA for my reports in 1970 on the exercises of its elite units, were now being used on my bookcases as "sand bags" against the murderous ammunition of the same army. From time to time, I would reposition or reinforce our barricades and retrieve a mass of bullets of various calibers as well as shrapnel that had collected under our windows.

Vesna lived in a perpetual state of anxiety. On my way to *Oslobod-jenje* every day I had to pass all the points which were constantly being mentioned in radio reports of artillery and sniper attacks across the city: from Ivana Krndelja Street, to Dolac Malta, to Velepekara (bakery), Nedžarići, Marindvor, Tršćanska (where my father lived), and Omladin-ska Street (where we rented few offices for *Oslobodjenje*). She was afraid for the children, for me, and preoccupied with the daily battle to get what we needed to survive. "This is not going to end well," she would say in warning when I would return from work late in the evening or the early hours of the morning. I shared her fears but I could not stop, not even on Sunday, because *Oslobodjenje* was a seven-day-a-week paper.

Thus on Sunday, July 5, 1992, I had three things to take care of. First, there was the meeting with Gordana and her team in the offices at Omladinska Street; second, I had an appointment with my friends Dževad Tašić and Miroslav Prstojević, who wanted to discuss the possibility of publishing a collection of my "Letters from the War." (Colleagues from *Oslobodjenje*, they had inaugurated their own publishing company just before the war with the publication of a book by Prstojević, with old postcards and his knowledgeable commentary about the old town of Sarajevo, which was to become a valuable document on the cultural and historic heritage of the city that was now being destroyed.) And, third, in the afternoon in our building in Nedžarići, I had to get together with Salko and the commander of the B-H Army unit responsible for *Oslobodjenje*'s defense.

Salko stopped by to pick me up about 9 A.M. He lived in the same hell, just a hundred yards or so from me, on Heroes' Square, and we went along the usual route to the center of town. After our editorial meeting, Gordana told me that the Bosnian government was considering establishing some sort of censorship of the press, and the vice-president at the time, a young and educated man, Dr. Zlatko Lagumdžija, wanted to know our opinion on the matter prior to taking a decision.

"Well, tell him that I think that censorship would strike at the people's right to know what was going on, it would alienate the public, and would be harmful for the newspaper, and even for the government itself, and its image in the world. They can pass whatever laws they see fit concerning the rules of service, to decide who can and who cannot speak to the public concerning the work of the government and state institutions, including the Army, and that will be understood for a country which is in a state of war, but it is our responsibility to find out what is happening and to inform our readers about it. We cannot accept censorship," I told her.*

---

* Lagumdžija affirmed the rightness of our position to me when I later met him in September 1993 at an unusual place and under unusual circumstances. He was badly injured in a mortar shell explosion on a street in Sarajevo and, after being in a critical condition for some time, was evacuated for medical treatment to Stockholm. I was there, together with my colleagues Branko Tomić and Goran Jovanović,

After the editorial staff meeting, I discussed my book with Tašić and Prstojević, gave them the manuscripts of all the letters, wrote out in longhand the dedication for the book ("To my closest mates in the trenches—Vesna, Tarik, and Mirza—with love"), and then set out on foot with Salko and Gordana from our offices on Omladinska Street for FIS, formerly a sports center where the first rock groups of Sarajevo had become famous and made the city the rock capital of Yugoslavia. Now, in front of that location, they were serving beer in mugs, the first in wartime Sarajevo, and we wanted to try it. The group at our table kept getting bigger: in addition to the three of us, we were joined by the artist Mladen Kolobarić; the writer Abdulah Sidran; the university professor Zdravko Grebo; and the actor Miodrag Trifunov. Some of them were among my closest friends and, for a few ephemeral moments, in the darkest days of our lives, we could sit, talk, and laugh together—and almost forget the war. While we were still there, the television producer Pero Filipović showed up with a camera crew and my favorite singer and good friend, Kemal Monteno, to film a video spot of perhaps the most beautiful song composed in the war in Sarajevo, "Pismo prijatelju" (A letter to a friend). We wanted to get up to leave, to allow them to do their filming, but Pero insisted: "Stay, please, I'd really like to shoot the video with all of you." So we stayed for another ten minutes, singing all together with Monteno: "If you ask where I am now, I'm not leaving this town, everything I have remains here. . . ."

Afterwards, Salko and I got into the car, the company Renault 21, and headed for our offices in Nedžarići. He drove the way everyone else did in those days, through the "Sniper Alleys" of Sarajevo along the Marindvor-Pofalići-Dolac Malta route—as fast as possible to evade the bullets. At Pofalići, going past the wrecked building of Elektroprivreda, I noticed that the speedometer was at 130 km/hr (90 mph). To our left, was a metallic silver police Audi. He caught up with us and, as we were approaching the bridge at Dolac Malta, moved into the far left exit lane from which one would normally turn left onto the bridge. But he did

---

to receive the Freedom Award given to *Oslobodjenje* by the leading Scandinavian dailies *Dagens nyheter* and *Politiken,* and Branko and I went to visit Lagumdžija in hospital. He was recovering, studying the most recent computer literature, and was expecting to go back to Sarajevo after the surgery which would enable him to walk again.

FRIENDS TOGETHER IN WARTIME SARAJEVO, JULY 1993. LEFT TO RIGHT: MLADEN KOLOBARIĆ, PAINTER; MAHIR PALOŠ, SINGER; KEMAL KURSPAHIĆ AND GORDANA KNEZEVIĆ, JOURNALISTS; KEMAL MONTENO, SINGER; ABDUL SIDRAN, WRITER; ADEMIR KENOVIĆ, MOVIE DIRECTOR; AND ZDRAVKO GREBO, UNIVERSITY PROFESSOR.

this only to be able to pick up speed and, probably losing us from his sight, he suddenly turned right across the intersection at Jugokomerc, cutting us off. There was a horrible crash. We collided into him in the area of the rear right wheel and, spinning around several times, he ended up on the sidewalk beside Jugokomerc. Our smashed car was stranded in the middle of the most dangerous intersection in town, constantly under sniper fire. Salko had been hit in the chest with the steering wheel, and his head had smashed into the windshield, but he jumped out of the car and, holding his head in his hands, shouted:

"Get out! Get out before they start shooting!"

"I can't, my leg is broken!" I answered, feeling unbearable pain in the knee and hip of my right leg. After years of lying in a cast, and two operations because of tuberculosis of the bone in my childhood, this leg was already stiff in the hip and shorter and weaker than my left leg. Unable to move, I was a perfect target for the snipers on Hrasno hill. Fortunately, within the same minute, some Bosnian Army soldiers materialized with a van and moved me from the wrecked car to the floor in the back of the van. On the way to the hospital, whenever the van turned a corner, my entire body slid across the floor, further injuring my already bad leg. We finally arrived at the Orthopedic Clinic where the surgeon on duty, Dr. Edib Jerlagić, checked me in. The x-ray confirmed my own diagnosis, which I had based on the pain: a serious break, the knee, and bone above it, practically smashed to smithereens, with a painful contusion in the area of the thigh and hip of the right leg. On my way out of the x-ray room, I asked them to wheel me over to a telephone so I could call Vesna.

"I knew it," she said, in a scolding tone.

I spent the night in great pain. The hospital did not have any electricity that night, so the surgery had to be postponed until the early morning. It was a complicated and time-consuming operation: the smashed bone above the knee could barely be put back together; it was reinforced with a number of screws, and then surrounded with a metal plate which would permit it to grow back together. This was followed by a two-month stint in a cast—a month in the hospital, another month at home. Vesna brought me the small electronic typewriter that I had bought some ten years ago in New York because it claimed in the advertisement to be "quiet as a whisper." I had always wanted a quiet typewriter so that I could work at home even late at night, after midnight or in the early hours of the morning or in a hotel room while traveling, without disturbing anyone. Now I could use the machine to write my articles in the hospital.

The stay in the hospital kept me off the streets of Sarajevo but still allowed me to carry on as best as I could with my work. My copy of *Oslobodjenje* was delivered to me every morning by my prewar secretary, Alma Sijerčić, who, like many other members of the staff, was then selling the newspaper on the streets in her neighborhood not far from the hospital. Gordana, Rasim and I regularly conducted our editorial meetings in my room and, since I now had enough time to read every single word of the paper, on one occasion we even convened a meeting of the wartime *Oslobodjenje* editorial board around my hospital bed for a comprehensive analysis of the strengths and weaknesses of the paper.

During those weeks at the Orthopedic Clinic, I was also reminded, in a very special way, of the many wonderful friends I had in Sarajevo. A steady stream of visitors, bearing manna from heaven and good cheer, flowed through my room. The very first evening, I was visited by Goran Milić, who brought a bottle of whiskey, which we agreed should be left unopened until a more salubrious occasion presented itself. Abdulah Sidran and the film director Ademir Kenović came together. Kenović's sister, Nermina Ćorović, was an experienced physiotherapist who helped me in my gradual learning to walk with a cast on my leg. Ivica Puljić, a television reporter, together with my friend Željko Devčić, brought me the sweetest of sweet cherries in the summer of 1992, "just picked at Vratnik" (an old part of town). Arina Šarac brought me cherry cake which her mother had baked, as wonderful as could have been made in the best of times. I have not forgotten the apples of Enver Demirović, the lunch Emina Kečo brought, nor the visit of Jovan Divjak, the second-in-command of the Bosnian Army, and Safet Tokača, who was the commander of the unit in my neighborhood.

But the war could not be conjured away, even in the company of good friends. News came over the radio that Salko Hondo, our photography editor and satirist par excellence, had been killed on assignment. Only three days before he died, he had come to see me, bringing a dessert made by his wife, Nura. The night before his visit, the hospital had come under artillery attack (the Serb forces made a point of targeting Koševo Hospital repeatedly through the years of the siege). It was a terrifying experience to hear the explosions and feel the hospital building tremble, as you lay immobile in your cast. The Orthopedic Clinic itself was hit by a shell from a tank, which destroyed the walls of five rooms one story beneath mine. It was a miracle that no one was killed, thanks to the fact that those rooms happened to be offices and examination rooms and it was a night when no one was there. I sent Salko to take pictures for *Oslobodjenje* of the destruction wrought by the attack, and that was the last time that I saw him. Three days later he was dead, killed while photographing a group of people standing in line for water.

But even while the war devastated Bosnia, there was always something or someone, to remind us that we had not yet been dehumanized by it all. On the second day after my operation, after the Bosnian Radio had broadcast an interview with me in the hospital, a small, elderly woman entered the room which I shared with two other patients, looked around at all three of us, and checking out first one, then the next, finally she approached me.

"Mister Kurspahić?" she asked.

"Yes, that's me."

THE DESTROYED SHELL OF SARAJEVO'S MAIN POST OFFICE WAS TURNED INTO AN ART GALLERY FOR AN EXHIBIT BY THE CITY'S ARTISTS.

"Ah, my name is Šefika R.," she said, taking out a dish of baby okra and half a bottle of beer. "This is all I could manage to find. Accept it, please," she said.

I knew who she was. Some time during the second month of the war, while my "Letters" were appearing in *Oslobodjenje*, she had called and introduced herself. "Mr. Kurspahić, this is a rat that was once a human being. Now I am, like everyone else, living in the cellar on nothing. Until yesterday, I had enough to buy *Oslobodjenje* and bread; today I have just enough to buy *Oslobodjenje*. Tomorrow I have absolutely nothing. I can't get to where my son is—it's too far to Sedrenik (a part of the old town on the eastern side of Sarajevo)—and I don't want him to come visit me, it's too dangerous. I don't have any hope left, except that you will write to that Ghali (the Secretary General of the United Nations) and tell him that he should be ashamed of himself, both he and the whole world!" she said, and I could feel the pain in her heart and tears in her eyes. I talked with her and listened to what she had to say, with little to offer her except words of encouragement and hope. Afterwards, I checked in the phone book and found her phone number and address—she was in Alipašino Polje, a working-class neighborhood on the western side of Sarajevo. From my colleagues who were sitting in the editorial conference room, I collected some money—little more than the average monthly salary of an *Oslobodjenje* journalist,—scrounged up a bag of coffee, a box of cookies, and a bottle of juice, and together with the two most recent issues of *Oslobodjenje* and a letter of encouragement, sent a colleague to deliver the package to her address. And now, here was this woman, for whom it had been too dangerous to visit her own son or for him to come to visit her—she had walked the entire length of the city in order to reciprocate in this very special way.

While I was still in the hospital, my collection of *Letters From the War,* was published. When the managers of the printing company brought me the first copies of the book, they also brought beverages and sweets to share with the hospital patients and staff, and we thus had a small celebration. The first book to be published in wartime Sarajevo, it was launched at a press conference at the International Press Center which was attended by my family, including my father, and my friends and colleagues. Since the press conference was broadcast on Bosnian television, I could watch it from my hospital bed.

"Boy, you must be an important person when you have been lying here for a month in the hospital and every day you are on television: either you're singing in that video with Monteno or they are advertising your book or re-broadcasting your appearances on television," the young man in the next bed commented. His name was Zaim Muftić, and he had both his legs smashed when the Serbs opened up with an antiaircraft gun as he stood guard at Heroes' Square. His brother, Izet, who was in the Bosnian Army, came regularly to visit him, but one day, instead of his brother, there were some other young men from his unit who came and told him, "Izet was killed yesterday in the battle at Poljine. He took some of the wounded into the cellar of a nearby house to wait for the shelling to let up, and there they were hit and killed by a shell."

The hospital was one of those places in Sarajevo where you were directly confronted with the tragedy and pain of the war. The doctors were performing true medical miracles. Without electricity even for xrays, there were times when they were forced to operate by the light of miners' lamps. Often there was no water, making it difficult to have enough to clean out the wound and to wash the sheets. There was not enough food either for the patients or for the staff, and every day the numbers of seriously wounded grew. While I was there, many of the victims of the May 27 bread-line massacre on Vase Miskina Street were still there: all of them had had their limbs blown off by the mortar attack. There was also a young man who had lost both legs while defending the city in one of the worst battles at Žuč. And there were children, women, and old men brought in from all parts of the town every day and night, maimed by an enemy who made no distinctions.

There were far too many who were much worse off than I was and, although I was grateful for the care I received from the doctors and nurses, I did not need the time and attention they gave me as much as the others did. I was also anxious about my family, fearing the worst, and wanted to go home as soon as possible. In my absence, every time that Vesna had gone out, usually in a fruitless search for something to buy (there was nothing available anywhere—not a single egg or liter of milk or any fruits or vegetables or bread), she left Mirza with a list of telephone numbers and addresses of our friends to contact, just in case she did not come back. Tarik was with his unit and often out on the defense lines at Hrasno Hill. And so, as soon as I could get across the hallway on crutches, I asked to be allowed to go home to convalesce. Back in my apartment—the snipers and artillery on the hill notwithstanding—I was much more settled and calm. I could see every day that my family members were still alive and well, and I could continue working and writing for *Oslobodjenje*.

My convalescence, however, turned out to be a more complicated matter. I was advised by medical specialists that, due to the seriousness of the injury and the prior weakness of the right leg, my progress was dependent on further treatment which was not available in wartime Sarajevo. As a result, the board of *Oslobodjenje* began making contacts with UNPROFOR and UNHCR to arrange for my evacuation to Croatia or Slovenia. Colleagues at Slobodna Dalmacija in Croatia wanted to help, and Joško Kulušić, the editor of the paper, as well as others recommended that I should go for therapy to the Orthopedic Hospital in Biograd-na-Moru on the Adriatic coast.

But I was not prepared to go anywhere leaving Vesna and my sons behind in one of the most dangerous zones in the city where I would not be able to reach them even on the telephone. "I will go only if they can accompany me," I told friends who wanted to help with my evacuation. If they stayed, I would stay, and carry on with my work as best as I could. And so, while still on crutches, I began to go to work, once or twice a week. By the beginning of September, it appeared that we were going to have all the necessary papers issued and approved for my evacuation, together with my family, from Sarajevo, But, while we were waiting to be notified of the specific date for our departure, an Italian airplane bringing in humanitarian aid was shot down near Sarajevo causing UNPROFOR to cancel all flights for nearly two months, and my therapy had to be put on hold. Finally, one evening towards the end of October, I was contacted by the Sarajevo UNPROFOR headquarters and told that our travel to Zagreb had been approved. This message came at the same time as the news via Austrian television that Gordana Knežević and I had been awarded the Courage in Journalism Award by the International Women's Media Foundation, and we were invited to come to receive that award on December 1, 1992—my forty-sixth birthday—in New York.

Thus it was that on October 31, my family and I set out, after seven months of the hell of war, to enter a world where life went on as usual. On that day, the city was once again being inundated with mortar shells and several people had been killed and maimed near the Sarajka department store. Given those conditions, I did not know if there would be anyone who would be crazy enough to be willing to try to drive us to the airport.

"Because of the shelling, UNPROFOR's armored personnel carrier will not be able to come into town to pick you up today. But if you can get transportation to the UNPROFOR building, we would provide you an ambulance carrier to the airport," I was told at the Sarajevo command post of the peacekeepers.

"Don't worry, we'll find a way to arrange it. We're not going to let this opportunity go by, after two months of delay and postponement," Gordana said, when I called to tell her that it looked like it was once again going to be impossible. "You be ready and waiting; someone will come to get you."

In half an hour she arrived with our driver, Ervin Algajer. They had risked driving through the city where the UNPROFOR armored personnel carrier did not dare to go! We all managed, somehow, to stuff ourselves into Ervin's Volkswagen Golf, and, with mortar shells exploding in the near distance, we made it to the UNPROFOR building. There my family and I transferred to the white armored personnel carrier with medical markings and flag, and we headed for the Sarajevo airport. This was the first time since the beginning of the war that I had gone any further than the *Oslobodjenje* building. We now crossed the front line at Stup and went past formerly beautiful houses which had been completely destroyed, cars which had been fried, and even a few chetnik tanks which had been gutted with fire. We went past the Serbian barricade (where, a few months later, members of the Serb forces were to stop the UN's personnel carrier transporting Bosnian Vice Prime Minister Hakija Turajlić and shoot him dead at point-blank range over the shoulder of his UN "protectors") to reach our destination at the improvised cafeteria of the French battalion in the completely destroyed airport building. From there we had to cross the runway, protected by mountains of dirt and sand bags, to make our way to a German transport plane.

"Who would have ever said, in reading and studying our history, that we would one day be saved by the Germans from the "Partisans"(the Yugoslav Army)!" I said to Vesna, as we buckled into the canvas and metal seats which ran along the walls of the empty fuselage of the plane which was to carry us to Zagreb. With the deafening noise of the empty Hercules, we finally took off.

Vesna wept for the entire hour and a half of the flight. It was extremely painful for her and for Mirza to realize that they were being forced to leave Sarajevo. From the beginning of the siege, I had wanted the two of them to go somewhere safe, so that I could do my work and not have to worry about them. I had only managed once, on May 19, to convince them to go with the convoy of the organization "Children's Embassy" to Split and, from there, to my brother in Čakovec, Croatia. But the convoy was stopped as it was departing from Sarajevo by Serbian forces which included "Arkan's men," and 3,000 women and children were taken captive and held in the Sports Palace at Ilidža. I did not dare to try to get any information or special protection for them, for fear of what might happen if the Chetniks found out that they were my wife

Man's brothers-in-law disappeared in the chetnik death camps, and after receiving the threat that their house would be bombed, and finally being told that a Serb family would move into their home, my parents had decided to ask for a permit from the police to leave the city. They left everything behind, their beautiful home in the center of the town, all their possessions and their memories, as well as the old family home and estate in Ljubija, and a new car, a Ford Fiesta, which the Old Man had just bought in Germany, paying 25,000 marks for it. He had been looking forward to driving it to Sarajevo to visit us: "It does great mileage—it wouldn't take me more than seven to eight liters of gas to come to you!" he told me buoyantly less than two weeks before the siege of Sarajevo began, not knowing that his car, with all his life's savings, would soon become "Serbian." In addition, in order to get the permit to leave, they had to pay 2,000 German marks each.

When my stepfather went to the police station to get this fascist "ausweis" to exile, the policeman on duty strolled over to the computer, entered his name, and pulled up his entire dossier: "Kemal Kolonić, retired financial director of the Iron Ore Mines of Ljubija, stepfather of Kemal Kurspahić, editor-in-chief of *Oslobodjenje*, who is, together with Goran Milić, a favorite journalist of Alija Izetbegović. One brother-in-law, Muhamed Ćehajić, was mayor of Prijedor, and another, Mehmedalija Kapetanović, a hotel director. The latter was killed." They were allowed to leave, but as they were going out of the office, a Serbian officer began shouting at my mother: "Hurry up, get your Ustasha butt out of here; we know who your son is!"

The Old Man was a Partisan fighter, and my mother had actively supported the anti-fascist liberation struggle. After working hard their entire life, they retired—my mother was a school principal and my step-father as one of the managers of the largest company in town—and were looking forward to the much deserved quiet years ahead. And now, like hundreds of thousands of Bosnians, they were just desperate refugees, in a small apartment in Čakovec my brother and I rented for them, crying for the lost home far away and hoping that some day—before they died—the Bosnian Army would liberate Prijedor and they would return. The Old Man spent his afternoons in Čakovec visiting Bosnian refugees who lived in railway cars with no place to go, trying, together with them, to track a weak Bosnian Radio signal and to hear the latest from Bosnia's front lines. I had been unable to get any news of them from the time Sarajevo's telephone connections with the rest of the world were severed. My mother told me how encouraging it was for them to listen to the Bosnian Radio in occupied Prijedor on the publication of my book: for them it was like a coded message that we were still alive.

This family reunion did not last as long as I might have wished. On November 5, I received a telephone call from Paris. It was Pascale Delpech, "the wife of Danilo Kiš [the celebrated Yugoslav writer]," she said, in case I did not recognize her name. She insisted that I should come the very next day to Strasbourg, to a literary and cultural event. Why? "To tell us about Sarajevo and Bosnia-Hercegovina—as you have experienced it." She told me that they had hoped to have some of Sarajevo's writers attend the meeting but their visit could not be arranged. I tried to decline, explaining to her that I was on crutches and barely able to get around, and that it was difficult to get to Zagreb from Čakovec—a distance of a hundred kilometers—so as to get to Strasbourg the next day. The next morning she called again, and this time convinced me to come.

It was a punishing schedule. At ten in the morning, my brother drove me to the French Embassy in Zagreb (struggling through the traffic jam we encountered at the outskirts of the city) to obtain an emergency visa, to the accompaniment of a grumbling bureaucrat who wanted to know why we could not "have taken care of it earlier"; then on to the correspondents offices of *Oslobodjenje* for an interview for *Slovenske novice,* an Slovenian paper; and then to the Swissair counter at the Zagreb airport where I had to pick up the airplane ticket for the Zagreb-Zurich-Strasbourg flight. By 9 P.M. I was at the official ceremonies in Strasbourg, seated with the mayor, Catherine Trotman, who was asking me: "What can we concretely do for Sarajevo?"

During my two days in Strasbourg, in my conversations with the mayor and many others, I talked about the life we lived in Sarajevo, the reality—or unreality—of which could not leave me no matter how far I traveled away from it: the struggle for survival in a country in the grip of aggression and a city under siege; the terror, the hunger, the cold and the destruction or paralysis of everything that makes life possible. "For many of us, it is already too late, for many more it will soon be, because the people in my country and my city are being killed, massacred, humiliated every hour and every day. But do something urgently for your own sake: Europe, the world, and civilization will not be able to live with the shame of indifference towards one of the greatest human tragedies of our times"—it was a message I kept repeating in meetings with people and in interviews for several papers, including the French daily, *Liberation*, which had just published a special issue on Sarajevo, and in which I found, among many pictures from the city, a picture of my father running for cover in a street under sniper fire.

The questions and my responses covered the ground which would be covered over and over again, among other people in other places, as the devastation of Bosnia-Hercegovina proceeded unchecked and in full view of the world…

How was it possible that we kept a daily paper going in a besieged city?

I told them how the journalists of *Oslobodjenje* from the beginning of the war were also the driver-distributors and the paper carriers, and how, in a ruined building without water, electricity or telephone, every day they produced their newspaper which, in the long weeks and months, was usually the only source of news, since few had sufficient batteries to listen to the radio or watch television, and how as many as ten families would share one copy of *Oslobodjenje*.

How do I view European participation in bringing an end to the bloodletting in Bosnia?

Europe has done its part in facilitating "ethnic cleansing" in Bosnia, since European mediators were the ones who introduced the idea of ethnic partition—as well as the maps of "Muslim," "Serb," and "Croat" regions—in a country which did not have a single settlement which could be regarded as strictly Muslim, strictly Serb, or strictly Croat, because everywhere people had lived together—until the beginning of this slaughter and exile.

Had Europe made a mistake by recognizing Bosnia-Hercegovina too early?

Recognition was not too early but rather late and overdue. After the breakup of Yugoslavia, the prompt recognition of the Republic of Bosnia-Hercegovina might have gone a long way in discouraging the appetites of larger neighbors for its territory. The war itself was unavoidable because the "Greater Serbia" project had been in preparation for a number of years.

Since your president, Alija Izetbegović, wants to create another Islamic state like Iran, how would Christians manage to live in such a state?

There is not a single serious politician in Bosnia-Hercegovina or in public life who has proposed the creation of an Islamic state (today, I would add, "until this time") and Izetbegović himself has directly stated: "Write a constitution that is based upon European standards and we will sign it."

What does it feel like to be here among us, after living for seven months in the terror of Sarajevo?

Uncomfortable. I am sitting beside this big window which faces the square and constantly thinking to myself how I would not dare to do this in Sarajevo. First, there are no windows left in my city—all of them have been shattered by explosions, and second, if I were to sit with my back to the window, some mercenary would have, by now, earned another 500 German marks—the prize, we've been told by captured snipers, they get for every Sarajevan that they kill.

How do people manage to continue to live in Sarajevo?

It is getting more difficult every day. All summer long there was not a single liter of milk available to be bought, nor a kilogram of tomatoes or potatoes. For weeks there was no electricity and no water. The humanitarian assistance which is constantly being promised to us is cut off as soon as some chetnik chooses to fire on a convoy or at an airplane, and the city is not receiving even a third of what is declared to be the minimal supplies needed, the hospitals do not have basic operating conditions...

And so it went late into the night.

NEW YORK, NEW YORK. . .AND BACK
TO HELL

ON THE MONDAY FOLLOWING MY RETURN to Zagreb, I had to leave for Split for two weeks of therapy at Biograd-na-Moru. In late November, Gordana and I were flying to Washington at the invitation of the International Women's Media Foundation to receive the Courage in Journalism Award. While we were to be the recipients of the award, we saw it really as a recognition of the struggle of all those who worked together at *Oslobodjenje* to get the paper out in the worst of times.

The flight from Zagreb via Frankfurt to Washington was scheduled to depart in the early afternoon of November 27. The big problem was how to insure that Gordana would get from Sarajevo to Zagreb, since it was not as easy for Bosnian journalists as for foreign ones simply to show their UNPROFOR accreditation and get a place on the UNHCR flights. They had to get the approval from Geneva. For Gordana, this arrived practically as the last airplane from Sarajevo on that Thursday evening was rolling down the runway. Had it not been for the intervention of the UNPROFOR officer, Colonel Sartre, who canceled the takeoff from the control tower, she would not have managed to make the flight. Only after her plane landed did she realize that she was in Split, not in Zagreb. Then, with me offering guarantees over the phone—since we Bosnians had had our credit card privileges revoked months earlier because the postal system was paralyzed and we could not be billed—she had to rent a car and drive all night to get from Split to Zagreb. I had already arranged with a friend, Susan Hovanac, at the American Embassy in Zagreb to get her an American visa "in the time it takes to have a cup of coffee." Thus, traveling on our new Bosnia-Hercegovina passports, we boarded the Lufthansa plane for Frankfurt to find ourselves—two shell-shocked travelers from the dark underworld that Sarajevo had become—transported to a place filled with Christmas trees, light, and festivity. The pre-Christmas atmosphere at the airport was as beautiful as it was unreal. "Do people here have any reason to think about other people's misfortunes?" we wondered, as we shared a drink before getting some sleep to be ready for the next day's flight across the Atlantic.

That evening, lingering over my cold beer—as on subsequent short trips out of wartime Sarajevo—I could not but think of those countless, very ordinary things we took for granted in the past and which had now vanished. On those trips I would stay longer than ever before in the shower in my hotel rooms, because there was no running water in my Sarajevo apartment for a year and a half; whenever I landed at the first airport out of Sarajevo—Zagreb or Split in Croatia or Ancona in Italy—I would look for a bar to have a real scotch on the rocks because at home there was no electricity and no ice for many months; traveling back by train from Ancona to Trieste to be picked up by someone from *Oslobodjenje*'s Ljubljana office, I would take along a few cans of cold beer, thinking with a touch of bitter humor of the "1,000 percent discount" I got on each beer that I bought, since a can of beer in wartime Sarajevo would cost me 15 German marks and on the train no more than 1.5 marks; and at every train station before boarding the train—in Ancona, Bologna, Venice—I would look for the nearest phone booth to call friends around the world and to celebrate with them the very fact that I was still alive.

We arrived at the Dulles Airport in Washington on the evening of November 28 to a warm welcome complete with flowers, television cameras, and a delegation of the International Women's Media Foundation to meet us. The following day was a day of recovery from our journey, a day to tour the city, and to meet friends. On that first day, we also met an unusual taxi driver. When Gordana and I exchanged a few words in Bosnian, he immediately reacted: "Oh, Yugoslavia? I've been there many times, at Rijeka, along the coast." When he discovered that our fellow passenger was from Kenya (Catherine Gicheru, who was also receiving a "Courage in Journalism" award for her series in the leading Nairobi daily, *The Nation,* about the corruption in the government), he broke into perfect Swahili. "That's one of the seven languages I speak," said the driver, explaining that he was an engineer out of work and his wife worked for National Public Radio. It was a marvelous encounter—the Bosnians, the Kenyan, and the American riding around in a taxi, speaking, as it were, in tongues—and, perhaps, possible only in America, that magnetic spot on earth where cultures, colors, and languages both collided and coalesced. For Bosnians, fighting for their own, more ancient multicultural heritage, the sights and sounds of America had a special resonance.

The following day we were in New York, making our way through a traffic jam to the PBS studios in west Manhattan, where we were to be the guests on public television's McNeil-Lehrer News Hour. We were asked the inevitable question: what can the United States, the world do? I was ready with my response, well rehearsed through all the other discussions of the preceding few days. And so I proposed the five steps which I believed would end the conflict: One, air strikes on specific military targets such as the positions of the Serbian artillery surrounding the cities ("If your military intelligence doesn't know where those targets are located, they can ask the children in Sarajevo—they know!"); two, lifting of the arms embargo on Bosnia-Hercegovina—like every country in the world, our country had the right to defend itself; three, continuation of economic sanctions against Serbia; four, a demonstration of political resolve to impose, and not merely to propose, a just political solution which was not based on apartheid; and, five, war crimes trials in accordance with international standards and under international supervision, to meet the demands of justice and to restore the conditions which would allow the return of refugees.

It was the first year of the war and we still nurtured the illusion that the Great Powers and the United Nations would surely support Bosnia in its struggle for survival. Disillusionment would come swiftly, but on that first trip to the United States it was hard to imagine that if the world knew and understood that an internationally recognized state was being destroyed—its people slaughtered and villages burned, so that an ethnically "pure" state could be built on its ashes—it would simply stand back and watch the spectacle. And so Gordana and I did the rounds—ABC's "Good Morning America," "CBS This Morning," talk shows, radio shows, interviews with various magazines and newspapers, talks at universities, meetings at the United Nations, discussions at public and private gatherings—for we saw our visit to the United States and Canada as an opportunity for us to inform the North American public of the Bosnian perspective on the war, its causes and possible resolution.

Thus our brief stay in the United States was a time of long days and equally long evenings during which we met and talked with countless people. During a meeting with Warren Zimmerman, the last American Ambassador to the former Yugoslavia, he told us, "You know that *Oslobodjenje* was my favorite newspaper from the time I became ambassador in Belgrade." We had a long, in-depth conversation on all the significant points: intervention, the embargo, Geneva, the role of Croatia, war crime trials, the legitimacy of the Bosnian government. Zimmerman was intending to discuss all of these matters with Secretary of State Lawrence Eagleburger, in the George Bush administration, and told us that he expected there would be some changes in United States policy. He was worried, however, by certain kinds of "refusals of humanitarian aid" in Bosnia. We explained to him that humanitarian aid was valuable, but not the most important thing: "If you're going to leave us to be locked up in a dungeon, condemned to die, it's all the same whether we die hungry or well fed!"

Ambassador Zimmerman did not see the changes he hoped for in the American policy towards Bosnia, either in the Bush or the Clinton administration. In the spring of 1994 he was to resign his high position at the State Department largely because he was disappointed by the lack of proper American response to the Serbian aggression.

An American who, at the time, had taken a strong and public position in support of Bosnia-Hercegovina was George Kenney. In August 1992, he was the first State Department officer who resigned his position on the Yugoslavia desk, protesting the Bush administration's passivity in the face of large-scale crimes in Bosnia. He argued for a massive military intervention and in 1993 he criticized Clinton's Secretary of State Warren Christopher for stating that the United States should support any peace settlement in Bosnia "that the parties can agree on," for it placed aggressors and victims on the same plane. I met him in Ann Arbor, Michigan, where I was the guest of two Sarajevo professors of mathematics, Naza Tanović and her husband, Harry Miller, and was there to give a talk at the invitation of the Department of Journalism and the Center for East European Studies of the University of Michigan. From the airport, I had gone directly to a party at the home of Jure Grahovac, a gynecologist, and his wife, Lidija. George Kenney was among the guests that evening and presented his scenario, which had been published in the *New York Times*, for an allied "Balkan Storm." There was a great deal of discussion and we agreed that such an operation would not be expensive nor dangerous as was feared by some in the West. After that, I left to get some sleep, with the hope that his scenario was not just science fiction. Whether it was or was not could never be tested, but what became clear a year later was that Kenney's principles could not stand the test of time. He changed his mind.

Relying on the moral and intellectual credibility he had garnered from his resignation from the State Department, he was to begin advocating the "recognition of new realities" in Bosnia, which would leave Karadžić's "Republic" in control over territories his forces had "ethnically cleansed." In a *New York Times Magazine* article Kenney was even to engage in denial that genocide in Bosnia ever took place: there were not 200,000 killed in Bosnia—as suggested in most internationally accepted estimates—but "only 25,000 to 60,000," as if sheer numbers and not the intention to destroy, in whole or in part, an ethnic group constituted genocide. (I was surprised that a prestigious publication like the *New York Times Magazine* would publish an article denying the perpetration of genocide in Bosnia on the basis of obviously unfounded estimates with almost a 300 percent margin of error: Kenney's "between 25,000 and 60,000.")

Among the Bosnians that I met there was, of course, a hunger to know how things were back at home. They wanted to do something, anything, that would help their country's defense. Among them was Istok Hozo, who had participated in organizing a network of computer information, "Bosnet," through which Bosnians in the United States and Canada could get the latest news from the Bosnian press as well as selections of articles from the rest of the world; Colleen London, a writer and teacher of foreign languages, who lived in Sarajevo in the seventies and was now editing a newsletter devoted to the cause of Bosnia, who said, "If that doesn't help, I have a pilot's license; maybe I can fly to provide some help for my beloved city"; Nada Rakić, the former theater critic for *Oslobodjenje* who had married an American, wanted to know everything I could tell her about the life of the theater in wartime Sarajevo. Some longed to return. Among them was Alica, the younger daughter of my hosts, Harry and Naza, who had just finished her degree in mathematics. She turned to me and said, "I have one serious question for you: can you take me back with you to Sarajevo?" I had to tell her that this was impossible, explaining that the UN airplanes would not transport civilians. "They tricked me into coming here, for my sister Lejla's wedding," said Alica bitterly, "but if I had known it would be this difficult to get back, I would never have left Sarajevo."

Predictable, and sometimes almost amusing in their absurdity, were encounters with the Serb view of the war such as the one that was in evidence in a question put to me—in a challenging tone—by a Serb at a public gathering. "Why is it that the world is only talking and writing about the Serbian, and not about the Muslim and Croatian, concentration camps?" he asked, as if there were a worldwide conspiracy to conceal the existence of such camps.

"The world media has one professional habit: to write about only what they have actually seen, what is proven, and not what someone tells them. I will give you an example. French Minister, Bernard Couchner, at the time of his visit to Sarajevo this summer, asked the leaders of the SDS to give him the addresses of some Muslim or Croatian camps that they were talking about. He then visited the first three places on the list, including the Koševo Stadium in Sarajevo, where they claimed that there was a 'huge camp'—and found nothing but long grass which hadn't been walked on for the entire spring and summer. That's why they're not writing about those camps," I answered.

Such fictitious allegations about the culpability of Bosnia could only be matched by the statements emerging from UN functionaries. I had been informed by some foreign diplomats that Yugoslav propaganda was especially strong, and partly successful, at the United Nations. Back in New York, I was therefore not surprised when a journalist from National Public Radio called me regarding the announcement of the American administration to enforce the no-fly zone over Bosnia. He asked, among other things, "Do you know that the UN is saying that all sides are violating the no-fly zone?" What did I think? "In our case, this must be the sighting of a flying saucer or a UFO. Bosnia hasn't got any airplanes, it's as simple as that—it hasn't got any!"

In the midst of all the hectic days and nights was, of course, the event in New York which had brought us to America: on December 1 Gordana and I received the "Courage in Journalism" award. At the ceremonies, which were attended by several hundred representatives of the media, the sound of shattering glass cut through the congratulatory remarks and applause and, for a surreal moment, transported me back to Sarajevo. As she was receiving the award, Gordana had tripped and the crystal eagle we had received fell from her hand, smashed against the marble, and broke into pieces. I broke the stunned silence saying lightly: "Nothing new, just another explosion from Sarajevo." One of the stars of American TV journalism, Barbara Walters, then jumped up and handed Gordana the eagle which she had received for her lifetime achievement in journalism. It was, to say the least, a very gracious gesture. "This is what she wanted—to get an achievement award without achieving it," I told Walters jokingly. We had barely managed to catch the airplane for Washington, exhausted by the long day that had begun at five o'clock in the morning, when Gordana asked, "How will we keep the eagle in Sarajevo?" I reassured her: "Don't worry. It doesn't eat anything, and since we have plenty of nothing there, it will be fine—it will even grow on us."

On December 12, the time to depart had arrived. Sarajevo beckoned and we were leaving: from a place where life was bountiful and taken for granted to a place where life was measured out moment by moment, and nothing was guaranteed. We left with promises of support—newsprint, supplies, etc.—for *Oslobodjenje*, and laden with letters and medicines from the scores of Bosnians we had met who wanted to send something home to their loved ones.

Back in Zagreb, waiting for the next UN flight to Sarajevo, I got a few days to be with my family again, and to attend, as best man, the wedding of my longtime friend Goran Milić with former Sarajevo Radio journalist Ana Lončar. Vesna, the boys, and I were able to spend that brief time together in the warm and convivial atmosphere of Goran and Ana's Zagreb apartment, and leaving them was not easy— for the return to Sarajevo was, in a way, also my family drama. Vesna, staying with the boys at my brother's home in Čakovec, was distraught: 'You still can't walk without a cane and you know how everyone in Sarajevo has to run to escape snipers!" she said, attempting to convince me to stay on, at least until I could walk without support. "But I have been away from Sarajevo and the editorial offices for a month and a half already," I said. "It's time for me to return."

She was never quite convinced that I was right in leaving her and the children and risking my life in Sarajevo. In Croatia she saw dozens of Bosnian government officials, including some ministers, who left the country and pretended to do some "useful job" far from Sarajevo. She knew about all those who were collecting humanitarian assistance for Bosnia and were renting luxurious offices and apartments in Zagreb, Ljubljana, or Vienna, spending large sums of money on expensive dinners with their friends. She also knew about journalists who fled Bosnia and kept selling their books or publishing magazines, with not a single correspondent in Bosnia, capitalizing on the misery of hundreds of thousands of Bosnians expelled from their homes and desperate for any news from their country. And then there were former leading Muslim and Croat party hawks, who were brave to quarrel with the Serbs in the Parliament but not brave enough to stay and defend Bosnia, "representing the country abroad" with no intention to go back to "that hell" which they helped to create. With such knowledge, she could not accept my explanation of why I, who was still on crutches, had to go back to Sarajevo.

"Just think, how would our boys grow up without you!" she faced me with the most cruel argument of all.

"But think also how it would be for them to grow up feeling ashamed of their father if he is remembered as the captain who was the first to abandon ship," I answered.

"The only question is: do you love them more or *Oslobodjenje*?"

"No, that's the wrong question. You can't make such comparisons. The three of you are all I have, but *Oslobodjenje* is my job, it's what I do: I want to do it the way I won't betray my profession and the public's trust."

I left her sad and not quite sure—we had been together since my early days in journalism in high school at Sanski Most—whether my professional obligations as editor of *Oslobodjenje* were worth the risk that I could be killed in Sarajevo and we might not ever see each other again. "Please, stay alive!" she whispered as we were saying good-bye at Zagreb airport.

In the first two years of the siege of Sarajevo that painful procedure was to be repeated several times on my brief trips (usually to attend some conference abroad or receive an award) out of Sarajevo. On one such foray, I had just enough time in Zagreb to have lunch with Vesna and Mirza in a restaurant since I had to be back in Sarajevo the next day for *Oslobodjenje*'s fiftieth anniversary. "You could give this much of your time to any woman you'd just met!" Vesna was filled with sadness, not really accepting any reason why I had to go back to Sarajevo so quickly and to leave her with Mirza, who, in the meantime, had undergone an appendix surgery with some unexpected complications which kept him in hospital in Čakovec for two weeks in critical condition. She was afraid for my life and for their future without me and was ready at that point to take Mirza and go as refugees to any country willing to accept them.

Staying in or traveling through Croatia as a Bosnian was itself becoming an increasingly unpleasant experience, typified by one encounter on a flight back from Germany.

"Where are you coming from?" the Croatian police officer asked when I gave him my Bosnian passport.

"From Berlin."

"What were you doing there?"

"A publishers' congress."

"And where are you going now?"

"To Sarajevo."

"How?"

"By the UN flight."

"Show me the ticket!"

I showed him the press credentials to board the UN plane.

"And how long are you staying in Croatia?"

"For three days, until Monday."

"Where are you going to stay: address, phone number . . ."

"At my brother's home, in Čakovec."

"Do you have enough money to stay in Croatia?"

"Yes, I do."

"You need 600 German marks."

"I have more than that."

"Show me the money!" the policeman insisted, cautioning me not to stay any longer than three days and demonstrating, in the manner of a police state, Croatia's worsening relations with Bosnia.

At the airport in Sarajevo, back in December 1992, it was cold, the mud was frozen, and I was greeted by the familiar whistling of sniper bullets. With one hand leaning on my cane and the other dragging my huge suitcase full of letters sent by Bosnians from America, Canada and Croatia, I was hurried along by the UNPROFOR soldiers to cross the ploughed area on the runway and get behind the protection of the hills of dug-up earth and sandbags. It was already late afternoon and in Sarajevo the telephones were not working, so I could not call anyone in the editorial offices to ask them to meet me and take me home. The UNPROFOR armored personnel carrier took me, together with the other passengers from Zagreb, to the Bosnian Presidency building.

"Welcome home!" I was warmly greeted by a security policeman from the Presidency. He told me that he would look after my suitcase while I went to the *Oslobodjenje* office on Omladinska Street a hundred yards further on. Fortunately, there were still some people at the office, including Fahro Memić, Vlado Šťaka, and the driver, Ervin Algajer. They

THE CHILDREN OF BESIEGED DOBRINJA, CUT OFF FROM SARAJEVO, WHO SUR-
VIVED BOTH THE BARRAGE AND THE BLOCKADE.

cades which divided Dobrinja from Sarajevo—Gordana and
I headed out to Dobrinja. Our route took us past the student housing
at Nedžarići on the other side of which the Serbs had deployed an anti-
aircraft machine gun, and long-range sharpshooter rifles were in
action; then past burnt-out trolley busses and cars; and then, finally,
the barricade. "This is the most dangerous place—we have to fly by!"
said the driver, and so we did until—to our amazement—we arrived at
the Press Center at Dobrinja. Dozens of citizens had gathered at the
Press Center and we spent several hours with them, talking and
answering numerous questions about our trip and encounters in
America. Afterwards, we visited the Dobrinja hospital organized by
Dr. Youssef Hajir, reports of which had spread beyond the besieged
district. The "hospital" was established in the basement of an apartment building, where an operating room and beds for the wounded
had been set up, since it was impossible to transport anyone to main
Koševo Hospital in town. It is hard to say how many of the hundreds

wounded in the attacks on Dobrinja would have bled to death had it not been for Doctor Hajir's hospital. His co-worker, Dr. Zlatko Kravić, took us around to visit the Dobrinja wounded, including children, women, and old men. "These are the most common victims in Dobrinja," Doctor Kravić told us. And so the slaughter continued into the new year.

I "celebrated" that New Year's Eve with a small number of colleagues from *Oslobodjenje* with my neighborhood army unit of Safet Tokača which was defending our part of Hrasno. We were joined for a while by the deputy commander of the Bosnian Army, Colonel Jovan Divjak, and later by Jusuf Juka Gojak, a commander of the commando unit on the hill of Žuć at which some of the most decisive battles for the defense of Sarajevo were fought. That night, while one played the accordion and another the guitar, this warm-hearted soldier sang one of the most popular songs of old Sarajevo: "Vratnik is singing, it is never sad; Sarajevo is echoing with its song . . ." Just a bit after midnight, he stood up: "Now I must go, Žuć is waiting for me." A few days later, a young soldier came to my office and, in tears, told me: "I'm Vanja Šantić, (the son of my colleague Slavko Šantić). My commander Juka Gojak was killed and I have come to place a death notice in *Oslobodjenje*." Vanja, who was just eighteen but had joined the defense of the city as a commando at Žuć, told me that Juka was killed while trying to get a wounded soldier out of the line of fire.

In Sarajevo, that is how it was through all the days of the siege. Life and death were bound together in a close embrace. While you sat and talked with your friends—in the editorial offices or in a cafe that still opened for business on rare occasions or in someone's apartment—you could, for a moment, forget. You could even tell jokes or sing songs if someone happened to be around with a guitar, but when you went your separate ways, it was always with a certain unspoken feeling that this could be the last time. You never knew if you would ever see those people again.

I remember my colleague, Željko Ružičić, from Radio Sarajevo. I had known him from our early days in the profession. In the first months of the siege of Sarajevo he had a program called "Broken Connections," on which he transmitted messages between divided families all night long, and always began his program with: "My dear ones." Listening to the program one night while my neighborhood was under fire

I had to laugh bitterly. A man called from Dobrinja with a message to his mother in Brčko: "We are all alive," he said. "So, you are all alive and well," said Željko who wanted to underline the good news for a faraway mother. "No, we are not well! There is no food, no electricity, nothing!" the man broke down and wept. I met Željko that winter in front of the UNPROFOR building. He was putting together the documents needed for a trip he was planning to visit Bosnian exiles in Australia.

"I'll stop by at *Oslobodjenje* before I leave," he said, "to figure out what I can do for you while I'm in Australia."

A few days later, Vinko Bošković, one of the four people who had made their cars available for use by *Oslobodjenje*, and who drove through fire delivering the paper and ferrying reporters across town, came to pick me up at the downtown offices of *Oslobodjenje*. "I have our assistant, Hajra, in the car. We need to drop her off at Baščaršija, and then we'll go to Nedžarići," he told me. As we walked towards the car, there was a flash of light, a blast of thunder, and Omladinska Street was filled with the presence of death. People were running in panic, attempting to find shelter in the entrances of the nearest building.

"What should we do? Go back to the office?" Vinko asked.

"I don't know; probably it won't hit again, let's keep on going," I answered.

We had almost reached the car, when there was another explosion, closer than the first one. (It was only then that I accepted a common wisdom among Sarajevans: if there is an explosion nearby, look for shelter because the next one is highly probable.) We opened the door for Hajra, who was shaking with fear, and returned to the entrance of the building that we had just left. There we waited for ten minutes. Then we set off again. Later I found out that the first explosion, in the park across from the Presidency Building in the center of town, had killed my friend, Željko. He never made it to our meeting, nor to Australia, nor to see his family—his wife and two children—in Croatia. On one of my visits to Goran Milić's home in Zagreb I met Željko's family and told them how greatly people in Sarajevo appreciated his voice in the long days and nights of the siege and how important his effort to reestablish "Broken Connections" between the people separated by the war was for hundreds of others. It was too weak a consolation for a grieving woman and children.

Death was everywhere, and we at *Oslobodjenje* of course had no insurance against it: it took away our friends and loved ones as it did those of others. Fahro Memić was leaving for work, as he did every morning, to deliver the newspaper around town. His wife, Željka, came out of the building at Čengić Vila with him to keep him company and to go in search of bread. While Fahro was heading towards Otoka, he heard an explosion from the area where he had been only a few minutes earlier. He returned. There were dead and wounded all around, and screams of pain. Željka was lying on the sidewalk, fatally wounded by shrapnel. Not far from her, lay Dragan Kadijević, the husband of the director of the children's section in *Oslobodjenje*, Svjetlana Kadijević, who was selling the paper in the neighborhood.

Karmela, the wife of our reporter, Dragan Stanojlović, was afraid to leave her apartment in Alipašino Polje. Prior to the war she had worked in the administrative offices of *Oslobodjenje*, but she would not venture out from the time the war began. One day, Dragan went to get water, and she locked the door and waited for him to return. When he got back, he pounded on the door but there was no answer. He got his neighbors' help to break down the door and found his wife lying on the floor in the kitchen, killed by a sniper's bullet. "She looked like she was sleeping: you couldn't even see her wound," Dragan told me.

Zuhra Bešić worked in *Oslobodjenje*'s finance department. She was returning by bus from work. As the bus passed by the destroyed gasoline station, at the spot where several people had been killed or seriously wounded by fire from Nedžarići, a bullet hit her in the neck. She bled to death in the arms of her colleagues before anyone could get her any help. This was a place I crossed at least twice a day on my way to and from *Oslobodjenje*. Someone had posted a handwritten sign there, Beware of Sniper—as if you could do anything about it! If you were in a car, you ducked to get your head out of the line of fire, and if you were on foot, you tried not to think about the sniper as you raced across that deadly ground, knowing that any of the bullets hitting the asphalt around you could be "yours."

"Sarajevo is the city of people who are missed" was one of the bitter jokes of the siege. People continued to die, but no one bothered any more to hide from the bullets or the mortar shells. If you stayed in the cellar all the time you would die just the same, because you would have no food, water, or firewood. And so you were forced to go out.

THE CROSSING POINT AT COBANIJA STREET IN SARAJEVO'S OLD CITY.

One evening, returning home from *Oslobodjenje* I found my neighborhood ghostly and deserted: a destroyed streetlight in front of my building, the flapping and snapping of the plastic on the windows torn by detonation, fresh traces of an explosion on the facade of the ground floor. "We have arrived just a few minutes after death's visit," my driver observed. There were traces of the explosion in my apartment: the ripped plastic on the windows in the living room, the mark of shrapnel which had hit the wall and torn the rug and then smashed the crystal ice bucket which was sitting on the buffet, broken the salt cellar on the improvised stove, and ended up on the floor.

Since I was now alone at home, my father urged me to move in with him. He and his wife Ensa had an apartment at Marindvor where they lived with my sister Nermina. (A writer, Nermina had published a novel, *The Disappearance of the Blue Riders,* and had stayed and worked in Sarajevo through the long years of the siege.) But I did not feel like withdrawing and yielding to the terror, nor did I want to leave the one place where, even through the long nights without electricity, I knew where everything was located, including every note I had made and every document I might need. And besides, they really were not any safer than I was, living on Tvrtkova Street, on the corner of Tršćanska, which was constantly the target of mortar shells and snipers. One day while waited for a lull in shelling of Marindvor, a huge, 120 mm mortar shell landed in their apartment, going all the way to the entrance into the hallway. It was an incredible bit of luck that it did not explode. They had to push it away from the door, risking the explosion, in order to enable my father to get out and go to the nearest police station to ask for the assistance of the explosives experts to remove the uninvited "guest."

In such an environment, every new day of life was a small victory. And all the days of the siege with always the same worries and risks, the organization of work, the writing, the permanent quest for paper, energy, food, and the means of transport from home to Nedžarići or to the center of town and back, sometimes made me feel as if it was just a single, long, and nightmarish day.

LAURELS IN THE DUST

THE WORD ABOUT *Oslobodjenje* had gone around the world. Its struggle for survival as well as its continuing support for a unified, multiethnic Bosnia at a time when the country was being destroyed in the name of competing nationalisms had won recognition for the paper internationally.* The irony, however, was that while the world bestowed various awards on *Oslobodjenje*, it became the target of vilification at home. Among its detractors were sundry hacks who hoped

---

* Along with "The Courage in Journalism Award," in 1993 Gordana Knežević and I were named "International Editor of the Year" by the World Press Review in New York. And that same year, Zlatko Dizdarević and I were given the "Human Rights Award" by the Bruno Kreisky Foundation in Vienna, Austria. BBC and Granada TV in London named us the "Newspaper of the Year" in 1992. In Scandinavia, two of the best known papers, *Dagens nyheter* in Stockholm and *Politiken* in Copenhagen, awarded us the 1993 "Freedom Award." At the United Nations headquarters in New York, Inter Press Service (of Rome) gave us its award for journalistic achievements in 1993. At the center of the European Parliament in Strasbourg, *Oslobodjenje* was awarded the Andrei Sakharov Award for Freedom of Thought (1993). In Cambridge, Massachusetts, the Nieman Foundation at Harvard University gave us their annual Louis M. Lyons award "for conscience and integrity in journalism"; In Vienna we were given "The Rothko Chapel Oscar Romero Award" from Houston, Texas, for maintaining freedom of the press.

to elevate their own stature by denigrating the work and success of *Oslobodjenje*, as well as nationalists of all stripes who found us guilty of all the sins in their book. For some we were "an Islamic fundamentalist paper" because we consistently supported the independence of Bosnia and the legitimacy of its elected government. For others, we were "anti-Croatian" because we were equally consistent in opposing the creation of the "Croatian Union of Herceg-Bosna" as we were in opposing the "Republika Srpska." For the Muslim extremists, we were "not a Bosnian newspaper" because we employed "too many Serbs and Croats" and were critical of the manifestations of Muslim extremism. And, finally, we were attacked by certain well-positioned representatives of the government who wanted to see in the paper laudatory reports on their performance.

One of the ugliest episodes of such vilification was provoked by a generous donation made to *Oslobodjenje* by Adil Zulfikarpašić, president of the Liberal Bosniak Organization (LBO). Mr. Zulfikarpašić was an interesting figure on the Bosnian political scene. He fought against the Nazis in the Second World War and also witnessed the original Chetniks' 1940s slaughter of Bosniaks in his hometown of Foča. Immediately after the war, he left a ministerial post in Bosnia's Communist-led government and became a political émigré in Switzerland. Eventually, he became a successful and rich businessman, investing much of his fortune in promoting the Bosniaks' name, culture, and history. He returned to Bosnia only at the time of the first free elections in that Republic in 1990. He originally intended to open the Sarajevo branch of his Bosniak Institute in Zurich, but very soon became involved in politics. With Alija Izetbegović, he was the co-founder of the SDA and, he said, they had agreed that if the SDA won the election, Zulfikarpašić would assume the office of the President of Bosnia. But before the elections, he split with the SDA, objecting to the growing influence, as he said, of radical Islamists within the party. Zulfikarpašić's breakaway party won just two seats in the Bosnian Parliament, but he once again attracted public attention by trying to broker a "Bosniak-Serb Agreement"—just before the war—which would keep Bosnia within Yugoslavia, providing it constitutional equality with Serbia. According to Zulfikarpašić, President Izetbegović encouraged and supported the agreement but later withdrew that support despite his warnings that without guarantees of some international protection Bosnia was heading towards catastrophe. Once closest political allies Izetbegović and Zulfikarpašić became bitter political enemies.*

I had met him in Washington while attending a conference on Bosnia in February 1993 before leaving for London to receive the "Newspaper of the Year" award for *Oslobodjenje* made by the BBC and Granada Television. At a dinner for the participants of the Washington conference Zulfikarpašić told me that he wanted to help *Oslobodjenje* because he was impressed with the work we were doing. "I want to send a personal contribution to its journalists. Can I do that through you?"

"Certainly, but I would suggest that we discuss this on my way back to Sarajevo from London a week from now, so I can see how we can manage it through our Fund for *Oslobodjenje* which we have just established."

Since there were no telephone connections with the editorial offices, I considered that it would be best to discuss that donation on my way back, when I was in Ljubljana, with the manager of the paper, Salko Hasanefendić, who was there for discussions with the Slovenian daily *Delo* about the printing of a weekly edition of *Oslobodjenje*. Adil Zulfikarpašić came to Ljubljana, where he has an apartment and often comes from his headquarters in Zurich, and—in the presence of Hasanefendić and two or three others present at the dinner in Ljubljana's old town—gave me an envelope:

"This is my donation of 500 German marks each for the sixty journalists of *Oslobodjenje*," he said.

When I looked over the list of those working in the wartime editorial staff, I realized that there were more than sixty. After talking with Hasanefendić, I called Zulfikarpašić and asked him if we could divide the money differently, so that everyone could get something, including the auxiliary staff, without which the wartime publishing of the paper would not be possible.

"You do as you think best. I'm giving the money to you and it's up to you how to distribute it."

Since at the time there were no banks or post offices working in Sarajevo, there was no way for the money to be sent through the usual

---

* Milovan Djilas and Nadezda Gace, *BOSNJAK: Adil Zulfikarpašić,* (Zurich: Bošnjak Institut, 1994).

channels. The only safe way was to ask someone to take with them the money and the mail that you wanted to send. Returning to Sarajevo from my trips abroad, I would carry bundles of letters with tens of thousands of marks and dollars sent by friends and relatives from America, Canada, Croatia for people whom I did not even know: I simply could not refuse to take a letter, a box of medicine or money which might prolong someone's life even though it was not easy to bring them and deliver them to the addressees in Sarajevo. First, you had to go through the UNPROFOR civil police's inspection. They had limited the number of letters you could bring into the city to just five and were obliged to check all those letters out of fear that someone might smuggle military drawings, blank ID's such as press cards or passports for those who wanted to leave Sarajevo or drugs or who knows what else. And baggage was limited to one piece no heavier than 20 kilograms. But, not being able to refuse those who were begging me to take something for their relatives or friends, I always had letters and few pieces of baggage which I managed to "smuggle" in with some help from foreign colleagues flying with me to Sarajevo or thanks to some flexibility on part of the UNPROFOR police—usually its Scandinavian members—who would pretend that they did not notice how heavy my suitcases were. The distribution was an even worse problem: there were no phone lines to call people and tell them about the letter or package they had been sent and, using volunteers among colleagues and friends to carry those letters, I risked that some of them would get lost and—on two occasions—I had had to compensate desperate people for the money lost in my "distribution network," some 1,200 German marks in all.

On a few occasions I had carried back to Sarajevo the money sent to *Oslobodjenje*. For instance, returning from Scandinavia in September 1993—where I had been invited to receive the Stockholm paper, *Dagens nyheter*'s "Freedom Award" for *Oslobodjenje*—besides the award money, I was carrying another 20,000 German marks that readers sent to *Dagens nyheter* for *Oslobodjenje*, as well as a voucher for twenty tons of newsprint.

In sum, knowing how crucial even the smallest source of sustenance was to people in the besieged city, I agreed—with the concurrence of the manager of the paper—to carry Zulfikarpašić's donation to Sarajevo. There, in accordance with the decision of the wartime editorial board, 400 marks were distributed to each of the members of the editorial staff who were on the weekly shifts, and 300 or 200 marks, and a minimum of 100 marks, were distributed to each of the other journalists and the workers in the auxiliary staff.

Earlier on we had established a Fund for the Renewal of *Oslobodjenje* to which donations were made by institutions and individuals who wished to help support the survival of the daily in Sarajevo. Without international solidarity and support, our survival would have been much more difficult if not impossible. I had asked Zulfikarpašić if we could list his name as a contributor to the fund and publish it in the newspaper. "That is not necessary. This is an expression of my respect for what you people are doing, and I do not need any expression of gratitude for it," he answered. Accordingly, at a meeting of the wartime board of *Oslobodjenje* it was decided that he would be listed as "an anonymous donor." For the sake of keeping our accounts straight, however, I asked all those who received a share of the donation to sign a receipt.

I could not have imagined then that this contribution would be used in a campaign to discredit *Oslobodjenje* and its editor-in-chief, but that is exactly what was attempted by Muhamed Filipović, Bosnia's ambassador to Switzerland and Great Britain. Filipović had been a representative of Zulfikarpašić in Bosnia before he broke with him to join the SDA. Presumably because he was unhappy with what was written about him or his party, he suggested that *Oslobodjenje*'s independence might be suspect. He also spread a rumor among some Sarajevo journalists that Zulfikarpašić had actually sent the money to all journalists in the city—not just *Oslobodjenje*—and mentioned larger sums of money. He was joined in his campaign of slander against the paper and against me personally by the president of the Union of Journalists, Enver Čaušević, who announced that he had learned "from reliable sources" that, of the 40,000 German marks which Zulfikarpašić had sent to *Oslobodjenje*, only 8,000 had been distributed to the journalists and the remainder was used "for travel expenses of the editor-in-chief." People in *Oslobodjenje*, fortunately, knew that it was not 40,000 but 30,000 marks, that every last mark had been paid out to the staff of *Oslobodjenje* as had been stipulated by the donor, and that a meticulous record of the contribution and its distribution was there for all to see. They also knew that their editor-in-chief had traveled abroad only at the expense of the organizations which had invited him to receive an award for *Oslobodjenje* or to participate in a conference.

Nevertheless, after this unpleasant episode, I wondered aloud whether it was politic to accept Zulfikarpašić's donation when such an otherwise decent gesture could become grist for the mill of *Oslobodjenje*'s detractors. "Of course, you should have and you had to!" said Hamza Bakšić, a commentator and board member. "What would the people in *Oslobodjenje* have said if you had refused to accept it, when we are working for virtually no pay, and when the monthly take-home wages are no more than eight marks?"

But the attacks continued. Thus Senad Avdić of *Slobodna Bosna* (*Free Bosnia*), a magazine printed in free Zenica and sold in besieged Sarajevo for German marks, wrote to the effect that the editor-in-chief of *Oslobodjenje*, after being completely smashed up in an automobile accident in which "everyone was dead drunk," was traveling around the world claiming that he was wounded by the Chetniks, and gathering donations for his newspaper. This sordid fiction spread with utter disregard for the fact that the most prestigious world papers, including the *New York Times* and the *Washington Post,* had published the story of the automobile accident which resulted in my injuries exactly as it happened. In a similar vein, the Muslim weekly *Ljiljan*, which was edited by refugee journalists in Zagreb and Ljubljana, and which clearly had strong support in the ruling circles of the SDA—hundreds of copies were distributed free at official Bosnian locations in London and at conventions of Bosnians in Chicago and Toronto—a certain Nedžad Latić included me in his list of "traitors of Bosnia," with the comment that I was being bought off by significant international awards to be "neutral like UNPROFOR."

Ljiljan seemed to nurse an almost pathological hatred for *Oslobodjenje* and its multiethnic staff. When that paper attacked our columnist Slavko Šantić, calling him a "chetnik," even though his son as a Serb was defending Sarajevo at the most dangerous defense lines, and when it condemned intermarriage among Bosnians of different ethnic and religious backgrounds as "ideologically oppressive," I could not resist—even though at that time I was already in the United States—responding to the rise of Muslim racism. Writing in *Oslobodjenje*, I said that by attacking that most intimate expression of our centuries-old Bosnian culture, *Ljiljan* was practically doing the work of

Serbian propagandists. And to its attempt to discredit *Oslobodjenje* as a bolshevik paper—because for decades it had been controlled by the Communist Party—I reminded the readers that *Oslobodjenje* was the first paper in Yugoslavia which, through its decision to remove the oath of allegiance to Tito, had renounced loyalty to dogma and opened its pages to political and intellectual pluralism. "But you did so only after it was obvious that Mr. Izetbegović would win the election!" was the response written by *Ljiljan's* editor-in-chief, Džemaludin Latić. In his devotion to his new leader and new party in power he had not even bothered to check the fact that the ideological slogan on the front-page of *Oslobodjenje* had been removed in January 1990—five months before Izetbegović even formed his party! But any argument, even an invented one, was good enough for those who hated us for not accepting hatred.

Such attacks, however, could not simply be dismissed as harmless exhibitions of envy or even unconcealed hatred, by obscure writers who were polishing their own credentials as "patriots" by spitting on others. In a country at war, in which far too many people had experienced indescribable suffering, lost their loved ones and all their earthly possessions, there were many who wanted to get their revenge on whomever they could blame for their misery, and especially on those who were tarred by the brush of treachery. In such conditions, the drivel that issued regularly against *Oslobodjenje* and other independent journalists made for dangerous execution lists. Incitement to murder was not beyond these born-again nationalists as was exemplified by a certain Haris Zulić in the newsletter *Bošnjak,* published in Los Angeles, who raised the alarm against the dangerous "troika" of Milić-Kurspahić-Pejić (the other two, respectively, were the prewar editors of *Yutel,* the most popular TV news hour in Yugoslavia, and Television Sarajevo), and went on to suggest that, in order to prevent them from running amok, this noxious threesome ought to "be beheaded."

Such "journalism" is just a short step away from all manner of bigotry, violence, and terror. Those who were never much given to reading or reflection were judging the events in Bosnia through the lenses of the nationalist, extremist press, which began calling for the liquidation of all those who disagreed with its view of the world. Such readers were truly capable of accepting the claim that *Oslobodjenje,* in spite of its consistent support for the independence and territorial integrity of Bosnia-Hercegovina, was "neutral" like UNPROFOR. That such a view was held by those closest to the highest circles in government was obvious from the reaction of a member of Alija Izetbegović's security detail who accompanied the Bosnian president on his visit to those who had been wounded in the Marketplace Massacre of February 1994. "Do you in *Oslobodjenje* now see who is shooting at us?" said the man angrily, in the inflamed tone of an ill-mannered bully who accepts without further thought what he reads in "our side's newspaper," as he turned upon the *Oslobodjenje* reporter, a Serb who was the most outspoken witness to the suffering of Sarajevo's citizens, and who had gone to cover the visit.

While I had the highest appreciation for the UN's humanitarian efforts and the risks its people took to deliver much-needed food and other supplies to Sarajevo and some other besieged towns in Bosnia, the worst insult anyone could hurl at me was to accuse my paper of UNPROFOR-like neutrality. The UN bureaucracy's refusal to make a distinction between the victims and the perpetrators of genocide and its insistence on the peacekeeping nature of UNPROFOR's mission in a country where there was no peace to keep was an exercise in lunacy.

The grotesque notion of neutrality in the context of the Bosnian war was first introduced by the Canadian UN commander in Bosnia, General Lewis MacKenzie. I had had the opportunity of confronting his version of the war in the course of my meetings with Canadian journalists and editors and in an appearance on the evening television program, *Newsworld,* during my short trip to Canada from the United States in January 1994. From the people I met I learned that the picture of events in Bosnia as presented in the Canadian media was greatly influenced by the "MacKenzie factor." Canadian journalists were not sent to Sarajevo as often as American and European journalists were. Many Canadians tended to see MacKenzie as their heroic general braving the firestorm in Bosnia and unquestioningly accepted his description of the conflict. "Dealing with Bosnia is like dealing with three serial killers. One has killed fifteen, one has killed ten, and one has killed five. Do we help the one who has only killed five?" he had asked in a Congressional hearing in Washington in May 1993. The General entirely ignored the explicit finding of the UN Commission of Experts on War Crimes in former Yugoslavia that there was "no factual ground for moral equivalence" in responsibility for the atrocities committed in Bosnia: there was nothing to compare with the genocidal nature of Serbian "ethnic cleansing."

In his persistent campaign to prove that all sides shared the blame for the atrocities, MacKenzie even promoted the canard that it was the Bosnian Army that planted the bomb which killed twenty and wounded more than a hundred Sarajevans in the notorious bread-line massacre of May 27, 1992. In doing so, he was supporting Serb propaganda, repeated on the occasion of every massacre in Sarajevo, that "the Muslims [were] killing their own people in order to provoke Western military intervention." In his book *Peacekeeper: The Road to Sarajevo*, MacKenzie thus asserted that there was "strong but circumstantial evidence that some really horrifying acts of cruelty attributed to the Serbs were actually orchestrated by the Muslims against their own people for the benefit of an international audience."* To check the General's evidence, Tom Gjelten, correspondent for United States' National Public Radio, took a Dutch expert on crater analysis to the the site of the bread-line massacre. After examining the sidewalk on Vase Miskina street, the expert told Gjelten that there was no evidence of a ground device; whatever had caused the crater had come out of the sky. At the time of MacKenzie's campaign in both Canada and the United States to "educate" the public on Bosnia no one knew that he was paid at least $15,000 by SerbNet, a Serbian lobby in the United States, for his two media tours to Washington in May 1993.**

Meanwhile, confronted with the monumental failure of the UN to stop the genocide in Bosnia, Boutrous Ghali would insist that they "did not have the mandate to impose, just to keep the peace." But they had the clear mandate to protect Bosnia's "safe zones" and they failed, allowing unspeakable crimes to be committed against civilians in Srebrenica in July 1995 when the town, supposedly under UN protection, was taken by the Serb forces and hundreds of people were tortured and

---

* Lewis MacKenzie, *Peacekeeper: The Road to Sarajevo,* Toronto: Douglas & McIntyre.

** Dele Olojede and Roy Gutman in *Newsday,* June 24, 1993. Eric Margolis, "My Advice to Lew MacKenzie," *The Toronto Star,* August 19, 1993. See also, Roy Gutman, "Serbs Bankroll Speeches by ex-UN Commander," in Gutman's *A Witness to Genocide,* New York: Macmillan, 1993, p. 168, and Tom Gjelten, *Sarajevo Daily, A City and its Newspaper Under Siege,* New York: HarperCollins, 1995 p. 147.

summarily executed. There are credible reports on the direct complicity of the highest civilian and military representatives of the United Nations in the Balkans—Yasushi Akashi and General Bernard Janvier—who refrained from using air power against the Serbs in exchange for the release of UN soldiers taken hostage. They also had a clear mandate to keep Serb heavy artillery away from Sarajevo's "exclusion zone" but they allowed the Serb forces to operate freely, massacring Sarajevans on a daily basis. They had a mandate to keep Sarajevo airport and the roads in and out of the city open but they allowed the strangulation of the Bosnian capital to last for more than three and a half years. And some of the UN personnel—such as the British general Michael Rose—holding on to their perverse neutrality between the victims and victimizers—did all they could to prevent any action against Serbian terror in Sarajevo, Bihać, Tuzla. When the "safe zones" of Goražde and Bihać came under brutal Serbian attacks while he was the UNPROFOR commander in Bosnia, Rose persistently played down the magnitude of the crimes and the number of those killed, refusing requests to act even when his own troops were attacked and his soldiers killed. "We are here on a peace-keeping, not on a war mission," he kept repeating the UN bureaucracy's favored mantra and then proclaimed that it was "too late" to do anything to save some 180,000 civilians in Bihać. If it were not for the defense of the area by the Fifth Corps of the Bosnian Army, people in that "safe zone" would have been slaughtered like those in Srebrenica—under the "protection," and in the presence, of UN troops.

There was never any doubt at *Oslobodjenje* as to the sources of the Bosnian tragedy: we knew from the beginning of the siege that Bosnia-Hercegovina was attacked because its population had voted for independence in a free and internationally monitored referendum with a clear majority of 64 percent, and that Bosnia-Hercegovina was the target, first, of the Greater Serbia project, and then of Greater Croatia. Nor was there any confusion in the paper over whom to blame for the terror—every child in Sarajevo knew that the city was being demolished and burned and its citizens massacred by the fire that came from Serb artillery positions in the hills; nor was there any nonsense about equating "all sides in the conflict"—because on the one side there was the legitimately elected government of an internationally recognized state and on the other the paramilitary forces of Serbia and the self-appointed "Republika Srpska" responsible for mass slaughter and wholesale expulsion of populations.

And yet the Muslim extremists kept attacking us for not being "sufficiently Bosnian" or—as in an article written by the minister of culture in the Bosnian government, Dr. Enes Karić—for being "the chetnik's paper," even though the Chetniks had leveled *Oslobodjenje's* building to the ground and had still continued their attacks. The ascendant Muslim faction wanted to reduce all Bosnia, and all its interests, to those of the Muslims or Bosniaks, readily finding their justification for Muslim exclusivity in the horrible crimes committed primarily against Muslims and on the basis of the widespread—and legitimate—belief that the West had abandoned Bosnia to its executioners. But, by abandoning the ideals of a pluralist multiethnic society, they were advancing the agenda of the perpetrators of "ethnic cleansing" whose main propagandistic claim was that the peoples of Bosnia could not live together. The propagation of a "Muslims/Bosniaks only" policy would, in fact, justify the creation of not only "Republika Srpska" and "Herceg-Bosna" on Bosnian soil, but also—and this is what the Muslim extremists wanted—the creation of a separate Muslim statelet. Such a partitioning of Bosnia would satisfy the nationalistic dreams of all three nationalistic movements and would destroy not only the centuries-old culture of interethnic and interreligious cohabitation but also the state of Bosnia-Hercegovina itself. Unfortunately, not only Serbia and Croatia, both neighbors greedy for Bosnian territory, but also the international community—contrary to their publicly expressed fears of the creation of an Islamic state on European soil—were directly encouraging such an outcome: by not intervening to stop the genocide of Muslims, by denying Bosnia the right to arm and defend itself, and by consistently trying to impose the division of the country along ethnic lines as the solution, they too were complicit both in the destruction of the country as well as the rise of Islamic extremism as a response to the devastation of Bosnia's Muslim people and heritage.

The one thing for which we at *Oslobodjenje* were "at fault" was our refusal to abandon, to "cleanse" our minds of our memories and our beliefs, as well as our dream, of a Bosnia-Hercegovina "which will be neither Muslim nor Serb nor Croat but rather altogether Muslim and Serb and Croat," as it was defined in the Constitution written by those who liberated it from fascist occupation in the Second World

War. It was the commitment to such a Bosnia that continued to define the work of *Oslobodjenje*: while the nationalists heaped abuse upon the paper, we held fast to our position that Bosnia could not be divided and were therefore categorically opposed to the successive peace plans and maps that were being drawn up by the UN and European Union mediators.

At a conference in Washington in February 1993, attended by academics as well as representatives of the U.S. administration and the United Nations, the principal topic under discussion was the Vance-Owen plan for the cantonization of Bosnia-Hercegovina as a means of ending the war. The plan was a prescription for disaster. Therefore, in my comments to the conference I could do no more than express the dissenting view, arguing that the international mediators insistently refused to comprehend that their maps for Bosnia were more a source of the tragedy than a solution. When the maps for the division of Bosnia were first presented in Lisbon, in March of 1992, the Serbian forces began "ethnic cleansing" in the areas which they wanted for themselves. Now when maps had again been brought to the negotiating table in Geneva, the same would happen in the territories which the Croats wanted to take. It was my conviction that the division of Bosnia, which the gentlemen mediators regarded as the easiest solution, could turn out to be the worst solution, because it would mean new years and decades of tension and conflict and even new waves of "ethnic cleansing."

And that, indeed, was what happened. After the Serbs did most of their genocidal work in creating "ethnically pure" Serb territory in Bosnia, Croat nationalists felt encouraged—even invited—by the new, Vance-Owen maps to "cleanse" territory for their own "Republic of Herceg-Bosna." The crimes they were to commit in the spring of 1993 in some of the places in Central Bosnia and in Hercegovina, with mass killings and torture of civilians in Ahmići, Stupni Do, Mostar, Dretelj, would not be less vicious than those committed by the Serbs in the spring and summer of the previous year, except that now they would face a Bosnian Army which would manage to defend huge parts of the territory. Tragically, in that campaign even some of the Bosnian Army units were to engage in random atrocities against Croat villages in Neretva Valley. The peace proposals of the mediators, and the academic conferences convened to discuss those proposals, were not likely to bring peace. Nor, it became increasingly clear, could one expect any better from the intercessions of the United States even as it emerged from the Cold War as the world's only superpower.

In the spring of the same year I had the experience, first hand, of the contradictory thinking that permeated the Clinton Administration's policy on Bosnia. Invited to attend yet another conference in Washington, I had had the opportunity of an extended conversation on Capitol Hill with Senators Bill Bradley of New Jersey and Daniel Patrick Moynihan of New York on what could and should be done for Bosnia-Hercegovina. I answered their numerous questions, mostly on the idea of lifting the arms embargo against the Bosnians and conducting an air campaign against Serbian strategic targets not only in Bosnia but in Serbia as well.

"I have answered many of your questions, would you answer just one: What do you think is going to happen?" I asked Senator Bradley, curious to know what he thought the Clinton administration might decide.

"Both lift and strike," he told me and I know that the two of them, among others in the United States Congress, were steadfast in their support of air strikes against strategic Serbian targets and the lifting of the arms embargo on Bosnia-Hercegovina. Later, as chance would have it, I met Bill Clinton himself. He was invited to the reception held at the Capital Hilton Hotel at the closing of the international conference I had been attending. The president of the National Endowment for Democracy, Carl Gershman, told the President that the editor-in-chief of the Bosnian-Hercegovinian newspaper *Oslobodjenje* was among the hundreds of guests there, and Clinton said he wanted to meet me. Together we left the large reception hall and went into an adjoining room. The President expressed his own admiration for our work at *Oslobodjenje*, and then asked directly:

"What do you think we should do?"

"Mr. President, I would suggest a cocktail with five ingredients," I said, and presented my favored prescription for a just peace. "First, air strikes against Serb artillery and other strategic targets around Sarajevo and other Bosnian cities; second, the lifting of the arms embargo on Bosnia so that the country is allowed its right to defend itself and then there would be no need for either American or any other country's ground forces, which is the kind of involvement very much feared over here; third, the tightening of economic sanctions against Serbia until they become not only cooperative but enthusiastic for peace; fourth, a demonstration of political will not only to propose but to impose a just political solution in Bosnia, and that would be a corrected version of the Vance-Owen Plan…"

"That plan looks bad," the President interrupted me at this point.

'Yes, because it is based on apartheid," I responded, "and if apartheid was not acceptable in South Africa, why should it be imposed as 'the best solution' in Bosnia? … And, finally, there must be a serious and declared commitment to hold war crimes trials," I continued with my five points, "so that the people who have been driven from their land and their homes can believe that one day they will be able to return."

Clinton appeared to be listening attentively. Of course, he did not promise anything; at the time he and the National Security Council were just considering their options in Bosnia and, besides, I was a mere journalist.

When I returned to the reception hall, the ABC television crew wanted to know: "What did the President ask you? What did you tell him? Did he ask for your advice?" "No, that would be pretentious. He asked me for my opinion, and he listened carefully to what I had to say," I answered.

In the next few days, the President did indeed announce his "lift-and-strike strategy," proposing the lifting of the arms embargo and the use of air strikes. But, in the end, not securing the support of the Western European allies—or perhaps not being able persuasively to demonstrate his own resolve, to himself or anyone else—he did not follow through. The Clinton administration's chronic confusion over what steps to take, together with the European powers' cynical abandonment of Bosnia, compounded our tragedy. Instead of the "lift-and-strike" strategy which Clinton had earlier appeared to favor, what we continued to get was more of the same: a refusal to allow the Bosnians to arm and defend themselves and a refusal to come to their defense. The high-minded rhetoric that regularly issued from Western capitals could not disguise the fact that the allied powers that fought the Nazis once could not muster the will to confront the petty fascists in Pale and Belgrade who were laying a country waste and slaughtering its population.

I often wondered why Clinton was unable to act coherently on the question of Bosnia. Apart from what some American commentators

have described as his politics of expediency—jettisoning any conviction that might get in the way of a second term in the White House—
one of the explanations was that at a time of crucial decisions he
simply read the wrong book or, more precisely, drew the wrong conclusion, from *The Balkan Ghosts* by Robert Kaplan, which led him to
the comforting thought that nothing much could be done in Bosnia
"until those folks get tired of killing each other"—the most offensive
words on Bosnia I found in Clinton's often contradictory statements.
If only he had read carefully the Central Intelligence Agency's own
reports he would know that at least ninety percent of the atrocities
were committed by Serb forces in a systematic campaign of "ethnic
cleansing" in Bosnia.*

Clinton was right in his initial resolve to use force to stop those
atrocities. Once his administration finally persuaded its NATO partners to use force against Serb military targets—in the summer of
1995—there was an immediate relaxation of the siege of Sarajevo and
the self-styled Serbian leadership readily endorsed essentially the same
Contact Group (United States, Britain, France, Germany and Russia)
plan they had rejected a year earlier. It proved how deadly wrong were
all those military advisers in the George Bush's administration—like
General Colin Powell—who warned Washington away from any action
in Bosnia, projecting the deployment of "hundreds of thousands of
U.S. ground troops" to stop the Serbs. All it took was an almost risk-
free demonstration of resolve in the form of a few days of an air campaign against strictly military targets to get Pale to sign on the dotted
line. How many lives could have been saved, and how vastly different
would have been the political and military outcome of the war, if Clinton's own "lift-and-strike" proposal had been implemented?

The history of this war was also to show that it took American
initiative for any movement towards a resolution of the crisis in

---

* The CIA and the U.S. Defense Department had detailed intelligence information on
the atrocities and mass killings being committed by Serb forces in Bosnia, but this
information was systematically withheld both from the public and from the United
Nations—and in some instances—even from the U.S. administration itself—
because sections within the Pentagon as well as the Government did not want to be
drawn into any action in Bosnia against the Serb forces. For a detailed exposé, see
Charles Lane and Thom Shanker, "Bosnia: What the CIA Didn't Tell Us," *The New
York Review of Books,* May 9, 1996, pp. 10–15.

Bosnia. There were some promising steps towards peace only when Washington took the lead from Europe: in February 1994, it was the American-initiated NATO threat that led to the first withdrawal of Serbian heavy guns around Sarajevo; in March that year, the Clinton administration brokered the Bosniak-Croat agreement to create a federation which helped to stop the fighting between the Croat forces and the Bosnian Army; and in late August 1995, U.S.-initiated air strikes helped to relieve the siege of Sarajevo and to open the way for a renewed peace initiative. But instead of building on his own initial successes, and pressing the Serbs to join the Bosnian federation which would have been more consistent with his stated goal of preserving Bosnian integrity and sovereignty, the President decided to join Europe in their failed policy to divide Bosnia, which only led to more bloodshed. The American peace initiative launched at Dayton in the summer of 1995, like the Contact Group's plan launched the year before, divided Bosnia roughly in half, giving the Bosnian-Croat federation control over 51 percent of the territory and Bosnian Serbs 49 percent. By conceding "Republika Srpska" to the Serb nationalists through a virtual partitioning of Bosnia the U.S. also undermined the Bosnian-Croat federation itself.

Was there a better choice? I believe, yes. Instead of offering the perpetrators of genocidal "ethnic cleansing" half of the country, the Clinton administration would have done better to insist on a federal arrangement for the whole of Bosnia. Serb leaders ought to have been faced with the simple choice: either they accepted the federal state with equal individual and collective rights for all citizens and all ethnic groups or they would face continued political and economic isolation while the arms embargo against Bosnia would be lifted, finally giving that country the means to defend itself. Instead, the United States opted for the policy that the European powers had long pursued and pressed on the Americans—the appeasement of the Serbs as a means to stopping the war. Legitimizing the carve-up of Bosnia in this manner could only have one consequence: the consolidation of power by the nationalists on all sides in their own ghetto states and an open season on the secular, liberal forces that still supported a pluralist, multiethnic state.

Small wonder then that as the Muslim nationalists gained ascendancy in the ruling SDA, the world view that *Oslobodjenje* and others represented became anathema—and akin to treason—in the Bosnia that was being defined on the peace tables of the international mediators. Speaking at a ceremony at the UN headquarters in New York on the occasion of the presentation of the Inter Press Service's Achievement in Journalism award to *Oslobodjenje*, I was struck by the sad irony of our condition: the world heaped recognition on this paper for its struggle and yet sat on its collective hands (there were ambassadors from 72 countries at the ceremony) while the spectacle of Bosnia's destruction unfolded. "We in *Oslobodjenje*," I said, "are touched by everything that the international press community has done for us: it has helped us to survive. At the same time, we are sad that the international community as a whole, whom you represent, has not done the same for our country."*

In the summer of 1993, when all diplomatic efforts were focused on the partitioning of Bosnia-Hercegovina into separate ethnic ministates, I had sensed a certain nervousness, an apprehensiveness even among the journalists of *Oslobodjenje*: what kind of a future did they have in an ethnically divided Bosnia, and what kind of a role would there be for a paper that had fought for multiethnic coexistence and still had a multiethnic staff? Deciding that it was time to contend with these questions, I called a meeting of the editorial staff. My own position was that there were certain professional standards, such as objectivity, openness to differences and criticism, and certain civilized values, such as tolerance, mutual respect, equal rights for all citizens, which were worth fighting for. *Oslobodjenje* would continue to do exactly that, regardless of any imposed territorial or constitutional "realities." The meeting went on for several days and resulted in the publication of an editorial document, entitled: "The Role of *Oslobodjenje* in the 'New Realities' of Bosnia-Hercegovina."

The document, in a sense, was also our answer to the pressures put upon us to abandon our "multiethnic utopia" and to admit that the Bosnia which we had known, loved and stood for was a "thing of

---

* At that time I was informed that even upon the occasion of our being presented with the award, the perverse logic of the "neutrality" of the United Nations was at work. Upon learning that the Journalism Achievement Award would be given to *Oslobodjenje* at his organization's headquarters, the UN Secretary General, Boutros Boutros Ghali, had stated his concern that this "might be awkward, because the representatives of Yugoslavia might object."

the past" and that now ethnicity would be the basis of all things. At one point, we feared that *Oslobodjenje* might be prevented physically from publishing by extremist forces which were active even in some institutions of the Bosnian government. This became an extremely serious problem on a certain day in August 1993. A unit of one of the Bosnian Army brigades, under the command of Mušan Topalović Caco, provoked an open conflict with the police in the Old Town district, and all the approaches to the newly rented *Oslobodjenje* offices on Vase Miskina Street were blocked off on that day. On the way to the office by car, I encountered armed police patrols at almost every corner.

"You cannot go further; the Old Town is a 'blocked zone'," they told me.

"But I have to—the newspaper has to come out tomorrow!" I tried my most convincing argument.

"You really should not go any further. It's dangerous. We don't know who controls the streets around Vase Miskina, but we'll let you through at your own risk."

The same procedure was repeated from the first to the second, third, and fourth checkpoints. When I got to the editorial offices, only a few, really insistent, staffers were there. With *Oslobodjenje* press cards in hand, they had managed to talk their way through the checkpoints; some had not been so successful.

"Caco's soldiers have picked up Tomo [Počanić], Vedo [Spahović], and our driver Ervin [Algajer]," I was told by our photographer Danilo Krstanović, who had been with them when they were checked for their identification and press credentials near the Sarajka Department Store. They were pushed into a truck together with other citizens who had been forcibly picked up from the streets of Sarajevo to be taken to dig trenches along the dangerous front line facing the Serb forces in the hills at the foot of Mount Trebević.

"I got off lucky," said Danilo. "They only took away my bulletproof vest."

The editorial board did not dare to intervene with the army to get our people released. Topalovic was a powerful force in the city whom no one dared to challenge. For months his units had been picking up people off the streets and carting them off to their most important military undertaking, "digging our way to victory." If anyone, using personal influence, attempted to intervene, the individual would be held longer than the others, as happened with the cellist Vedran Smajlović, who played the "Adagio" for days at the site of the bread-line massacre on Vase Miskina Street and at the Sarajevo cemetery. I was especially upset that they had taken Tomo Počanić, one of our oldest and most diligent journalists in *Oslobodjenje*'s wartime editorial staff, who was also looking after his wife, who was seriously ill. In those days, the capriciousness of Topalovic's brigade was reaching a culmination point with its open confrontation with the police and the blockade of a large part of the city. Eventually, after several days of public protests as well as intervention from the highest echelons in the government, all civilians who had been forcefully inducted, including the three from *Oslobodjenje*, were released. Later that year, Topalovic was killed in a Bosnian Army action against those renegade volunteers who had taken to terrorizing the citizens of Sarajevo under the cover of the "defense of the city."

The experience of having come so close to a point where the editorial staff could be completely disabled and the paper shut down, not by Serb artillery but by elements within Sarajevo meant that we had to prepare for the worst. Together with Deputy Manager Emir Hrustanović, I began work on a plan to insure the publication of *Oslobodjenje* even if all access to the editorial offices in the city and in the nuclear bomb shelter at Nedžarići should some day be cut off. We agreed that he should find a good printing machine which could print up at least several hundred copies of the paper prepared on the computer in the A-4 format, and that he should also locate an apartment which would not attract attention somewhere in the center of town where we could work for several days and let the world know that *Oslobodjenje* was in danger of being silenced.

How much this was, indeed, the aim of the faction that was angered by our opposition to its exclusivist agenda and annoyed by the recognition the paper had received abroad, was symbolically demonstrated at the awards ceremonies in the summer of 1993 organized by the Union of Journalists of Bosnia-Hercegovina. Although there were hardly any members of the *Oslobodjenje* staff who were members of the union—which had been formed and was led by several individuals who had never worked in daily journalism—they could not avoid recognizing some of *Oslobodjenje*'s writers, including Gojko Berić, who was voted "journalist of the year," Vlado Mrkić, "reporter of the year," Šefko Hodžić, "war reporter of the year" and Fehim Demir, "photographer of the year." But they did manage to ignore *Oslobodjenje*, giving the award for the publishing achievement of the year to *Muslimanski Glas* ("The Muslim Voice"), a magazine which published only a few issues during the siege. Foreign correspondents who attended the awards ceremony, commented in whispered asides:

"That's the way it goes. Worldwide recognition, but unacknowledged in Sarajevo."

"They will forgive you anything except success," I responded wryly.

The siege around *Oslobodjenje* was dangerously tightening as the fiftieth anniversary of the paper drew near that summer. The Bosnian government had removed us from the list of organizations which were sanctioned fuel distributed from their thin reserves by the Ministry of Energy. There was no electricity and we had to find at least a hundred liters of fuel every day just to operate our generator long enough—five to six hours—to type and print the paper. In a desperate search for fuel, at times some of the staff would stay on beyond the curfew hour of 10 P.M. And the price per liter on Sarajevo's black market was reaching 25 German marks which was more than we were able to earn selling the paper on the streets. We were spending our award money in order to keep it going and I was afraid that we might finally be forced to stop publishing just days before *Oslobodjenje*'s fiftieth anniversary in August. But that summer we received a life-saving infusion at the initiative of two senior UN officers.

First, the commander of the UN forces in former Yugoslavia, General Jean Cot from France, arrived on his first visit to Sarajevo and asked to see me. "You in *Oslobodjenje* have been heroes in my country," he said. "I've been reading and hearing a lot about you." He wanted to know how we managed to survive. Soon after, the commander of UNPROFOR for Bosnia-Hercegovina, Belgium's General Francis Briquemont, came to visit us in our atomic bomb shelter in Nedžarići. I was telling him about our plans for the paper's fiftieth anniversary at which we were to be joined by dozens of our foreign colleagues who were intending to travel to Sarajevo to express their professional solidarity with *Oslobodjenje*. But I also admitted my fear that we might not be able to continue publishing until that day. "We can't earn enough to buy the fuel on the black market," I told him.

That evening General Briquemont sent us a "top secret" gift of two tons of diesel, enough for almost three weeks of production. With that gesture of appreciation for the value of the press in the besieged city he distinguished himself from numerous UN and UNHCR officials who did not consider newsprint to be among the necessities which were allowed into Sarajevo. That summer they would not bring in even a single role of newsprint and we had had to use our "Italian connection"—our Italian colleague Piero Giudicci—to smuggle in a few tons of the paper with a shipment of medical supplies from Italy for Sarajevo's Koševo Hospital in order to survive. The embargo on newsprint, it seemed sometimes, was linked to the embargo on arms for Bosnia. At the anniversary celebrations at the Holiday Inn, General Briquemont was among our foreign guests when the machine gun from the armored vehicle in his escort was hijacked. "I'd like to think, General, that this might be the first step towards the lifting of the arms embargo against the Bosnian Army," I said, only half in jest.

On September 16, at an anniversary reception for foreign correspondents in our destroyed building, we were joined by editors and journalists from fifty international newspapers. Over the long months and years under siege, in our underground shelter we had received many of the distinguished visitors—writers, artists, statesmen—who came to Sarajevo to express their solidarity with Bosnia. There were long and friendly discussions with prominent French intellectuals such as Bernard-Henri-Lévy, André Glucksmann, and Pascal Bruckner, and American writer Susan Sontag who directed "Waiting for Godot" in the summer of 1993 in the Sarajevo Chamber Theater 55, was a frequent and well-liked guest at Oslobodjenje. The attention and recognition that Oslobodjenje received came, of course, from those countless citizens of the world who saw the war against Bosnia as an assault on our common humanity, and the resistance that Sarajevo embodied as, perhaps, civilization's last stand against the rising forces of barbaric tribalism. Oslobodjenje was therefore not a thing apart—its struggle was emblematic of the larger, more desperate, certainly more heroic struggle that the people of Bosnia were waging for a country and for a way of life that was being destroyed as the world watched.

And yet hope sprang eternal. We in Bosnia could not afford to surrender. Laughter, music, camaraderie, the ordinary rites of

The staff of *Oslobodjenje* celebrate the paper's fiftieth anniversary.

humanity sustained us through our darkening days. Thus I remember
a summer evening with a few friends from *Oslobodjenje*—Gordana
Knežević, Emir Hrustanović, Bećir Čaluk—who had gathered at my
apartment. We had been joined by Susan Sontag, her son David Rieff,
and the American photographer Annie Leibovitz. We talked, and
raged, and sang quietly old Bosnian songs to the accompaniment of
Čaluk's faithful guitar—and some of my neighbors came, one by one,
to greet my guests, offering to bring some coffee or even to bake a pie.

"What is this hole in your window?" Susan asked me.

"A bullet gate-crashed last night, but I didn't have the party
then," I said to Susan who was sitting next to the broken window
and reminded me of the episode when we met two years later in
Washington, D.C.

FAREWELL TO SARAJEVO

IN THE MIDDLE OF FEBRUARY 1994, after the massacre at the Markale Piazza and the threat of air strikes by NATO, Serb artillery was largely removed from around Sarajevo. Thus, after nearly two years, as the shelling of the city ceased, it briefly entered a period of respite, even though the siege was not lifted and, a few months later, the strangulation of Sarajevo had become even more systematic. (The reluctance of the United Nations to use force would encourage the Serb forces to bring back the heavy weapons they had withdrawn earlier.) For us in *Oslobodjenje* that short period of relative calm posed the question of how to best to function in a state that was neither at war nor peace. Rather than rely on emergency, ad hoc measures to circumvent the difficulties we faced, it was necessary to work out more stable solutions to a number of issues. We needed to ensure a steady supply of newsprint and other materials for the continued publication of the paper, and to provide the staff with a bare minimum of income so that they could purchase some food, which was now being delivered with greater frequency but was only being sold for hard currency, usually the German mark. We also wanted to revive some of the other publications, such as *Nedjelja* and *Svijet,* which had been discontinued during the war. And, finally, it was important to begin the repair and renewal of the editorial building so that, after nearly two years of living and working in a bomb shelter, the staff of *Oslobodjenje* could begin as soon as possible to work in more normal conditions.

When things were at their worst and our Nedžarići headquarters were under daily artillery attack, *Oslobodjenje* had established its Fund for Renewal. Confronted with the imperative of shutting down and going home, we had instead chosen to go out into the world and secured badly needed support for our survival. That is why, instead of being silenced and destroyed by mortar shells, we had undertaken the international edition of *Oslobodjenje,* which now is available around the world. Finally, towards the end of February 1994, the same reasons—the determination to keep the paper in print and so maintain its advocacy for a pluralist, heterogeneous Bosnia—led to the decision by the Managing Board and the wartime Editorial Board of *Oslobodjenje,* to send me as an editor-correspondent to the United States and Zlatko Dizdarević to Europe. Calculating that *Oslobodjenje* could

The Kursphahić family reunited at Harvard. Vesna, Tarik, Mirza and Kemal.

survive and start the process of renewal, it was deemed essential to maintain the international network of professional solidarity and support the paper had built up over the past two years of war.

During my short trips to Washington and New York, we had obtained donations for *Oslobodjenje*, both in cash and in computer equipment, of over 200,000 dollars. The assistance we were thus being able to raise was the largest single source of income for the paper in 1994. I had also come to the realization by then that in the current conditions of relative peace in Sarajevo, when *Oslobodjenje* was no longer confronted with the possibility of imminent death, I could be more useful to the paper in Washington than in Sarajevo. After all, I knew that there was little more I could do to devise ways of keeping the paper running, nor could I imagine difficulties worse than those we had already faced and overcome.

There were also personal factors which influenced my decision to leave. Vesna and Mirza were in Croatia and Tarik was in London, both children had been out of school for the second year, all of them were concerned for me in Sarajevo and I was deeply troubled about not being with them and therefore unable to take care of them abroad. Vesna grew so desperate that she had bought plane tickets for Mirza and herself to go to Norway as refugees and only at the last moment was persuaded by my friend Goran Jovanović not to leave: he assured her that he knew that *Oslobodjenje* would be sending me to the United States, even though the decision was not made at that time. Besides, I had been encouraged to apply for the Nieman Fellowship at Harvard for academic year 1994–95, which at that juncture represented the opportunity not only to benefit from the privileges of spending a year at one of the world's best universities but also to gather my family together after two years of war and separation, to put my sons back in school, and to work on my book. I could continue to write for *Oslobodjenje* (with the agreement of the Nieman's curator, Bill Kovach) without drawing a salary. With another grant, from the Tribune McCormick Foundation in Chicago, I would be able to continue my work as *Oslobodjenje*'s correspondent without being paid by the paper for a full two years. It was therefore agreed that my appointment as the U.S. editor-correspondent would be the best both for the paper and for me.

Thus the discussions began for selection of a new editor-in-chief. The Editorial Board first established the credentials which it would require of the new editor: professional experience and a strong reputation among the general public; acceptance and respect from the paper's workforce; and a good knowledge of English for the sake of maintaining its international connections. I considered it especially important that the head of the paper should be someone whose personal and professional qualities would be a positive force, holding the editorial board and staff together and guaranteeing the commitment of the paper to the principles of professional independence and interethnic tolerance. And finally, in addition to the official deliberations of the Editorial and Managing Board, it was important to ascertain the opinions of especially those journalists—Gordana Knežević, Gojko Berić, Hamza Bakšić—who in the past two years had made the greatest contributions to the survival and reputation of *Oslobodjenje*. And all were unanimous in their vote for Mehmed Halilović as the best candidate for the job.

Mehmed Halilović—known as Meho to his friends—had, like myself, spent his entire professional life at *Oslobodjenje*. He entered the world of journalism as a high-school correspondent from his home-town of Gradačac, and during his college days he worked for the student newspaper *Naši dani* in Sarajevo. He was a journalist and an editor of the political and foreign affairs sections at *Oslobodjenje*. In the days when Party control was paramount, he was among those who tried as far as possible to ensure that the paper would be edited along professional rather than political lines. As deputy editor-in-chief he had won the trust of the younger journalists as a strict critic and a strong supporter of their efforts. Meho did not really want the job of editor-in-chief and had not sought it but agreed to accept it if that was the wish, democratically expressed, of the entire editorial staff. An editorial staff meeting was held on February 27 at which the Editorial and Managing Board proposed Mehmed Halilović as a candidate for the job. The journalists at the editorial staff meeting supported the proposal and his election was unanimous. "I did not want the job, but I will work as if it's the one thing I've wanted all my life," he said at the time of his election.

Two days after the announcement of the election of *Oslobod-jenje*'s new editor-in-chief, we were invited to a reception at the offices of the president of the Presidency of Bosnia-Hercegovina, Alija Izetbe-gović. He congratulated Gordana and myself on having been chosen as "International Editors of the Year" in 1993 by the World Press Review of New York (the news of the award had just arrived), and he congratulated Halilović on his being chosen as the new editor-in-chief.

"I would like to add my vote in support of that choice," Izetbe-gović said.

"I am especially pleased, Mr President, that you are casting your vote two days after his election and not two or more days before, as has been the case with radio or television," I quipped, recalling the battle we had had even with this democratically elected government in order to maintain the independence of *Oslobodjenje*.

Izetbegović smiled, and acknowledged *Oslobodjenje* for its "consistent Bosnian orientation"—as he phrased it. "*Oslobodjenje* is a very good paper for all those who do not wish to read only their own opinion. Sometimes it criticizes me, and sometimes I don't agree with what it says, but that is the way it ought to be in a democracy."

Dissent at the heart of democracy—this had been the leitmotif of our struggle at *Oslobodjenje*. In its pages we had tried to practise as we

AFTER SIX YEARS, *OSLOBODJENJE* ELECTS A NEW EDITOR. LEFT TO RIGHT: SALKO HASANEFENDIĆ, GENERAL MANAGER; MEHMED HALILOVIĆ, THE NEW EDITOR-IN-CHIEF; AND KEMAL KURSPAHIĆ, THE NEW WASHINGTON BUREAU CHIEF.

preached, and hoped that those who governed Bosnia would recognize that a society that allowed no space for a multitude of voices would lapse into tyranny. As I said my farewells before taking leave of Sarajevo to take up my new assignment in Washington, my friend Hamza Bakšić referred to the long road I had traveled as the editor of *Oslobodjenje* and said: "Your five and a half years have been like someone else's fifty-five—long enough to last a lifetime."

When I was chosen, in December 1988, as editor-in-chief of *Oslobodjenje*, it was supposed to be a four-year term. At that time there was no way for me to know that the hurricanes of change in which a dying Communism would be replaced by a rising tide of virulent nationalism and war would cause me to remain in that position for nearly five and a half years. It was a time of tectonic quakes, in which the nature and the geography of the entire country changed, and during which the newspaper I edited held its own. It stood on the side of democracy and, not afraid of the risks, it opened its pages to the expression of a diversity of viewpoints while Yugoslavia still had a single-party system in power. It recognized quickly, and consistently pointed out, the dangers, first, of Serbian nationalism and then, the emergence in a chain reaction, as it were, of other nationalisms. It determinedly opposed the attempt to replace one-party dictation with the dictation of the three ethnic parties. And it did not permit itself to be silenced by mortar shells, tanks, and cannons. From a bomb shelter in the basement the voice of *Oslobodjenje* reached across the blood-drenched territory of Bosnia to the most distant countries and continents. And *Oslobodjenje* managed, in probably the most difficult conditions in which any daily newspaper has ever continued to publish, to remain faithful to its roots. It came into existence in the struggle against one fascism on August 30, 1943, as a newspaper of the anti-fascist movement in the Second World War, and it did not retreat in the face of a new fascism at the end of this century. It continued to use the means at the disposal of journalism—words, ideas, facts, and argument—to fight for the freedom of speech and freedom of the press in a free and pluralist Bosnia-Hercegovina. And it won, as a consequence of its struggle, the recognition of the world.

Not surprisingly, the positions that *Oslobodjenje* adopted were misunderstood—or travestied—in some quarters. The misperceptions were perhaps best expressed in the remarks by David Binder of the *New York Times*, in a televised debate in the United States on the press coverage of the war(s) in the former Yugoslavia, when he said that "even the once wondrously independent *Oslobodjenje*" was now more and more expressing the position of the Bosnian government. That statement did not really say anything about the independence of *Oslobodjenje*. If the views of the newspaper and of the Bosnian government concerning the causes, consequences, and possible solutions to the Bosnian tragedy were "more and more" or frequently the same, it was not because the government exercised any kind of control or influence over *Oslobodjenje*, but rather because *Oslobodjenje* had never pretended to be neutral between those who were destroying and those who legally represented Bosnia; between those who were creating their so-called Serbian state in Bosnia by means of slaughter and the "cleansing" of "others" and those who were seeking to defend an internationally recognized and legitimate state; between war criminals on the one side and victims of those crimes on the other. *Oslobodjenje* was able to be both objective and "one-sided" because the war of terror against Bosnia was completely one-sided. It was sufficient simply to record the horrors of a massacre of civilians in Sarajevo and elsewhere in Bosnia, simply to record the conclusions of the most respected international institutions for protection of human rights concerning mass murder, rape, exile or deportations to concentration camps, sieges and strangulation of cities and shelling of civilian targets, without having to worry about whether or not the paper's reporting might correspond to the point of view of the government.

Was it conceivable for American or British journalists during the Second World War to talk in terms of neutrality, objectivity, and "balanced" coverage when it came to "taking sides" between Nazi Germany and their own governments? As frequently as some of our well-intentioned acquaintances worried that *Oslobodjenje* might lose its "once wondrous independence," we were likewise worried, and felt offended, that the international institutions, including even some in the press, were almost perverse in their insistence on neutrality between genocidal killers and their victims. They would sometimes accept at face value, and as fact, the propaganda issuing from the headquarters of the aggressors, such as that which would have had the world suspend all reason and believe that "the Muslims themselves were engaged in massacres of civilians in Sarajevo"—in the bread-line massacre of Vase Miskina Street, in the lines for water and humanitarian aid at Bistrik and Dobrinja, at the Piazza Markale, even though no proof was ever furnished to substantiate these accusations. On the contrary there were international experts who established the falsehood of most of these wild claims and concluded that the atrocities were committed by Serbian artillery.

We were not able, as the Western media did upon occasion, to write about "negotiations among the warring parties of Bosnia" as if this was a matter of negotiations of equal legitimacy and significance when one of those "parties" represented the legally elected government of an internationally recognized state while all the others were simply self-appointed representatives of "states" created through seizure of power and property and the perpetration of war crimes.

Oslobodjenje, which had always advocated a Bosnia of citizens with equal rights regardless of ethnicity or religion, and had represented exactly that kind of Bosnia on its own editorial staff, could not allow itself to be simply neutral with regard to the determination by armed local fascists or pathologically neutral international mediators that everything that was Bosnia should be carved up by a division of this ancient land into three ethnic statelets: Muslim, Serbian and Croatian. We consistently opposed such a dismemberment of the state on the grounds that it was illegal and immoral because it would legitimize the stealing of territory and changing of borders by use of force, and reward genocidal "ethnic cleansing" by leaving in the hands of aggressors half of the country. We also knew that such a partitioning of Bosnia would be an invitation for more years, perhaps even decades, of ethnic tensions, conflict, and even "ethnic cleansing": people driven from their homes and villages would fight for the rest of their lives for their right to return, and no Vance-Owen-Stoltenberg plans would erase the memories of their stolen homes, towns and country. No, *Oslobodjenje* in such matters had never been, and never wanted to be, neutral. But it did try, and I think with fair success, to be objective.

For me, just as it was for some of my Western colleagues, those criteria of objectivity and neutrality were often rather puzzling. I didn't know whether to weep or to laugh at some of the "objective" reports from my homeland even in the American media, (who for the most part deserve the credit for informing the world about some of the most horrible atrocities committed in Bosnia). The reports would say "the Muslim forces are attacking the Serbian town of Brčko," but there would be no awareness of the fact that in Brčko, according to the census of 1991, there were 55.8 percent Muslims, 6.9 percent Croats, and 20 percent Serbs, and that this town became "Serbian" only after thousands of "others" were killed or driven out. They said, "women and children stopped the humanitarian convoy for Goražde in the Serbian small town of Rogatica." But two years ago that town was 60.4 percent Muslims and 38.4 percent Serbs, and only after Serb forces accomplished their genocidal "final solution" with the expulsion of the last remaining Muslim families did that area become "all-Serbian." They said, "the Bosnian government and army are hindering the peace process because they refuse to accept the proposed cease-fire or the proposed map for division of the country." But they did not say that for the Bosnians the acceptance of such a cease-fire and division meant the freezing and legalization of Serbian occupation and that a responsible government could not sign such a deal. Or consider the media treatment of the "president of the Republika Srpska," Dr. Radovan Karadžić. They described him as the "leader of the Bosnian Serbs," but he was not even a leader in the Western democratic sense of the word, because in the first and only free election in Bosnia-Hercegovina in November 1990, he was not on the ballot for any public office whatsoever. Nor was he Bosnian, because he came to Bosnia as a teenager from a mountain village in Montenegro, and he was not a Serb, because by his birth and ethnic origin he was a Montenegrin.

This kind of "objectivity"—which would mean neutrality between those who killed our correspondent, Kjašif Smajlović, while he was sending his report from Zvornik, and whose artillery had bombarded us, set fire to and destroyed the places where we lived and worked, and the legally elected government of the state of Bosnia-Hercegovina, which was trying to defend Bosnia against formidable odds—is not something which could be expected from *Oslobodjenje*. At the same time, we have had, even during the horrible time of the war, a healthy quantity of disagreement with that same government. We criticized their inability to solve any of the problems faced by the citizens of Sarajevo under siege. We spoke out against the manifestations of lawlessness in our capital. We wrote against those at the top of the government who were ready to accept the ethnic division of Bosnia because they would be able to have their own Islamic mini-state.

Throughout a quarter century of professional work in journalism in a country where one's fate and success were decisively dependent upon how close one was or how obedient, to those who were in power, at the time when there was only one-party in power, and at the time when nationalistic governments took over, I was never a favorite of those in power. At a time when the favorites among journalists were chosen to sit on committees and assemblies or appointed as ministers or ambassadors, I was not for one single day a member of even a neighborhood committee of the ruling Party, nor of the regional or Republic Assembly, although there were stories told to this effect by those who wanted to destroy my reputation. There were always plenty of folks who were unhappy with my commitment to my work. The only ones who had a right to complain were my wife and children: Vesna, Tarik, and Mirza.

It was not always easy for them, sometimes not even possible, to explain why it was necessary for me to be at work first and to leave last from the editorial offices, when there were so many others who had a lot more money and a lot more time doing less important things. They never were able to completely understand, even though they gave me their support, that I would spend even the weekends working on the paper, when the other kids were able to spend time with their fathers. It was especially difficult for them, leaving Sarajevo after seven months of living in the free-fire zone of Hrasno, to comprehend the reasons why, for another full year and a half, I remained in the city and went to work during a time when almost no one who managed to get out ever came back. Very simply I was doing my job and fulfilling my obligations as a journalist and as a citizen. I could not leave as long as I was the editor-in-chief—to do so would have been to abandon ship while I was at the helm. I believed that by devoting myself to my work and sticking to my own moral principles, I was doing the best I could do for my confreres, my family, my country, and myself: I wanted to leave as my legacy the record of a man who had lived, and who had left— standing up.

For me, the fight to preserve the multiethnic nature of Sarajevo was not just a political platform for maintaining the unity of the capital of Bosnia, but for maintaining the very essence of life there. Sarajevo was indivisible. Muslims, Serbs, Croats, and Jews all lived on the same streets and in the same apartment buildings; a large number of them intermarried and raised children of mixed "ethnic origin." For them the maniacal logic of Karadžić's minister, Aleksa Buha, that for Serbs "it is better to commit collective suicide than to live with others anymore" had absolutely no value. All of its absurdity was best seen in the event which was described in the Western media as the "reopening of the Bridge of Brotherhood and Unity" between the residential community of Grbavica, under Serbian occupation, and the rest of the city in March 1994. What appeared to foreigners as an opening of the bridge, appeared to me as the erection of a new Berlin Wall. The sight of Serbian border guards, with a flag and a border marker of the "Republika Srpska" and Serbian police in the heart of Sarajevo, conjured up images of the infamous line of division in Berlin. The only difference was that there people of the same nationality were divided by an ideology, whereas here people of various nationalities were being divided by the fascist logic of "ethnic purity." In order to cross the bridge one had to spend days gathering documents and getting approvals. Even then, not everyone could go across: only women with very small children and old folks. Europe and the world, which had only recently celebrated the dismantling of the Berlin Wall and the ending of apartheid in South Africa, were now imposing upon Sarajevo and Bosnia—as the best of all possible worlds—exactly the same thing: partition and walls.

In the name of peace in Bosnia-Hercegovina, they were destroying the very thing which constituted the essence of the land: the freedom to be whoever you were, to practice whatever faith you wanted; the acceptance of and respect for differences; and the melding of cultures which made life infinitely richer. A Bosnia in which we, its citizens, in order to go from one to another part of the city of Sarajevo, would need to get police passes, to be met at control points by the very men who for more than three and a half years had been maiming and killing us with their big guns; a Bosnia in which cities such as Zvornik, Foča, Višegrad, Banja Luka, Doboj would be in the "Republika Srpska" and everything that my mother and my stepfather, like tens of thousands of others, had in Prijedor and Ljubija would belong to Karadžić plunderers, while the two of them, and all the others who were forced to leave, would spend their old age in exile, in Croatia or elsewhere around the world; a Bosnia in which—in Mostar, Banja Luka, Foča, and many other towns—those in charge would be the ones who destroyed living monuments which were among the most beautiful architectural and cultural heritage of the country: the Old Bridge, the Ferhadija mosque, the Aladža mosque and other landmarks; a Bosnia whose million and a half refugees would have no right to return to their homes or to the now desolate places where their homes used to be. Such a "peace," should it come to pass, will remain a bloodstain on the map of Europe at the end of the twentieth century, a shameful defeat by a new fascism in the same century of those who had vowed, "Never Again."

Is there then any hope for Bosnia? Perhaps the Bosnia which we knew and loved will not be the same on the geographic and political maps of the world. But it will, without any doubt, continue to live in the memories of the children who had to escape from chetnik knives to seek refuge in other people's homes and other people's countries, in their letters and their dreams, in their longing and the eternal call of their first toys, their faraway yards and homes, streams and hills, their first loves. They have carried Bosnia with them into the faraway places of exile so that they can always dream of her and return to her pristine nature, unsullied by the evil and mammoth crime of "ethnic cleansing."

As for *Oslobodjenje*, let there be no surprise if on its pages and in the work of its reporters and writers in the future you continue to recognize the dream of the Bosnia in which they were born, which belongs equally to all her children, and which cannot be so easily destroyed. Bosnia is not just a mark on the map of the world, it is a condition of the spirit, a way of life, a culture of deep roots which will outlive its murderers and the indifference of the world—until a new liberation.

POSTSCRIPT

Iᴛ ɪꜱ ʟᴀᴛᴇ ꜱᴜᴍᴍᴇʀ ᴏꜰ 1996. *Oslobodjenje* has survived the war without missing a single day of publication. In this year, using the fragile peace in the country, the paper took two major initiatives to reach its prewar readers, many of whom were expelled from their homes and towns in Bosnia and, together with some two million Bosnians, now live in yet another diaspora across the globe. And so *Oslobodjenje* has revived the publication of its magazine *Svijet* (The World). Edited by Zlatko Dizdarević, it is designed to rival the best international weeklies and represents the best in *Oslobodjenje*'s tradition of open debate and a free expression of ideas as well as its support for a multiethnic and multicultural society in Bosnia. The paper has also begun the simultaneous publication of a daily edition in Frankfurt for the large number of Bosnian refugees in Germany and other parts of Europe.

However, in my frequent conversations with colleagues at *Oslobodjenje*—who always tell me "everything is fine"— instead of expected joy and optimism, I detect untold feelings of disappointment and uncertainty. Sarajevo has finally been opened up to the world beyond and you can bring in all you need—but only if you have the money. In the forty-three months of the siege, *Oslobodjenje* could not earn anything from sales due to its reduced circulation, and especially not from advertising since all business activity in the city had been destroyed by the war. The postwar revival, with the publication of Svijet and the international daily edition, will take many months before producing any income badly needed for renewal and for decent salaries for the journalists who have been doing mostly unpaid work.

In the worst days of the shelling and the killing, struggling to keep the presses rolling just for another day, another week, another month, I allowed myself the luxury of a dream. I dreamed of peace and calm returning to Sarajevo and hoped that the international press, which had witnessed our fight for survival and had helped us with numerous gestures of solidarity, would pitch in to help rebuild "the paper which refused to die" and in its resistance became a symbol of a worldwide struggle for the freedom of expression and of the press. Today I do not know if it is still possible that editors and journalists around the world, in their newsrooms and on the pages of their papers, can muster the enthusiasm and take the initiative to organize a day or a week of international press solidarity to support their embattled colleagues who survived the war survive the fragile peace as well. Or it might well be the case that we were just another dramatic story and now the story is deemed to have ended. But for us the story is not over yet.

As I expected, Mehmed Halilović who succeeded me as editor-in-chief in March 1994 kept the spirit of *Oslobodjenje* alive through all the remaining months of the war. In late summer of 1996 the Editorial Board is not the same as the one I led but, reading the Sarajevo-Frankfurt edition, I see the same commitment to the idea of open debate and multiethnic coexistence. Of the team that I worked with in the first two years of the siege only one, the political editor Rasim Ćerimagić, is still on the Editorial Board. Gordana Knežević has only this summer managed to reunite her family, her husband Ivo, her sons Igor and Boris and her daughter Olja, after four years of separation. Unable to find stable jobs in Croatia, Gordana and Ivo are now living in Toronto with their children as yet another Bosnian refugee family. Of my three editors who led the weekly shifts in the bomb shelter, the first, Zlatko Dizdarević edits *Svijet,* the second, Branko Tomić has joined his family as refugee in Sweden, and, the third, Feto Ramović is back at another Sarajevo daily *Večernje Novine* (Evening Newspaper) which he successfully edited before the war. Foreign News editor Mirko Šagolj served as Moscow correspondent but with no guaranteed salary from *Oslobodjenje* had to go back to Sarajevo and still writes commentaries pleading for reason to prevail in the shaky Bosnian-Croat federation. "The Sarajevo Chronicle" editor Josip Vričko spent three years as correspondent in Croatia before accepting a job with the leading Zagreb daily *Vjesnik*—the mouthpiece of Tudjman's party. But all people on Halilović's Editorial Board are some of the finest journalists from my years as the editor: his deputy is Emir Habul, Newsroom editor Slobodan Stajić, International Edition editor Mugdim Galijašević, editor for culture Nada Salom, "Sarajevo Chronicle" editor Dragan Stanojlović, and sports editor Tomo Počanić—still Bosnian Muslims, Serbs and Croats working together in a country whose wells have been poisoned by rabid ultranationalism.

And in the summer of 1996, as in my years at *Oslobodjenje*, the paper is under renewed attack by the nationalists on all sides of the divided country. In the most recent polemic, papers under the control of nationalistic Muslim SDA—led by the weekly *Ljiljan* but followed by other publications as well—attacked *Oslobodjenje* as the "traditionally chetnik paper," listing a number of Serbs who used to work for *Oslobodjenje* and are now "on the other side." But, at the same time, one of few former *Oslobodjenje* journalists who really are "on the other side," Miroslav Janković, in a book published by Karadžić's propagandistic agency SRNA at Pale, attacks us as "Muslim fundamentalists led by Kemal Kurspahić." These extremes that characterize the descriptions of *Oslobodjenje* in the nationalistic press are, ironically enough, a source of reassurance for me for they are a confirmation of the fact that *Oslobodjenje*, in my time as editor and since, was and is merely a collection of people brought together by their profession. It represents a state of mind, a way of thinking and being, an institution which draws its sustenance from Bosnia's centuries-old cultural heritage and is not simply made or unmade by changes in personnel, no matter how richly deserving some individuals might be for their contribution to the survival of the paper or the culture.

Sometimes people ask me: what was the point in keeping the paper alive when you lost the country? Bosnia-Hercegovina as we knew her, and as was internationally recognized as an independent state in April 1992, no longer exists. The American-brokered Dayton Peace Agreement, signed in Paris on December 14, 1995, formally still recognizes Bosnia as a single country, only internally divided into two entities: the Bosnian-Croat Federation constituting 51 percent and the Republika Srpska 49 percent of the territory. In practice, it is much worse. The ultranationalistic leadership in Republika Srpska that organized and perpetrated genocide in the territories it now occupies, openly defies Dayton by treating its "Republic" as a separate state with no connection to the rest of Bosnia. As for the Bosnian-Croat Federation, it is far from being a single entity. Croat ultranationalists still keep all territories they managed to occupy in their campaign of "ethnic cleansing" as part of an exclusively "Croat" zone and do not bother to disguise their intent to annex it to neighboring Croatia while the influential extremist faction within the ruling SDA, in territories under the control of the Bosnian Army, reinforces the drive for a permanent partition of the country by exercising totalitarian control over "Muslim" Bosnia—the Sarajevo-Zenica-Tuzla region and the Bihać and Goražde enclaves.

The international community which wrung its hands while Bosnians were being slaughtered and their country destroyed, in many ways supports partition even while its leaders still shed crocodile tears for a multiethnic and multireligious Bosnia. After the ceremonial signing of the peace agreement, a 60,000 man, NATO-led Implementation Force (IFOR) was dispatched to Bosnia which set about impressively executing the military provisions of Dayton: the separation of forces, the creation of the 2.5 mile-wide zone of separation, the withdrawal of troops into designated barracks and the withdrawal of heavy artillery into designated warehouses. But with no political will in Western capitals from Washington to Paris to take even the smallest risks in the implementation of the civilian aspects of the peace plan—such as the free movement of civilians throughout Bosnia, the right of return for the two million Bosnians expelled from their homes and towns in campaign of "ethnic cleansing," the apprehension and extradition to the Hague of indicted war criminals—IFOR's presence has in fact made a peaceful zone of separation into a bitterly contested border between the new entities of the state which was supposed to be reunited.

The West's calculation in enforcing the partition instead of the reintegration of Bosnia is obvious. And, as always, utterly wrong. They believe that the recognition of "new realities," even though these have been created by genocide, will finally end the suffering of Bosnians. What they never understood while introducing endless series of maps of a partitioned country—beginning with the Carrington-Cutillero proposal for ethnic cantonization in 1992, followed by the Vance-Owen idea for ethnic provincialization and the Owen-Stoltenberg "union of three ethnic republics," all the way to the Contact Group's two entities sanctioned in Dayton—was the elementary fact that maps for ethnic partition of a country of deeply interwoven ethnicities and religions was more an invitation for further terror than a solution for tensions created by virulent ultranationalism.

For Bosniaks from Eastern Bosnia, from Zvornik to Foča, from Višegrad to Bijeljina, from Vlasenica to Srebrenica, or those from Prijedor and Banja Luka in Bosanska Krajina, or Stolac and Čapljina in Hercegovina, there is no peace in their hearts as long as those who tortured them and who destroyed their lives and all their cultural and religious heritage control their towns without allowing them even to visit the graves of their dead on Muslim religious holidays. But this "peace" is no less painful for Bosnian Serbs from Sarajevo, Drvar, Bosansko Grahovo, Glamoč—forced to leave their towns either by advancing Croat-Bosnian forces or by their own political and military leaders seeking to claim representation of the whole Serb nation—who will always dream about their previous life. Imagine, for a moment, the plight of a Serb from Sarajevo who spent his entire life in that lively cosmopolitan city, but who is now expected for the years to come to rejoice in the great "Serb victory" while resettled in someone else's looted and bloodstained home in Srebrenica. Equally grim are the prospects for Croats who had to sacrifice their centuries long presence in the beautiful, fertile regions of Central Bosnia or Bosanska Posavina in order to populate the mountainous terrains of Western Hercegovina which have been newly designated as "Croat." Once they all awake from the stupor of nationalistic madness induced in large part by a decade of progaganda in the media in Milošević's Serbia and Tudjman's Croatia, and recently by the Muslim extremists in Bosnia, they will fight for their right to get back to the only places they can call home. Perhaps, by ballots, more realistically by guns.

Instead of sanctioning new realities created in crimes which still might ignite conflicts in the entire Balkan region—since the racist concept of ethnic purity undermines the permanence of many borders in that area—any wise and responsible international leadership would do all in its power to help reintegrate the country so brutally torn apart. Instead of endlessly appeasing the murderous drive for "Greater Serbia" and "Greater Croatia" the world should honor its own commitment to Bosnia as a single state. It can do so by isolating Serbia and Croatia, politically and economically, as long as their regimes do not demonstrate a full appreciation for the integrity and sovereignty of their neighboring state; by supporting Bosnia's economic renewal and defense capabilities without spending a single dollar in regions or entities in which there is no respect for human rights, freedom of movement, and right of return of those expelled to their homes and property; and, as the highest moral priority, by arresting and extraditing for trials in the Hague those most responsible for war crimes in order to give their victims the hope for reconciliation and coexistence among those innocent on all sides. They were all sacrificed at the altar of maniacal drive for territories, for power and historic greatness of the leaders who used the vocabulary of democracy, liberty and self-determination to perpetuate a new totalitarianism.

This is also my response to the question on saving the paper while losing the country. The war did not kill Bosnia in us. As the idea of coexistence of all its faiths and ethnicities, Bosnia cannot be destroyed or rebuilt by force or by cynical peace formulas. She lives in the soul of her people, no matter how far the terror forced them to go—from Scandinavia to America, from New Zealand to Australia. Tortured, raped, looted . . . Bosnia is still alive, like the paper which reflects and defends her essence and keeps faith with memory.